Tom Fort worked as a journalist f
for more than twenty years. He w
Financial Times. This is his ninth bo
of *Eels, Downstream* and *The A303:*

Praise for *Casting Shadows*

'Tom Fort's wonderful social history of angling is the ideal book for
fish fanciers ... A wonderful and unsnobbish social history of angling
by a master fisherman' Max Hastings, *Sunday Times*

'His writings cover a wide range of subjects ... he therefore brings
to this book a more practised pen than most angling writers bring
to theirs' *Literary Review*

'*Casting Shadows* is a beautifully written, unexpectedly humorous and
fastidiously researched expression of gratitude for creatures and for
a sport. Fort recreates vivid vignettes of moments in angling's heritage
with novelistic flourish' Patrick Galbraith, *The Times*

'Tom Fort ... leads us into all sorts of fishy places, with their delightful sights and smells, and introduces us to rough-hewn, fishy
characters – and we love it ... His writing must give any fisherman
nostalgic thoughts. Equally, any non-fisherman will surely be enticed
by the scenes he depicts, and amazed by the facts of history and
natural history he reveals' *Oldie*

'Marvellous' Jeremy Paxman, *Saga Magazine*

'Tom Fort's *Casting Shadows* ... offers garrulous witness to a fine
passion ... [Fort] is a sort of aquatic anthropologist, an angler with
an infectious curiosity about all things fishy ... The aroma of wonder
seeps through his sentences. Buried beneath the anecdote and the
arcana is the poignancy of the fisherman's encounter with nature ...
A plea for attention to the radiant world' *London Review of Books*

'An essential antidote to a modern world'
Fly Fishing & Fly Tying magazine

Also by Tom Fort

The Book of Eels
The Grass is Greener
The Village News
Channel Shore
The A303
Against the Flow
Downstream
Under the Weather
The Far From Compleat Angler

CASTING SHADOWS

FISH AND FISHING IN BRITAIN

TOM FORT

WILLIAM
COLLINS

William Collins
An imprint of HarperCollins*Publishers*
1 London Bridge Street
London SE1 9GF

WilliamCollinsBooks.com

HarperCollins*Publishers*
1st Floor, Watermarque Building, Ringsend Road
Dublin 4, Ireland

First published in Great Britain by William Collins in 2020

This William Collins paperback edition published in 2021

2022 2024 2023 2021
2 4 6 8 10 9 7 5 3 1

A catalogue record for this book is available from the British Library

ISBN 978-0-00-828348-3

Typeset in Adobe Caslon by Palimpsest Book Production Limited,
Falkirk, Stirlingshire
Printed and bound in Great Britain by CPI Group (UK) Ltd, Croydon

For my two fishing brothers, James and Matthew,
who first showed me the path to the water.

Contents

Introduction

As the tide ebbs the netsman stands on the sandbar, 'the place' as he calls it. The water, thick with sediment, is above the knee seams of his chest waders, pushing insistently at his legs. He scans the smooth water, searching for the mark, where the surface is furrowed by a salmon finding its way upstream.

The waiting and watching begin when the falling tide makes it possible to reach the place. The fisherman wants calm weather, to aid visibility. Too much wind is bad, rain is bad. He needs to be able to scan the surface intently. Then he sees it, a 'V' parting the smoothness. He moves fast but without hurry. He knows from experience that as long as the fish does not detect his presence, it will move steadily up against the flow, holding its course.

He wades just faster than the tide, so that he leaves no wake. The net, shaped like a great 'Y', looks cumbersome. But he handles it with ease, leaning it against his shoulder as he moves, then extending it where he judges he is intercepting the salmon's course.

He braces himself against the rush of the stream. Behind him, across the width of the river, the water is draining seawards. It pushes itself across the bars and banks of sand, seeking the channels, surging and seething in its haste, setting up a dry, insistent, rustling sound, 'the ruts', the fisherman calls it. He is intent on the one channel, where the fish run.

He can see nothing in the brown water, but he has followed the mark as the back of the fish steals upstream, and he knows it is close. The net is thrust out before him and his hands are firm on the ash staff. He dips it down then sweeps the frame up. There it is, like a flash of silver light or a sunbeam, but solid flesh and muscle, twisting and kicking against the mesh. He reaches for his knobbling pin, a short, heavy stick, smooth and with a slightly rounded head, and strikes the fish hard at the back of its head. Its life journey, which began on a bed of gravel on one of the nameless spawning streams that form the headwaters of this river – the same nameless stream it is seeking today – is over.

Mike Evans, one of the last of the Severn lave netsmen.

The implement described is known as a lave net. The origin of the word 'lave' is unknown, and its use in this country has been restricted to sections of the Severn estuary where the movements of the tides and the accessibility of sand and mud banks with deeper channels between made it effective. But the principle behind it is universal. The great ethnographer James Hornell –

who studied ancient fishing methods in all parts of the world
– found a fairly exact version of the lave net in use on the lower
Ganges in Bengal,* the one significant difference being that the
mesh was made from bamboo mat instead of cord or thread.

Across the world prehistoric societies exploited the rich food
source available in lakes, rivers, estuaries, lagoons and along
shorelines. They trapped, netted, speared, noosed, stunned, tickled
and lured every species of fish they could find. The methods they
used evolved in response to particular circumstances. But – as
with the lave net – the responses were often very similar because
the circumstances do not vary that much. James Hornell, travelling and inquiring among what were still primitive and isolated
communities at the end of the nineteenth century and into the
1930s, described many of these methods in his indispensable
Fishing in Many Waters. He was able, for instance, to observe
Chinese and Japanese fishermen deploying trained cormorants
to catch fish on the Yangtze and Nagara rivers; and the use of
toxic plants to stupefy fish in a lagoon in Fiji and in pools on
the Benue River in northern Cameroon.

It may be that these techniques were used somewhere in the
British Isles in the dim and very distant past (poisonous plants
such as *Verbascum phlomoides* and *Euphorbia villosa* were still being
resorted to on the Danube delta and in the Carpathian region
of Romania post-1945). But if so, that use can be presumed to
have lapsed well before the start of what we regard as recorded
history. So for knowledge, we depend on remnants. Once we
have those, it becomes possible to reconstruct what they formed
part of, what that implement was used for, and how and when.

The oldest known fish traps in Europe go back 7,000 years
to the Mesolithic era, examples of which have been discovered
as far afield as Ireland, Denmark and Russia. The earliest
confirmed trap in Britain, at Cold Harbour Pill on the western

---

* The lower Ganges and its delta in the Bay of Bengal are now in Bangladesh.

船鴛魚

A Chinese illustration of cormorant fishing, 1872.

side of the Severn estuary near Newport, has been carbon-dated to the late Bronze Age (perhaps 1200 BCE). These and other prehistoric structures revealed their existence because the wooden posts and other materials used can survive many centuries if buried or half buried in mud. Archaeologists love them, because they represent fact, data, proof. The fact that visually these pieces of blackened wood and fragments of basketwork are extremely unexciting matters not at all. They can be photographed, subjected to carbon dating, minutely described and compared with equally unexciting bits-and-bobs from elsewhere to build timelines and arching narratives, thereby justifying the whole laborious process of discovery and excavation.

But these finds are not the story. The fish trap at Cold Harbour Pill on the Severn represents one point in a timeline extending long before and long after. It was preceded by other devices installed for the same purpose – to intercept fish, chiefly salmon, eels and shad – so that they might be killed and eaten by the communities that managed the trap, or traded and bartered by them for other needs. It was followed by other traps used for the same purpose. Two thousand years later the same principle was being followed in both sides of the estuary in the form of fixed ranks of baskets known as putchers or putts – more elaborate, more time-consuming to construct and maintain, more effective in terms of fish caught, but essentially no different. These survived until living memory, when the sudden collapse in salmon abundance put them out of business.

There were two terms in Anglo-Saxon for these fixed traps – *haecwer* and *cytweras*, meaning fish weir and fish weir with baskets. The concept would have been recognisable the world over: a V-shaped barrier on a gently shelving stretch of foreshore covered and uncovered by the tides, generally facing upstream to take fish that moved in with the flood and dropped back on the ebb, with a net or basket at its apex. In London the remains of fish weirs of this type have been uncovered close to the banks of the Thames at several locations including Chelsea, Vauxhall, Isleworth, Kew, Hammersmith and Brentford. The arms consisted of wattle hurdles fixed between oak or elm posts, and the apex trap was made of woven willow. Carbon analysis dates them to between 650 and 890 CE – but, again, it is certain that traps of a similar design would have been in use in roughly the same locations – generally across a channel between the shore and a sandbank or mudbank or an eyot, a river island – going back to the earliest human occupation.

By its nature a fixed trap is only effective in catching migrating fish – primarily salmon and eels (although on the Severn lampreys and shad came into the equation as well). In tidal waters Atlantic salmon returning from the sea to spawn in their birth rivers move up with the incoming tide and drop back on the ebb, biding their time until the river flow is strong enough for a decisive move upstream. Eels are intent on an opposite path. In autumn, in high water and in stormy conditions, they forge their way downstream seeking the open sea and – eventually – the immensely far distant Sargasso, where they mate and die. The migratory impulses of both salmon and eels means that they are also vulnerable to exploitation at any point in fresh water, from nets and other kinds of traps, as well as spearing, snagging and – in the case of eels – being caught on bait.

Prehistoric communities adopted multiple strategies for survival. Along the Severn shore Megalithic men, women and children left their footprints in the mud, alongside those of wolves, aurochs and birds. They grazed their animals, panned salt, hunted and devised various ways to catch fish. Some of their methods lapsed with them, others survived into the era of written record, evolving along the way. Some – but not all – even survived into our time. On the tidal Thames, for instance, the fixed shore-line traps of Anglo-Saxon times fell into disuse or were dismantled in the medieval period because they interfered with a more pressing requirement, navigation. But on the weirs that were built upstream to accompany the navigation locks, traps for migrating eels – known as eel bucks – were in use until the end of the nineteenth century.

For most of our history we have been untroubled by the notion of sustainability or the concept of a need to conserve natural resources. People helped themselves to fish by whatever means the available materials and their resourcefulness made possible. Generally, the abundance was such that they could not imperil its future. Fishing was a matter of life for societies living or maintaining seasonal camps by the water, and death for the fish. Later it evolved into a business, the fish into a commodity.

Lowering eel bucks on the upper Thames, 1875.

Expanding markets and more sophisticated methods enabled an ever-increasing proportion of the resource to be exploited. But as recently as the second half of the nineteenth century the respected authorities who advised the government on fisheries policy were continuing to assert that the abundance of fish of all species was such that it could never be overexploited – that the very idea of overfishing was flawed. It is only over the past century that the full extent of that disastrous misinterpretation has been exposed.

In 1976 – when I was twenty-five years old – that lave netsman on the Severn caught and killed and sold more than three hundred salmon during the season. Twenty-six of them he netted on a single tide. He made more money that year from salmon than he did from his full-time job in a factory in Gloucester.

For the season of 2018 his licence allowed him to take one fish, which he did one day in August on the great horseshoe bend upstream from Newnham. He took it, not to sell or trade, but just to demonstrate that the tradition in which he grew up and plied his craft is not yet dead. Maybe not, but it is dying and nothing can save it. The salmon still come, but the scale of the run has diminished from a steady stream to a trickle, to the point that those charged with safeguarding what is left have decreed that no significant exploitation can be permitted. The netsman I have described at work is now eighty years of age; within a few years there will be none left.

In January 2019 the commercial fishery for wild salmon on the north-east coast of England, using fixed nets on the shore, ceased operations after the Environment Agency announced it would no longer give licences to the handful of remaining netsmen. It was the last significant wild salmon fishery in Britain. The relentless decline in the numbers of salmon returning to these shores from their North Atlantic feeding grounds had finally forced the hand of the authorities. What Thomas Huxley and those other Victorian experts had asserted could not happen – and which had already happened to herring, cod and plaice at sea – had now happened to the salmon, our most valuable and charismatic freshwater fish. The reasons for that collapse continue to be argued over. What is certain is that the exploitation of the species for food for us – which has lasted for millennia, sustained communities and local economies, and nourished a rich heritage and store of knowledge – is finished. And barring a cataclysm that brings about a reversion to a hunter/gatherer existence, it will never return.

The harvesting of our other main fish-as-food freshwater species – the eel – is going the same way. As a commodity it was never as important as salmon, but it was systematically exploited in those parts of the country where it thrived – chiefly East Anglia, the Somerset Levels and the Severn system – and was traded in significant volume at the Billingsgate Market in London. Its popularity as a food item in Britain waned some decades ago (although it is still warmly favoured in much of continental Europe). Over roughly the same period there has also been a sustained fall in eel populations across Europe, causing it to be declared an endangered species. Fishing for adult wild eels – always a localised, low-level and marginal activity – has declined almost to vanishing point. The Environment Agency now follows a policy of issuing licences only to existing fishermen, thereby virtually guaranteeing that eel fishing will die out within a generation.

Now is a suitable time to look at the very long history of how we have made use of our freshwater fish as a source of protein – a history that has not been celebrated, nor even hardly told, because fish are fish and not much regarded by society at large. But there is another dimension to this story of the fish of our rivers, streams, brooks, becks, burns, lakes, lochs, loughs, meres, ponds, canals, estuaries and other assorted waters. There has been a third stage in the evolution of our relationship with them, one that is far from finished. First, it was a matter of fishing to eat and survive. Second, the need to fish became a business and the fish a trading commodity. Later still – but not that much later – the business gave birth to a desire to pursue, outwit and catch the fish for the pleasure of it. This is what we called angling.

This birth was one minor aspect of that Middle Ages blossoming of the human spirit that embraced writing, painting and other visual arts, dress, manners, chivalry, philosophy, scientific inquiry – the notion (among the privileged few) that there should be more to life than merely the struggle, often unavailing, to maintain it. But how did that refinement, fishing for fun, evolve from the business?

There are places and circumstances in which a net or trap or spear is not so much inefficient as useless. But you might still want a fish to eat – a trout, say, feeding in fast water, or a pike lurking by a reedbed. Then the rod (or angle, hence angling) comes into its own. It is a uniquely effective way of delivering a bait or lure to a particular spot for a particular fish. That is what the Roman historian Claudius Aelianus, in the first recorded reference to angling, described the Macedonians as doing on the River Astraeus around 200 CE – deploying a rod and an artificial fly to catch 'fish with speckled skins'.

Those Macedonians were definitely not motivated by a sporting impulse. They devised (or maybe borrowed) the technique because they worked out that this was the best way to catch the trout they wished to eat. In time, that desire – I am surmising here, but what other answer is possible? – became tinged by another, more subtle emotion, excitement. And the excitement was followed by another, the pleasure in success (and its antithesis, bitter disappointment).

Thus angling grew into a diversion, a sport. It beguiled poets and painters and philosophers, soldiers, statesmen and scientists. In time it embraced the Sheffield knife-grinder eager to escape from his poisoned city to a quiet bend on the river in the countryside where he might watch his float in peace. It embraced the highborn Scottish aristocrat, descended from Highland land-grabbers, lording it over his river and jealously watching over the silver salmon as they came in from the sea. It entranced film stars, dictators, American presidents and British prime ministers, terrorists, murderers. It touched all classes of men and women, who found that – if they had nothing else in common – they shared this passion to feel a fish on the end of their line.

It is no coincidence that Jesus should have recruited four fishermen – the brothers Simon (called Peter) and Andrew, and the brothers James and John – as his first disciples, to make them fishers of men. In their first calling they required particular qualities: patience, of course, resilience in the face of adversity and disappointment, endurance, determination, courage, versatility. These were qualities that would stand them in good stead in their second calling.

They would also have learned from their fishing that the

important things seldom come quickly. They would have learned to take their time, to be aware of what lies beneath the surface, to know that there is always more to know and that learning is never complete. Peter and Andrew and James and John and all the fishermen and women before and after them have been bound together in sympathy for the element of water and the life it sustains – 'the mythic plane', as the poet Ted Hughes called it. For Hughes the acquisition of polaroid glasses was a revelation, enabling him to penetrate that plane to a degree. But even with the glasses no one can see it all. The picture must be filled in as far as possible by intuition, experience, understanding, and the exercise of the imagination.

The water lover – often an angler – will deploy those slowly acquired skills to grasp the wholeness of the life above, on and beneath the surface. It is a complex entity. There is movement, stillness, clarity, obscurity, light, darkness, depths, shallows. There are plants: willows, alders, reeds, sedges, flag irises, ranunculus, ribbon weed, tough-stemmed water lilies. There is the insect life: water boatmen, damselflies, a host of invertebrates. There are frogs, snails, newts, coots, ducks. And there are the fish. The water lover will have an apprehension of all that, and those who do not share that sympathy will know very little and hardly understand what they are missing.

The passion gripped me when I was a boy. More than sixty years later I am still gripped by it, although the focal points have changed somewhat over the intervening period. The mind and imagination of my eight-year-old self were concentrated on the bright orange top of my float, the pink worm suspended unseen below, my savage longing for the float to tremble, glide away, disappear, and for the upward lift of my rod tip to be answered by the desperate, vital resistance of a perch. Now, as I write these words on a morning in early June, I picture a minute chalkstream threading its way through rough meadows grazed by black cattle, mayfly air-dancing in search of mates in the shade of the hawthorn or veering towards the water to lay their eggs, wild brown trout on station above the golden gravel ready to raise a snout and intercept the struggling prey.

What has not changed at all is the sense of fulfilment that comes from studying and deepening my understanding of the medium of water, still or moving. I have spent a significant proportion of my years on, beside or in fresh water. The declared purpose has always been to catch a fish. But I recognise that operating beneath that purpose has been an inexhaustible inquisitiveness about the wholeness of the watery sphere and how it nourishes itself, how the many communities of life forms within it fit together and how we – its custodians and exploiters – relate to it.

For many years I wrote copiously about angling, until I found that I had pretty much said all I had to say and was beginning to repeat myself. I wrote on other subjects instead, while occasionally yielding to a weakness for introducing watery or fishy matters into other contexts. I always had in the back of my mind the awareness that one day I would come back to what has been one of the determining impulses of my life; and try to pull together in a single narrative everything (or almost everything, because some of its inevitably gets left out) about it that I had learned from experience and study and reading and talking to others, and from thinking and letting my imagination work. This is that narrative. I hope that it expresses something of the gratitude I feel for the way in which our waters and their creatures have enriched my life and the lives of countless others.

CHAPTER ONE

In from the Sea

The old grey town of Dingwall stands near the head of the Cromarty Firth, a few miles north of Inverness. It was a place of some importance once, one of the royal burghs and the county town of Ross and Cromarty. Although it was never wealthy, the leading townspeople who sat on its council took their duties seriously. Despite being a mile or so from the shore of the firth, it had a harbour of sorts and the council had ambitions to expand its sea trade. To that end it commissioned the most celebrated engineer of the age, Thomas Telford, to upgrade the River Peffery – actually no more than a stream – into a splendid canal that would connect Dingwall with its harbour and allow cargo boats to unload and load near the centre of town.

Amid familiar scenes expressing civic pride – bands playing, feasting, pompous speechifying – the canal was opened in 1817. For a time small vessels did use it to deliver and take on cargoes of timber, grain, coal and so forth. But Dingwall struggled to compete with other, more favoured ports. By the mid-1830s the harbour was taking no more than £130 a year in dues, not enough to pay to keep the canal in good repair and the ever-encroaching sands away from the mouth. No one wanted the job of Collector of Shore Dues, and despite an expensive refurbishment, which included removing silt from the canal and extending the harbour piers, the combination of the coming of the railway and the silting-up of the harbour mouth finished it off in the 1880s.

Dingwall's efforts to improve itself had been a disappointment, and the failure of the canal was a heavy burden on the council's finances. But not as heavy, nor as galling, as the fiasco over Dingwall's salmon fishery.

The town slumbered in the half-light of a cool, overcast September morning. The road to the harbour passes the hospital and ends at a car park close to the Cromarty Firth. The area beyond has been grassed and landscaped for the benefit of dog walkers and lovers of the open air, although the closure of the footbridge over the defunct canal on safety grounds has severely truncated the Round Dingwall Walk promoted by the community council.

At low tide, the remnants of Dingwall's disappointed maritime ambitions are very evident. Blackened posts rising from smooth grey mud mark what must have been the approach to the harbour from open water. The harbour wall itself is still sound, but what would have been a safe anchorage, even a port in a storm, is now filled high with fat mudbanks between which the meagre Peffery creeps towards the firth. When I was there two dirty, uncherished fibreglass dinghies lay on the slope of the mud nearest the wall, tethered by long greasy ropes.

I looked out across the firth to the fields of the Black Isle, richly dark where recently ploughed. The tide exposed flats of mud on the near and far sides. Between them the current of the River Conon pushed purposefully in the direction of the sea. This is one of the prime rivers of Highland Scotland, draining four hundred square miles of upland mountain terrain and moorland, gathering in tributaries great and small, its final few miles flowing through rich grazing and arable land.

On the mudflat in front of me there was a line of black, weedy rocks regular enough to suggest deliberate arrangement. This unexciting structure was what I had come to see. The line comprised deposits of stone placed to support or revet the alder stakes and willow panels that formed the Dingwall yair – *yair* being the Scottish term for a fish trap. Radiocarbon analysis of one of the eroded stumps revealed that it had been driven into position sometime in the second half of the seventeenth century.

The principles of the Dingwall yair are the same as for fish traps built by primitive and developing societies all over the world – a permanent structure arranged to intercept the passage of migrating or feeding fish in shallow water. In Scotland they were generally installed along the shallow, shelving edges of sea lochs and estuaries where they were covered and then made accessible by the fluctuations of the tides. The usual shape was a rough V, or that of a harp with one straight side and a longer curved one, and they were generally aligned to intercept fish on the ebbing tide. Fish would enter the wide mouth and would make their way along the walls of wattle panels without being aware that their space was being confined until they reached the apex, where they generally hit a net or entered a kind of holding basket from which there was no escape.

We know the Dingwall yair was in use 350 years ago, but it is a sure bet that a similar trap was working there or thereabouts for centuries and quite possibly millennia before that. The awareness of the movements of salmon – how they come in on the tide towards the river mouth then drop back on the ebb, the pattern repeated until there is a sufficient flow of fresh water to draw them upstream – is as old as time. The availability of construction materials for a trap – stones, posts, withies – presented no difficulty. And until modern times the abundance of salmon was such that even this primitive technology, if in the right place, could justify the effort required to maintain it.

But not all yairs were equally effective, and the history of the Dingwall yair, chronicled briefly and spasmodically in the records of the town council, shows that the effort was considerable, and, as time went on, increasingly regarded as not worthwhile. The first mention of the yair is dated 1732. One William Fraser proposed that its condition 'having been ruinous for several years', he would rebuild and maintain it. The tack, or rental, was awarded to him for ten years, but no charge was made, presumably because the yair was in such a state of dereliction.

It is not known how William Fraser fared with it, but thirty years later he – or one of the same name – had other fish to fry. He proposed to the council a five-year lease 'of a coble fishing' at a yearly rent of sixty marks, but on condition that the council lend him one hundred marks 'to set up the fishing'. A coble was an open boat, and coble fishing involved shooting a net several hundred feet long from its stern while it was rowed in a semi-circle, the two ends then being gathered and pulled together by a tow-rope either from the shore or another boat. It is also an ancient method, highly efficient (and still in use today), but obviously more labour intensive and therefore expensive. The way the Dingwall minute is worded suggests that a net-and-coble operation was a novel concept; all the councillors asked for in return was that Mr Fraser should 'furnish and sell to the inhabitants . . . preferable to all others as much salmon as the said inhabitants will have occasion for during the fishing season at one penny for each pound'. Had they any inkling of the trouble they were storing up for their successors, they might have debated William Fraser's offer more thoroughly.

Two years later someone, possibly Mr Fraser, was evidently trying to keep the yair in business, as the council accepted a supply of alder wood cut by Alexander MacKenzie 'for wattling to the yair . . . and stakes to the said yair'. But its fortunes clearly

A traditional Yorkshire coble being pulled up from the sea in the early 1800s.

slumped, as in December 1791 the use of it, 'which has remained unoccupied for some years past', was snapped up by Mr John Simson at a yearly rent of one pound eleven shillings and sixpence on condition that he 'shall build and erect a sufficient yair'. The value was clearly going in one direction, down, as six years later 'Mr Patrick Hay, merchant' secured it at eight shillings per annum on the same condition as Mr Simson.

By then the focus had clearly switched from the old and generally unproductive yair to the far greater economic value of net fishing. In the same year that Mr Hay forked out a few shillings to rent the trap, the council agreed to rent the 'stell fishings belonging to the Burgh' to Forbes and Co. of Aberdeen at £25 a year, on the condition that they would provide salmon for the locals at preferential prices.

The term 'stell' – derived from the word for a sheep enclosure – simply meant fishing rights. In 1813 the council reached a deal with a Berwick-upon-Tweed businessman, Mr Landles, for him to rent the fishery at the same rate as Forbes and Co., but with a lump sum of £860 added; he also got the yair thrown in for an extra £20 a year. Mr Landles also agreed to provide cut-price salmon to the town, and the good burghers must have congratulated themselves on their canny management of the resource on their doorstep: a steady income in return for no expenditure or effort, and cheap salmon steaks to boot. But six years later an ominous note was sounded in the minutes with a passing reference to 'a dispute having arisen between the Tacksmen of the Town's Stell Fishings and the Tacksman of Culcairn's Fishings with regard to the extent of the respective rights of parties . . .'

In fact the argument over who had the right to catch the salmon of the Conon – and by extension, over whom the salmon arriving from the seas off Greenland actually belonged to – had by then been rumbling along in the background for almost a century, since the Earl of Cromarty had attempted to take 'by violent possession' fishing held by Munro of Culcairn. The magistrates of Dingwall (appointed by the council) maintained that they exercised the right to fish by royal charter granted by James VI in 1587, confirming two earlier charters from 1497 and 1226. But in 1825 Mrs Anne Hay-Mackenzie of Cromarty brought an action against Dingwall's magistrates claiming that she and her tenants had sole rights to the lower section of the river. The complications of the case were enormous and it took the Court of Session seven years to find in favour of the rich and powerful Mrs Hay-Mackenzie, and against the town of Dingwall.

At this point in a protracted and tedious legal saga, the magistrates of Dingwall made a fateful decision. Instead of retreating to lick their wounds and pondering the maxim that standing up to the bigwigs almost never pays, they resolved to fight on. In the words of Dingwall's historian, Norman Macrae, they 'foolishly – may I not say inexcusably – appealed this decision to the House of Lords'.

The appeal was dismissed and further litigation was embarked upon, while the council continued to let the fishing, and even tried to sell it outright. All the time the legal bills mounted. By 1850 they exceeded £3,000 and Dingwall council did not have the means to pay. The repayments were strung out over many years, a heavy burden on a town that had never been wealthy, while the Mackenzies and their tenants helped themselves to the salmon. Of Dingwall's age-old yair, nothing more was heard. Like the harbour, it rotted away until nothing more than the stumps or the old posts and the stones used to fix them were left for the tides to wash over and the salmon to swim past.

No other fish – with the possible exception of the rare and freakish sturgeon – was as sought-after for the banquets of the rich and powerful as the salmon. Being able to offer it to prestigious guests was, of itself, a mark of high standing. When the mute monks at the great Burgundian monastery of Cluny required salmon, the sign they used connoted both pride and the fact that they were used to such fare. Ninth-century documents from Prüm Abbey in Germany show that the abbot had rights to take salmon from the Rhine and the Moselle for the monks' feasts.

But as early as the thirteenth century the runs of salmon into the rivers of France and Germany were in decline as a result of overfishing, the installation of mills and other barriers to migration, and changes in land use. No such problems were encountered in Scotland, which increasingly assumed the role of major supplier of salmon to the rest of Europe. Power in Scotland lay with its kings, and below them with the lay lords and religious houses, and at each level a surprisingly tight grip on the exploitation of salmon was exercised. Successive Scottish kings asserted their control over the major rivers and granted rights to take salmon from them – initially the Tweed, Forth, Don, Tay, Spey and North Esk, subsequently others including the Ness, Border Esk and Leven.

Often these rights were split between the secular and religious sectors. The Cistercian monastery of Coupar Angus, north of Perth, had extensive fishings on the Tay nearby, but also on the Deveron, North Esk and Ericht. Monastery records from 1508 refer to the pool at Stanley on the Tay as being ideal for the use of a seine net. Naturally enough the monks did not haul the nets themselves, and the fishing was usually let to tenants who were licensed to sell a portion of their catch on condition that the best of it went to the monastery. On the Ericht, Thomas de Camera was obliged to provide eighty salmon a year as part of his rental agreement.

Where the river was suitably wide and the flow not too fierce, nets were used. But in the narrow channels and the necks of pools, the preferred method was to install a cruive, a rectangular, box-shaped trap held in place by stone dykes. The Black Friars of Inverness were granted fishing rights on the Ness by Alexander II in 1240; subsequently they devolved to the town's Burgh Court and to Lord Huntley, who controlled the fishery below the castle.

The channels between the islands on the Ness were ideal for the use of cruives; a map of 1744 entitled 'Views of the Cruives' shows multiple installations through the town. The salmon trade was important and poaching from the traps was a serious offence. In 1559 Donald Yet was sentenced to have his ear nailed to a beam in the marketplace for nine hours after he was caught filching six salmon from one cruive. John Crom (Bent John) fared even worse for a similar crime – he was left to tear his ear from the nail.

The international trade in pickled and salted salmon packed in barrels developed from the late fourteenth century onwards. In 1426, for instance, eight thousand fish were shipped out of Aberdeen. Some went to London, some to the ports of Hull and Kings Lynn en route for the Continent. It was a lucrative small-scale trade: a barrel retailed at thirty to fifty shillings, with a tax of a penny per fish going to the Crown.

The authorities in Scotland were alive to the importance of

their salmon fisheries, and the need to conserve and protect the stock. In the thirteenth century William I, known after his death as 'the Lion' but nicknamed 'the Rough' during his lifetime, ordered that all weirs on Scottish rivers – used to divert salmon into traps – should have a permanent mid-stream gap 'so large that a well-fed three-year-old pig should turn about without touching its tail or snout' so that a portion of the run would be sure to get through. They were sufficiently familiar with the salmon's life cycle to know how crucial it was to ensure the safe passage of smolts downriver – hence the statute of 1318 prescribing a three-by-two-inch minimum mesh size for nets. Fishing was not allowed between Saturday evening vespers and dawn on Monday, and a close season of varying length was enforced, with exceptions, to let the late-spawning fish through.

The eminent Canadian historian of pre-modern European fishing and husbandry, Richard Hoffmann, labelled the various Scottish statutes protecting the salmon as an example of 'precocious state intervention' – even a precursor to the European Union's Water Framework Directive. It reflected an acute awareness of both the economic value of the fish, and the need to look after it at crucial stages of its cycle. With that awareness came jealous guardianship that – because of the extended nature of the salmon's journey, necessarily taking it past the properties of multiple landowners – inevitably led to the kind of dispute that bankrupted poor Dingwall.

The chronicles of Scottish history are littered with accounts of quarrels and lawsuits between the owners of land on major rivers. Many centred on fishing and the taking of salmon at one point on the migratory route, thus preventing them from reaching the next. The exploitation of water power for emerging cottage industries created a new bone of potential conflict.

In 1755 long-standing rivalry between two branches of Clan Campbell based at Ormidale and Glendaruel near the Kyle of Bute erupted into a notorious pitched battle in and beside the

River Ruel. Campbell of Glendaruel's jealousy of his cousin at Ormidale was intensified when the latter installed a weir and dam to power the wheel of a mill used to dress cloth produced by local weavers. Glendaruel asserted that the dam was blocking the passage of salmon to his stretch of river, and sent men in the night to breach it. Ormidale had it repaired under a hail of stones from his cousin's retainers. It was breached **again**, repaired again. Then Glendaruel sent this stirringly worded challenge: 'Sir, I will have no more child's play . . . I will bring one hundred men and you will bring the same, otherwise you are a coward and devoid of honour . . . I will drown you and all your unspirited men in your dam and make your bodies food for the fishes.'

Next morning the horn was sounded along the glen and both chieftains led their men, armed with cudgels, into the water by the dam where they set about each other with vigour until the Reverend Mr Forbes, the minister from the nearby village of Clachan, intervened to implore the parties to separate in the name of God. No one was killed, but there was a fine display of cuts and bruises. Eventually the dispute was resolved in court, with Ormidale undertaking to put in a fish-ladder so that the salmon could ascend the dam in high water.

The foreshore at Sudbrook Point, in the shadow of the bridge that takes the M4 into Wales, is – like the car park at Dingwall harbour – a mundane location from which to consider the distant history of fish exploitation. The village of Sudbrook was built to house workers hired to dig the Severn railway tunnel in the 1870s and 1880s, and is still dominated by the redbrick bulk of the pumping station in which the six engines needed to suck the water out of the tunnel were housed. A path leads from a car park past a football pitch to the top of a low, much-eroded sandstone cliff from which the intimidating vastness of the Severn estuary stretches towards a distant, indistinguishable England.

Severn Bridge at Sudbrook Point.

I timed my visit to coincide with a low spring tide. The bridge was going about its noisy, monotonous business high in the air, infinitely divorced from the intricately sculpted world of water, rock, mud and sand below. Downstream, partially visible through the arches, was Avonmouth Docks. The grey sky spread over distant clusters of wind turbines, standing like sentinels, their blades motionless on this still afternoon.

The liquid component of the estuary was wonderfully reduced, allowing the mudbanks and sandbanks to reveal themselves like lost kingdoms. The water in the web of channels was glass-like, going nowhere, untouched by current or wind. Immediately below me the mud extended a hundred yards or so from the stony beach. Its surface was like skin seen under a microscope, grooved by complicated networks of tiny runnels and studded with black, greasy rocks. I would not have wished to take a step anywhere on it, yet long ago men who knew what they were doing ventured forth securely on it to gather food to eat and trade.

In January 2007 an unusually potent winter storm combined with exceptionally strong tidal currents to sweep away a layer of long-established sediment from the shore at Sudbrook Point. Across the country trees were uprooted, lorries were sent skidding off roads and trains ground to a standstill. At least nine people were killed and millions suffered transport delays, power cuts and general inconvenience. But for archaeologists interested in ancient fish traps, the cleansing of Sudbrook Point was an extraordinary stroke of luck.

Exposed at the surface of the mud were the upper parts of an array of fish-trap components in a remarkable state of preservation despite being, in some cases, almost a thousand years old. They included stakes, hurdles, a withy tie and – most precious of all – sixteen baskets or parts of baskets woven from hazel and willow. Having taken measurements and tiny samples for radiocarbon analysis, the archaeologists judged that the baskets would have made up one or more of the traps known as putts, a Severn speciality in which three baskets of varying sizes are fitted together as one, with the prey – anything from a salmon to a shrimp – detained in the innermost and smallest one, known as the forewheel, which had a wooden stopper so nothing could escape.

It is thought that this was an example of the trap referred to in Anglo-Saxon charters as *cytweras*. It was the Severn way to fix them in ranks three or four deep and thirty or more wide, each trap being five or six feet in diameter at the open end, and twelve to fourteen feet long. Generally they were fixed facing upstream to take fish on the ebb tide, and they presented formidable barriers. Putts and their smaller, simpler relatives known as putchers were mentioned in legislation in the sixteenth century and were referred to as 'ancient fisheries' in a parliamentary Act of 1778. They continued in use until very recently – indeed until the runs of salmon declined to such a point that the Environment Agency in effect closed the Severn fishery down.

Also found in the mud at Sudbrook Point were three much smaller and more closely woven baskets – one with an integral throat, which prevented captured fish getting out. These were

An old Severn fisherman making conical willow putchers,
used for catching salmon and eels, 1932.

probably eel traps, which would have been baited – perhaps with
a tasty bit of fresh rabbit or offcuts of salmon – weighted with
stones and laid in the river with a tether to the shore. Traps of
a similar conical design were staked out in shallower channels
to catch that much-appreciated delicacy, the lamprey.

The finds at Sudbrook Point were all the more delightfully
unexpected because the area had been extensively surveyed by
archaeologists sixteen years earlier in advance of the building of
the bridge. That study uncovered the remains of fish traps in
sixteen places – including post-settings, hurdle panels and fragments of baskets dating from the eleventh and twelfth centuries.
Remnants of a similar kind were found a little way up the same
shore at Magor Pill. The oldest yet found in Britain was located
a few miles downstream at Cold Harbour Pill, where a section
of Bronze Age fence and a bit of what may have been a basket
were recovered.

Pretty much wherever archaeologists have poked around on both sides of the estuarial Severn, they have found the remains of fish traps. Investigations on other estuaries all over Britain and Ireland reveal a matching picture. In the Anglo-Saxon era the mudbanks of the Blackwater estuary in Essex were lined with V-shaped fish weirs, some with walls three hundred metres long. The shores of Strangford Lough in Northern Ireland have yielded evidence of numerous fish traps of the standard design dating from between the eighth and thirteenth centuries, which caught salmon and eels as well as various sea fish, including cod and skate. On the Shannon estuary in south-west Ireland, surveys revealed multiple traps, generally smaller than those in Essex, with walls thirty to forty metres long.

The exploitation of the freshwater fish resource took place in every suitable location. In general the fragmentary surviving records merely note who owned those locations, while revealing little or nothing about those who did the work and formed those fishing communities. An exception is the documentation from the two great estates of Berkeley and Thornbury that controlled the land and shorelines along the eastern, English side of the Severn estuary. This does furnish fragmentary glimpses of that artisan fishing dimension at a local and even individual level. In 1255 Peter de Wike is recorded as leasing the fishery at Berkeley Pill – now the site of Berkeley power station – from St Augustine's Priory in Bristol, although by 1370 this had been taken over by the Berkeleys of Berkeley Castle. In 1594 an educated lawyer, John Smyth, became steward to the Berkeleys and made it his business to study the deeds and papers accumulated since the twelfth century.

Smyth eventually produced a family history in three weighty volumes. It is clear from this that fishing was not of great economic importance to what was, in effect, a mini-kingdom within a kingdom. But Smyth was a dutiful recorder, so he did not ignore the great expanse of water that formed the western boundary. For example, he listed the fifty-three known species

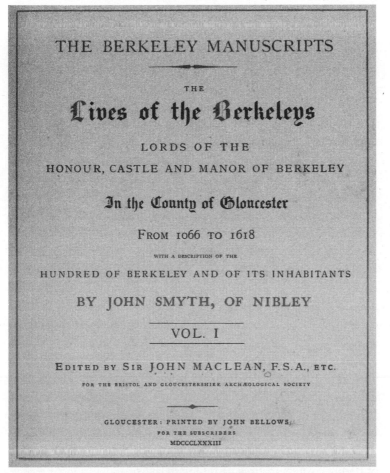

THE BERKELEY MANUSCRIPTS

THE

𝕷𝖎𝖛𝖊𝖘 𝖔𝖋 𝖙𝖍𝖊 𝕭𝖊𝖗𝖐𝖊𝖑𝖊𝖞𝖘

LORDS OF THE
HONOUR, CASTLE AND MANOR OF BERKELEY

𝕴𝖓 𝖙𝖍𝖊 𝕮𝖔𝖚𝖓𝖙𝖞 𝖔𝖋 𝕲𝖑𝖔𝖚𝖈𝖊𝖘𝖙𝖊𝖗

FROM 1066 TO 1618

WITH A DESCRIPTION OF THE

HUNDRED OF BERKELEY AND OF ITS INHABITANTS

BY JOHN SMYTH, OF NIBLEY

VOL. I

EDITED BY SIR JOHN MACLEAN, F.S.A., ETC.

FOR THE BRISTOL AND GLOUCESTERSHIRE ARCHÆOLOGICAL SOCIETY

GLOUCESTER: PRINTED BY JOHN BELLOWS,
FOR THE SUBSCRIBERS
MDCCCLXXXIII

The frontispiece to the 1883 edition of
The Lives of the Berkeleys

of fish from the channel, which included such fictitious oddities as the horncake, the roucote and the thornpole, as well the more familiar salmon, eel, sturgeon and so forth. He also mentioned some of the families involved in the fishing. Among them were the Atwoods, several generations of whom had the fishery known as The Shard at Blackstone Rock between 1548 and the 1620s at annual rents varying from six shillings and eight pence to seven shillings and two pence.

The fishing 'places' changed with the seasons, as the sands shifted with the tides, covering and uncovering the rocks and channels. Some were easier to get at than others. Grove's Hole on the Oldbury estate – recorded in 1696 as having paid tithes 'time out of mind' – was a mile from the access point and was reached by horse and sledge.

Complex rules governed the obligations of tenants. One tide a week was known as 'the lord's tyde' and all the fish taken on it went to the estate. Under the so-called Gale Tax, the lord could appropriate a salmon from the fisherman and pay him half the set price, or require him to pay the same sum to keep it. But if the fisherman managed to move it from the place of capture to somewhere above the high-tide mark and put grass in its mouth, the fish was regarded as exempt. To protect the local interest, all fish had to be offered at Berkeley Market Cross for one hour before they could be taken further afield to be sold.

The estuary is a world apart. It is made from river and sea but belongs to neither. To the eye, the land and sky merge with each other and the water, so that – as Philip Gross put it in a poem about the Severn – 'the hills were clouds and the mist was a shore'. The toing and froing of the tides, covering and uncovering the land, create a realm suffused with dynamism and inconstancy, a wide shifting amalgam of river, sea, land, sky, space and light, shaped by what someone once called 'the never-ending *pas de trois* of earth, water and moon'.

Inevitably those who lived on and from the estuary formed a race apart, geographically and culturally. The rhythms of their daily lives were very different from and more complicated than those of the peasants who worked the land, who rose with the sun and lay down when they could no longer see what they were doing. For the estuary fishermen, the tides – ebb and flow, neap and spring, all the variations between – dictated how they expended their energies. Their inner tide tables would have been spliced into awareness of the seasons: when the spring salmon were running, when the eels would migrate in the first storms of autumn, the arrival and departure of the migrating waders, ducks and geese, the nesting times when eggs would be ready for taking.

They inherited knowledge and added to it. Making and maintaining a fish trap required a major communal effort. It had to be in the right place, and the inconstancy of the estuary meant this changed. A trap would have a limited life span; sometimes it was rebuilt in the same spot, but often the location was shifted, reflecting the impact of erosion on the shorelines and the movement of channels and mudbanks. As the Irish archaeologist Aidan O'Sullivan put it in an illuminating paper, 'Place, Memory and Identity among Estuarine Fishing Communities', they were archaeologists themselves and 'would actively have built their knowledge by their observation of ancient wooden structures on the mudflats'.

These communities would have had contacts with the outside world to trade their catches and pay their dues. But the inherent bias resulting from reliance on written sources – suggesting that the anonymous working classes were closely controlled in their daily lives by the ruling class and regarded their first duty as being to serve the interests of the ruling class – is particularly wide of the mark in this context. These fishing families were geographically and culturally isolated and must have felt themselves so. They had their own language – there are countless Severn words for different aspects of the fishing heritage. They were born, they married, they procreated, they died within the sound and smell of their salty, shared place. They pursued their own interests with not much more than a nod towards wider obligations. Their knowledge and experience were matters of life and death to them, but of no use elsewhere.

With their passing, all that dies with them.

CHAPTER TWO

Night Harvest

Just west of Glastonbury and its myth-laden Tor, the River Brue diverts abruptly from its northern direction and turns north-west in a straight line beside the road to Meare. It is termed a river but it owes very little to the processes that first shaped this soggy landscape.

There are several obvious clues to its artificial provenance. Much of its course is in straight lines or flattened regular curves with none of the normal riverine meanders. It is raised above the surrounding countryside, so that it actually flows above the level of the Meare road. Its embanked sides shut it in, blocking any view from a distance. It has its tributaries, but these – like the mother flow – are drawn in straight lines, their contributions controlled by multiple sluices.

Meare is three miles or so from Glastonbury. The Brue is directed around the north of the village, close but keeping its distance. On the eastern side of Meare there is an irregular tongue of lush green meadow between the river and the road. The land slopes a little up from the river, enough to keep the curious old building that stands on its own in the meadow safe from the floods that have always troubled this region.

I cycled out from Glastonbury on a clear, mellow October evening to see Meare's celebrated Fish House. You cannot miss it: a very plain, upright oblong with pale, worn grey stone walls and a tiled roof, and a very beautiful decorated window in each of its gables. Across the meadow is its companion, the manor house. They were both built in the early fourteenth century, quite possibly by the same hands. With its orchards, vineyard, dovecote and windmill – and the chapel a stone's throw away – Meare's manor house formed an integrated complex.

Meare Fish House

It was laid out for the pleasure of a notable prelate at a time when abbots and bishops were as powerful a force in the land as the lay lords. The manor house, the chapel – subsequently church – and a portion of wall survive, but the orchards, gardens, vineyard, dovecote and windmill do not. Even so, it is quite easy to picture it as it was: a place of ease, even luxury, where the retired Abbot of Glastonbury, Adam of Sodbury, could pray and stroll and receive his guests in his great hall and reminisce about the challenges he faced in keeping Glastonbury pre-eminent among the great religious houses and its assets and estates intact.

But the Fish House does not tell such a straightforward tale. Standing beside it as the light faded, I tried to work out its context, what it was doing there, what its purpose had been and who used it and how, and what the view from it would have comprised. I had read about it at length but relating the words of archaeologists and historians to what was in front of me required an effort of the imagination, as there are few landscapes in Britain that have been more thoroughly transformed over the ages than the Somerset Levels.

Fifteen hundred years before Abbot Sodbury was planning his rural retreat, the region to the north and north-west of Glastonbury Tor would have seemed a forbidding place. The Brue – the 'old' Brue, bearing no resemblance to the regimented watercourse of today – wandered north and found its way through a gap into the Axe valley, where what there was of it joined the Axe itself. It crawled through a swamp, thicketed with scrub, with the occasional patch of slightly raised and drier land covered in alder and birch. There were innumerable ponds and meres, shallow and reedy. Towards Meare the swamp was bounded by a raised peat bog covered by moss, cotton-grass and heather, pitted with hummocks and, again, dotted with pools of water. On the edge of the bog were two substantial humps, drier (but by no means dry) and therefore offering the possibility of human occupation. Around 300 BCE the two humps became the sites of seasonal camps for Iron Age migrants. A little after that – fifty years or so – a similar but drier and more stable bedrock island just north of Glastonbury was occupied and became a permanent settlement of roundhouses with clay walls and floors, hearths and thatched roofs.

Collectively, but misleadingly, all three were dubbed the Somerset Lake Villages when their existence was revealed towards the end of the nineteenth century. The Glastonbury site was certainly a village, occupying almost 1.5 hectares (3.5 acres) and housing as many as two hundred people. Meare was much less stable and congenial, and although brushwood, timber and clay were spread across the bog surface to make temporary floors, no sign of permanent occupation ever came to light.

The excavation of the lake villages was a heroic enterprise instigated, organised and overseen by a Glastonbury-born doctor, Arthur Bulleid, which lasted more than half a century until halted by the imminent outbreak of war in 1938. Vast hoards of Iron Age remains were recovered, which gave a remarkably full picture of how the villagers lived. It is clear that by the standards of the time they were well equipped, well fed, possibly even well content. They had axes, billhooks, sickles, slings, cookpots, wooden ladles, mallets, ladders, metal-toothed saws and doors with iron latches. They wove cloth and worked metal, bone and antlers into useful tools and ornaments. They knew how to rivet sheets of bronze and how to hollow a boat from a trunk of oak. They had iron spears, and some had swords; they had horses for travel and vehicles with spoked wheels. They had necklaces made of amber and glass beads, used tweezers and polished bronze mirrors for personal care, got their whetstones from the shore of the Severn, played games with counters and dice.

They reared sheep, pigs and a few cattle. They hunted red and roe deer, otters, beavers and foxes. They shot or netted a wide range of birdlife including ducks, geese, herons, cormorants and gulls. They foraged nuts, berries, herbs and plants and grew emmer wheat, spelt, barley, rye, oats, peas and beans.

And, of course, they fished. Among the objects found in the camp sites were considerable numbers of sinkers used to hold nets in place. The nets would have been set from their slender shallow-draught boats which were the only practical way of getting around. The villagers would have eaten the occasional salmon traded with fishermen from the Bristol Channel. But their focus closer to home would have been the local species – roach, perch, pike and, much the most important, the abundant, ever-present, tasty, protein-packed freshwater eel.

The Shapwick canoe, discovered in 1906 in an early excavation of the Somerset Lake Villages, is an iron-age dugout canoe.

The lake villages lasted a couple of centuries or so before being abandoned – almost certainly because of rising water levels. Storms raged, the rivers overflowed, the swamp became a patchwork of lakes, and the hummocks and bedrock outposts were invaded. In time the floodwaters closed over where the lake villages had been, covering the sites in silts and clay.

Thereafter this part of the Levels reverted to being an uninhabited watery wilderness. But sometime in the centuries after the end of the Roman occupation, someone – there is no more precision than that – began to tame it for the purposes of human occupation and exploitation. It is likely that the monks of Glastonbury Abbey – founded early in the seventh century CE – directed the process. Certainly by the time the veil obscuring the Anglo-Saxon period was lifted in the histories of William of Malmesbury (twelfth century) and John of Glastonbury (mid-fourteenth), the landscape had changed drastically. By then the draining of the more accessible and amenable parts of the Levels was well advanced.

Most strikingly, the northerly wandering of the Brue towards the Axe valley had been cut off, and a new course engineered to the west that took it to the Bristol Channel at Highbridge. Several other streams had been canalised and new ditches and watercourses constructed to create a network of drainage channels.

One of the consequences of this aquatic rearrangement was the creation of a considerable lake just north of Meare. This was known in the Anglo-Saxon period as the *Ferlingmere*, later as Meare Pool. This haven for fish and wildfowl was the reason Abbot Sodbury had seen fit to commission his Fish House.

The pool was a medium-value asset for Glastonbury Abbey. The Domesday survey lists it as supporting three fisheries paying twenty pence a year each, with ten fishermen. Fish traps along the neighbouring stretch of the new Brue were valued at 100 shillings. By the early twelfth century the manor of Meare, including the pool, was within the Glaston Twelve Hides, an area granted to the abbey in a succession of charters between 670 and 975 CE and subsequently confirmed by Henry I and Henry III.

The legal and fiscal privileges enjoyed by the Hides aroused the envious avarice of successive Bishops of Bath and Wells, Savaric (1191–1205) and Jocelin (1206–41), who intrigued over many years to annex the abbey and its lands. In 1218 a commission awarded a quarter of the abbey's estates, including Meare and eight other manors, to the bishopric. The ruling was subsequently reversed, but there was continuing bad blood between the two Christian power blocs which periodically spilled over into open conflict. There were allegations of trespass, and the mutual rights of turbary – to cut peat for fuel on each other's land – caused endless trouble. The abbot's men destroyed a piggery belonging to the Dean of Bath and Wells. The dean's men breached dykes and pulled down a fish trap belonging to Glastonbury. A fire was started on a Glastonbury peat moor, and horses, oxen, cows, bullocks and pigs worth £200 were stolen at Meare. Eventually the feud petered out, and in 1320 a comprehensive agreement on the division of lands and the protection of reciprocal grazing and other rights was reached.

In the more tranquil atmosphere, Meare became the favoured out-of-town refuge for the abbots of Glastonbury. Although the 'new' Brue acted as an important drainage outlet to the west, its prime function as far as Glastonbury was concerned was as a means of transport to and from Meare. One of the abbey's head boatmen, Robert Malherbe, was charged with bringing the wine from various vineyards, maintaining the waterways, and steering the boat that conveyed the abbot plus cooks, kitchen equipment, huntsmen and hounds to whichever of his residences took his fancy. A steady supply of pike, perch and eels was conveyed along the Brue to the abbey's kitchens.

The Fish House was built to organise and guarantee this supply. There were two floors, the upper of which – two rooms in which the fishermen are assumed to have slept and eaten – was accessed by an external staircase, later destroyed by fire. The three ground-floor rooms were probably used for making, repairing and storing nets and other gear, and perhaps for gutting and cleaning the fish destined for either the manor house or the abbey. Outside, between the building and the pool, were three modest-sized fishponds used for keeping fish alive and, possibly, breeding them.

The extent of the pool would have fluctuated according to the season and the rainfall. Three surveys from the first half of the sixteenth century refer to it as being about a mile long by three-quarters of a mile wide. One of them, carried out in preparation for the imminent dissolution of Glastonbury Abbey, records 'a great abundance of pikes, tenches, roaches and eeles and diverse other kinds of fish'.

In September 1539, on the orders of Thomas Cromwell, the last Abbot of Glastonbury, Richard Whiting, was arrested, subjected to a show trial at Wells, dragged on a hurdle to Glastonbury, hanged on Glastonbury Tor and drawn and quartered, his head being set upon the Abbey gate and the rest of him displayed at Wells, Bath, Ilchester and Bridgewater. It was a typical Cromwell display of ruthlessness and cruelty. 'Let the evidence be well sorted and the indictment well sorted', he wrote on the eve of poor Whiting's trial.

Within a few weeks, the most ancient and perhaps the most beautiful abbey in England had been stripped of its treasures by Cromwell's henchmen and left to rot, its stones dragged away to improve the road to Wells. Meare Pool was not among those treasures but its days were numbered. Attention was beginning to be given to the profits and increased food production made possible by reclaiming wetlands for growing crops. By 1630 a Mr William Freake 'had drayned manie acres of ground' near the pool, and a few years later it was described as 'lately a fish pool . . . drayned so that there is neither fish nor swannes in the same'. By then part of the complex network of canalised rivers and artificial watercourses we see today was in place. But the area remained an intractable one from the point of view of agricultural improvement, and it is likely that part of Meare Pool remained open water into the eighteenth century.

The halting progress of land-improvement schemes in the Somerset Levels was organised and funded by well-to-do landowners eager to augment their income and power. As always, the common people were not consulted, were indifferent to the concept of progress, did the hard labouring required, and put up with the consequences. They would never have shared the assessment of the pre-drainage Levels as a barren wasteland. Like those lake villagers of old, they would have acknowledged what the historian of the Levels, Michael Williams, termed the 'hierarchy of usefulness'. There were pools and sluggish streams abounding with fish and fowl and tasty eggs; beds of reeds and withies to be cut and used to repair roofs and make baskets and traps; deer and otter to be hunted, berries, nuts and plants to be foraged; and there were the drier patches where a few animals could be grazed and crops grown.

The techniques and strategies that enabled the people of the Levels to exploit the natural resources around them did not die because the Levels were drained, tamed and turned over to agriculture. They were always part-time activities, done on the side when other duties permitted, not economically vital but valued extras that contributed immeasurably to the texture of hard lives. A dish of rabbit or venison or grilled eel, a plate of duck eggs, a slug of home-made sloe gin – these were precious treats in an existence characterised by hard slog. Although the overall economy of the Levels was transformed by drainage projects, there was no compelling reason for the people to give up their hunting, foraging ways. They were woven into the tapestry of their world, cherished for helping define who the Levels people were and their heritage.

Meare Pool had gone but the rivers, rhynes, ditches and ponds were still full of fish. And of those fish none was more prized, more persistently pursued, or more deeply etched into the shared consciousness than the freshwater eel.

Almost twenty years ago I wrote a book about the eel and its improbable life cycle. I read everything that had been written about it. I travelled around England, to France, Northern Ireland,

Italy, Denmark and the USA to meet and talk to men who fished for eels, or who had become obsessed with studying them. I fished for them myself, not very successfully, and I dreamed about them persistently.

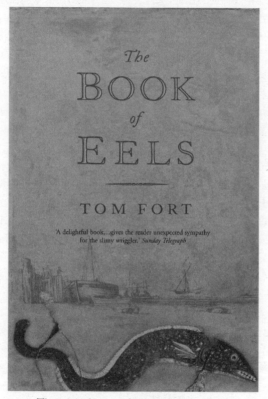

The original cover of *The Book of Eels*, 2002.

Researching and writing that book filled me with an immense sense of wonder at one of the truly astounding life stories of our planet, which I have never lost. The wonder springs from the physiological complexity of the creature; but perhaps more from the contrast between the epic, almost inconceivable migrations with which the life of the eel begins and ends, and the extended period of invisible, sedentary residence in between. I spent many happy library hours poring over the accounts published by the great Danish biologist, Johannes Schmidt, in which he described tracking the route of the eel larvae from the Sargasso Sea to the shores of Europe. Through Schmidt's dry, academic prose I glimpsed the spectacle of the birth in the deep, clear, warm, salty waters of the clouds of minute specks of eel life, and their slow drift on the Atlantic currents.

I stood in the darkness beside an ancient Severn elver fisherman as he dipped his net to intercept a portion of the silver stream of little fish borne inland on the tide. I went out with the last proper Thames eel fisherman and watched him lift his fyke nets from the grey estuary waters out from Erith. I sat with a retired US state trooper on his eel rack on the Delaware River in New York State discussing his dysfunctional family while waiting for the migrating silver eels to run downstream.

As I listened to him, I imagined that same instinct at work along the distant coasts of Europe: eels awakened from years, even decades, of placid, monotonous existence by the silvering of their bellies, the swelling of their sex organs, the widening of their eyes; slipping downriver one black, rain-lashed night to the salt water, and then out to and across the ocean. No one has ever followed that journey, but I could see it in my mind's eye: the meeting and mating and dying beneath the clods of sargassum weed that hang on the surface, the final drift down to the floor of the sea fifteen thousand feet down to be fed on by the outlandish lanternfish and hagfish.

I did my best to communicate that sense of wonder in *The Book of Eels*, as well as recording everything that was known then about the eel, and summarising the mass of informed speculation about what was not known – the unknown exceeding the known by a very long way. Since then the knowledge has increased very little, although the flow of guesswork has continued unabated.

Elver fishermen with their nets on the banks of the River Severn, near Gloucester. Photographed by John Tarlton.

We still do not know what triggers the migratory transformation or how they manage to navigate their way to the Sargasso Sea three thousand miles away, never mind what actually happens when they get there. We do not understand their gender division. We do not understand why some eels stay in salt water and eschew fresh water, while others do the opposite. The population dynamics remain a mystery: we have no idea how abundant eels are, or even where they are.

What has become much clearer since I wrote the book is that their numbers have declined very steeply in the freshwater systems where, until a generation ago, they were abundant. This vanishing from places where they were once common – to take one example, the chalkstreams of southern England – has understandably been interpreted by scientists as proof of a wholesale crash in eel stocks, threatening the very survival of the species. The consensus quoted by experts across Europe is that the population has declined 'by 90 per cent'. They may be right, but they do not know: the figure is an extrapolation. And it is an awkward fact that in some locations – the Thames Estuary, for instance, or Poole Harbour – there are still healthy populations of eel, as far as we know.

That is the nub. The reason we know anything about eel abundance in the past is that people went out to catch them – not because scientists studied them. Eels are easy to catch if there are plenty around and you have spent a lifetime catching them, but hard if you haven't. Scientists generally haven't and are bad at catching them. They used to rely heavily on eel fishermen for data. But for reasons I shall look at more closely later in this book, there are very few eel fishermen left. The data has become ever more sketchy, the temptation to engage in hypothesis more potent.

The Somerset Levels, like the Fens, constituted a perfect domain for the eel. The elvers were sucked into the great maw of the Bristol Channel in their fluttering silver hordes each spring. The majority were drawn onward into the Severn Estuary, but a good proportion were claimed by the north Somerset rivers, principally the Parrett, the Brue and the Tone. If they evaded the battery of predators – including the elver fishermen dipping their big nets in the darkness of night – they filtered inland, replenishing the populations along the rivers and spreading like blood through veins up the tributaries and the streams feeding the tributaries and the network of man-made channels that drained the moors, reaching the pools and ponds. Everywhere they found ideal eel habitat: somewhere to hide, to feed, warm water in summer, soft mud against their bellies to sink into when winter came.

Salmon and eels – throughout our history these have been the two chief food sources among our freshwater species. Although there has been a degree of crossover in the methods of catching them – the putchers on the Severn, for instance, took both – overall they required different approaches and engendered different attitudes. Building, maintaining and monitoring traps for salmon demanded co-operative effort, as did netting; and that effort was focused on particular times of the day as well as seasons, reflecting the limited nature of the opportunities. But the eel is there all the time, and in the half of the year that it is active – say May to October – it can be caught anywhere and at any time.

Eel fishermen do not need to be part of a team. They work alone or with a single partner. They are deeply suspicious of other eel fishermen, fearful that their special places and tricks will be spied on. By nature they are extremely stingy with information, and anything they tell you about their trade should be viewed with the same suspicion that they display to all and sundry. Eel fishermen are not as other men. They are solitary, they are accustomed to lonely, watery places and the night. They like eels.

On the Somerset Levels eels were extremely common and easy to catch. The methods were age-old and simple. You could walk along the edge of a rhyne with an eel spear – a long-handled fork with pronged tines – plunging it into the mud, and be sure to come up with an eel thrashing between the prongs before long. If you laid a sack of straw on the bottom with a length of clay piping stuck in it, the eels would creep in for cover during the night and could be tipped out into a bucket in the morning. Baited traps of woven green willow were put out for them. Another technique was known as rayballing or clotting: worms were threaded into a loose ball of wool and lowered at the end of a pole into a likely spot, where the eels would attack it and snag their teeth on the wool so they could be lifted and dropped into a bucket or sack. Nets were widely used, and in the first storms of autumn the migrating eels – silver, packed with fat for the journey, the best eating – were taken in the traps installed on weirs.

The one significant innovation denied to the old-timers was the arrival from continental Europe in the 1970s of the fyke net. This was neatly described by the celebrated elverer, eel catcher and smoker Michael Brown in his eel memoir *Moonlighting*, as looking like 'a windsock attached to a tennis net'. It is a peculiarity of eels that when they encounter a net on their nocturnal wanderings they follow it. Whoever invented the fyke net – I can find no record of its origins – exploited this tendency by putting together a wall of netting with holding traps at intervals into which the eels stray, and where they seem content to remain until removed and consigned to the food chain.

Leaving the fyke net aside, the continuity stretching back to time immemorial would have enabled the lake village dweller of Glastonbury or Meare two centuries before the life of Christ to know exactly what the eel fisherman on the Brue was up to two thousand years later, and the other way round. Everything else had changed, but not this helping yourself to what nature had provided on your doorstep. Michael Brown's chief helper, Ernie Woods, grew up in the 1930s close to the River Parrett, living on and off the moor. 'I've et everything that moved down on that there moor,' he told Brown. 'Fish, eels, elvers, swan, duck, rabbit, crow – you name en, I've had en.' As a boy Ernie speared eels, skinned them, and sold them around the village. When the elvers ran in the early spring, the family simply dug a trench from the river into their garden to divert a portion their way.

The writer Adam Nicolson went hunting eel fishermen for his book *Wetland: Life on the Somerset Levels*, on which he collaborated with the photographer Patrick Sutherland. One, Arthur Stuckey, described drifting along on the front of the boat poking a fifteen-foot eel spear into the mud. 'You'd catch four or five at a time, they couldn't get out past the notches,' he reminisced.

'But it was banned after the war.' Arthur's father kept an eel trunk in the river, six feet long and with a perforated cover, in which the fish were kept alive until there were enough to be worth sending up to London 'where the Jews wanted them', as Arthur put it delicately.

Although fishing for eels was in the warp and woof of Somerset Levels life, and the supply of eels and the maintenance of eel traps were matters of interest to Glastonbury Abbey and the other religious houses, it was never as significant economically as in that other great expanse of English marshland, the Fens. The tenth-century foundation charters of the Fenland Benedictine monasteries and abbeys illustrate how seriously the monks took their eels. Villages near Wisbech were recorded as catching 16,000 eels a year – half allocated by Bishop Aethelwold to Thorney Abbey, half to Peterborough. Ely's charter of 970 CE included 10,000 eels a year from Outwell and Upwell.

The Domesday survey provided a detailed breakdown of fisheries. The abbots of Ramsey and Peterborough were recorded as having a boat each on the great expanse of water known as Whittlesey Mere, north of Holme Fen in what is now Cambridgeshire, while Thorney had two. Ramsey also received rents measured in tens of thousands of eels from fishermen at Wells, on the Norfolk/Cambridgeshire border, and in the later Middle Ages snapped up eel fisheries all over the place.

The sheer abundance of fish in Fenland was evidently a standing joke. The chronicler William of Malmesbury wrote in the twelfth century: 'There is such a quantity of fish as to cause astonishment in strangers, while the natives laugh at their surprise.' The *Liber Eliensis* of about the same time recorded the capture of 'innumerable eels, large water-wolves [*lupi aquatici* in Latin, presumably pike] . . . roach, burbots [now extinct in Britain but still found in Scandinavia] and lampreys . . . together with the royal fish, the sturgeon.'

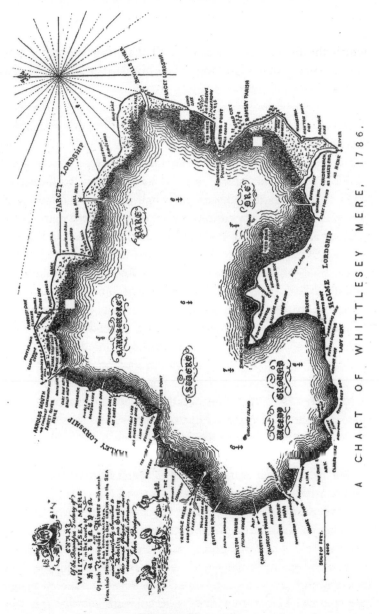

Whittlesey Mere, 1786.

It was common practice to calculate rents in 'sticks' of eels, a stick comprising twenty-five fish. The busiest time for transactions was Lent, for obvious reasons, even though at that time of year the eels would, most likely, have been salted ones from the previous season. When Ramsey agreed to pay four thousand eels per annum to Peterborough in return for a supply of Barnack stone to build its abbey, it was stipulated that the fish should be delivered in time for Lent.

The eel economy of the Fens was unusually valuable and therefore well documented. But wherever eels were found in England – they bothered with them much less in Scotland and Wales, where they had salmon – they were trapped, netted and speared, and eaten and traded. Monasteries and secular lords maintained traps all the way up and down the Severn and Thames, for example, which were used to take salmon when there were salmon, and silver eels in the autumn migration.

But the written records are dry and transactional. They show the fishing was happening, who owned it, how much it was worth, but reveal nothing about who was doing it and how. Records of court proceedings provide an occasional snippet: how at Littleport, north-east of Ely, one 'John Beystens drew the pool at Wellenheath by night and carried thence fish price 6d and that he ought to be removed out of the vill'; how 'Walter of the Moor against the peace of the lord came on such a night at the hour of midnight and entered the preserve of the lord . . . and carried off at his will every kind of freshwater fish . . . and carried the fish with him and made boasts of this . . .'

On the whole it was not until much later, when educated men and women discovered the excitement of travel and became curious about what was going on in distant places, that more information emerged. Many generations of Fenland families had fished Whittlesey Mere and helped themselves to its reeds, sedge and wildfowl before that tireless seventeenth-century traveller Celia Fiennes passed by and observed it to be '3 mile broad and

six long . . . in the midst is a little island where there is a great
story of wildfowl . . . the ground is all wet and marshy . . . ye
Mer is often very dangerous by reason of sudden winds but at
other times people boat it round with pleasure . . . there is abundance of good fish in it . . .'

Whittlesey survived the organised draining of the Fens and
continued to function as a valuable natural resource well into the
nineteenth century. Trading boats were able to ply between the
mere and the town of Whittlesey and a considerable business
was done in cutting reeds for thatching and sending them all
over the country. A reed merchant from Yaxley, Joseph Coles,
paid £700 a year for the fowling, fishing and reeding rights.
Gradually, though, the mere was silting up and in 1848 the local
bigwigs co-operated in having it drained and converted into
agricultural land. Great crowds gathered to watch Whittlesey
Mere's death throes, and to help themselves to the multitudes
of stranded fish − which included a vast eel 'with a head as big
as a dog's and teeth that bit through the heel of a gutter boot'.

The mere was no more and the Whittlesey fishermen − their
voice entirely unheard − presumably went off to try elsewhere.
There were plenty of alternative venues − the draining of the
Fens over the centuries had created a huge network of artificial
channels, all of them high-grade residential areas for eels. The
fishing went on, and just occasionally an eel-fisher made himself
heard.

One such was Ernie James of Welney, one of the last of the
true Fen Tigers, the term for those who lived in the remote
pockets of fenland that had survived the drive for reclamation,
and deployed diverse means to make their livings. Ernie James
was born in 1906 and brought up in his parents' cottage which
stood between the Delph and the Old Bedford rivers. He was
chiefly celebrated as a punt gunner, and one of his clients in that
capacity was James Wentworth Day, an assiduous chronicler of
Fenland life (also an extreme right-wing High Tory bigot whose

brief career as an early TV pundit was terminated after he offered his opinion that all homosexuals should be hanged).

In his *A History of the Fens* Wentworth Day reproduced a lengthy letter from Ernie James which gives a strong flavour of the Fen Tiger life. James's father had a line in selling eel grigs – traps made from withies from his own osier beds beside the Delph – and Ernie James recalled getting forty stone in a night during a summer flood, he and his father emptying the grigs at midnight and again at 4am. He described glaiving, their word for spearing: 'I used to do some glaiving . . . but since the Delph was dredged the eels don't stop like they used to . . . I have often glaived a stone out in three hours then skinned them and sold them in the village. Hard work, I can tell you.'

Wentworth Day also included an affectionate, even loving portrait of William Kent, from a family of 'punt-gunners, eel-catchers, reed cutters, pike fishermen and makers of things with their hands', crafting a six-foot eel grig using his own withies. 'When I was a boy', Wentworth Day sighed, 'every dyke and lode had its grigs, which one could see lying shadowy amid the forests of water weeds on the bottom. Nowadays you could walk through the Fens for a month and never see a grig set.'

That was 1954. Ernie James lived to be ninety-nine and was still trapping eels into his nineties. But they have all gone now, the last of the Fen Tigers, and the eel fishermen of the Somerset Levels. I do not mean that no one takes eels any more, because a handful do. But that way of life – a weaving together of different but complementary and sustainable ways of exploiting the natural world around – has gone and will never return.

I spent a while strolling around Meare's Fish House, trying in my mind to make sense of the past, to relate the tranquil flat meadows stretching away from the River Brue – the grazing cattle, the pylons, the functional farm buildings – to the fishy, watery history. I carted my bike over a gate and across a footbridge over

the Brue, then pedalled strenuously along some of the embankments, occasionally having to dismount and push when the grass
was too thick.

The map showed the various channels dug to keep the landscape in order and restrain Meare Pool from coming back to life:
Pitts Rhyne, Waste Rhyne, Decoy Rhyne, Galton's Canal, White's
River, James Wear River. They are quite mysterious, these ruler-
straight, sunken pathways of water – dark, steep-sided, reedy,
weedy, still.

The Brue, however – as befits the senior watercourse – boasted
a perceptible current. A little way below the confluence with
White's River and above the bridge taking the old road known
as the Blakeway over the Brue, I saw fish moving – not tiddlers,
but decent fish. At first I thought they must be chub, but they
did not behave in the leisurely way chub do. They seemed more
urgent, as if searching for something. I wondered if they might
possibly be an adventurous shoal of grey mullet – it is no more
than ten miles to the sea, and mullet do wander.

I saw no eels. But they were there, somewhere.

CHAPTER THREE

A Passion for Ponds

I like to picture Prior More of Worcester on a fine summer's morning in, say, 1521. He has said mass in the cathedral and had a series of conversations on administrative matters with certain monks under his direction. Now he is free to consider other things on his mind.

He walks slowly from the cathedral along the cloisters and out onto the green leading to the broad River Severn, deep in thought. He is of medium height, slightly plump, conspicuously well-fed, his cheeks coloured like the blush on a Worcester apple. He considers how well he has done for himself: born forty-eight years ago to parents of modest means in a modest village a few miles upstream, 'shaven into ye religion ye 16th day of June, St Botolph's Day AD 1488', his uphill path starting in the priory kitchen as a lowly servant.

William is now, by some distance, the most powerful man

in Worcester, powerful enough to be designated My Lord Prior. The city has a bishop, of course: Silvestro de' Gigli, an Italian who has never left the shores of Italy and would not know where to find Worcester on a map (his equally absent successor, Giulio di Medici, would become Pope Clement VII in a few years). But by ancient privilege granted from Rome, the prior is entitled to wear a mitre and ring, carry a pastoral staff, and give solemn benediction at mass and table. He is bishop in all but name.

He has wealth and power. His standing is that of a regional magnate. He entertains the gentry and the civic leaders. When a great personage such as the child Princess Mary Tudor comes to visit Worcester, she and her entourage stay with him and he is in charge of all arrangements and festivities. Most years he spends several weeks in London, where he entertains powerful prelates and courtiers. Otherwise he passes weeks at a time at one or other of the priory's manors, in which he takes a keen interest. In fact he is not often in Worcester itself, although he is careful to be present for Christmas, Easter, Quinquagesima, the Rogations and the other important Christian festivals.

This morning William's tonsured head is full of calculations and assessments relating to his native village, Grimley, and his plans for it. How much clay will be needed to build up the first dam? How will the spring be kept clear? Where should the sluice be best placed? How much should he pay for the stakes to reinforce the banks? When should the stocking be made and how many? How many eels should he require to be delivered at the wharf?

Prior More takes out a small book and makes some notes. Later he will itemise the work he is to commission and the cost in his journal. He is a man with a considerable passion for fish-ponds and in the England of 1521, with his position and power, he has ample means and opportunity to indulge it.

JOURNAL

OF

PRIOR WILLIAM MORE.

EDITED FOR
THE WORCESTERSHIRE HISTORICAL SOCIETY
BY
ETHEL S. FEGAN, M.A.
LIBRARIAN OF THE LADIES' COLLEGE, CHELTENHAM.

Printed for the Worcestershire Historical Society,
By MITCHELL HUGHES AND CLARKE, LONDON, W.
1914.

The frontispiece of the 1914 edition of the
Journal of Prior William More.

It is recorded that in 1257 Henry III and his court celebrated St
Edward's Day, 13 October, with a feast for which 300 pike, 250
bream and no fewer than 15,000 eels (I have my doubts about
that figure) were supplied. Where the organisers secured such a
vast multitude of eels is unknown, but it is a fair bet that some
of them, and some of the other fish, would have come from one
or other of the networks of artificial fishponds maintained at the
Crown's expense in various parts of the country.

Fishponds were symbols and expressions of status and wealth
– like bowling-greens in the seventeenth century, landscaped

parks in the eighteenth, follies in the nineteenth, or giant yachts and football clubs in our own time. The science of constructing ponds to breed and store freshwater fish can be assumed to have arrived here from France in the wake of William I and his knights. There was a royal pond or system of ponds on the north-east side of Stafford as early as the middle of the twelfth century; the records show it was let to William, son of Wymer, for half a mark. A later Wymer, Ralph, was allocated three oaks to repair it, and around 1250 the order came from London for one hundred bream, one hundred tench and thirty pike to be taken, salted and transported to Westminster without delay.

The pond at Stafford must have been highly productive. In 1281 the king's fisherman, the queen's saucemaker and 'a boy' were sent there for two weeks with instructions to send the catch to Edward I in Wales. The saucemaker was paid three shillings for his work, the king's fisherman and the boy shared four shillings and a penny.

The records of the palace at Woodstock in Oxfordshire are peppered with references to repairs to the fishponds fed by the River Glyme, and to stocking them. The bailiff was instructed to secure one thousand pike 'wherever he might find them' to stock the king's stew. William, the king's fisherman, was sent to get six pike and deliver them salted to his employer. The royal ponds at Marlborough were a notable source of bream for breeding, which were supplied – presumably at a price – to fish fanciers in Lincolnshire, Wiltshire, Gloucestershire and elsewhere.

Where the king led, lords and bishops and abbots tended to follow, in the matter of fishponds as in other tastes. The proliferation of fast days prescribed in accordance with the teaching of St Benedict was a distinct stimulus to the eating of fish and the trade in supplying them. But, as the social historian of the Middle Ages, Professor Christopher Dyer, has elegantly demonstrated, the consumption of saltwater fish – generally salted cod or herrings – greatly exceeded that of freshwater fish. That applied even when the consumer was far from the sea. For example, the accounts of Bishop John Hales of Coventry and Lichfield show that in 1461 he and his household ate two-and-a-half times as many sea fish as freshwater fish (overall consumption of fish was a little under half that of meat).

Fishponds were laborious and expensive to construct and laborious and expensive to maintain and clean. It took several years for fish stocked in infancy to reach a size fit for the feast, plus a considerable investment in planning. In many parts of the country the secular and ecclesiastical powers were in the happy position of owning fishing rights on rivers where the most prized species for eating – salmon and eels – could be trapped at comparatively low cost. It was often more convenient and cheaper simply to buy in fish caught elsewhere as and when they were available.

The rich and powerful liked the idea of fishponds for a while, but when the bills came in and kept coming their interest tended to wane. It took a true enthusiast to persist with them. One such was Prior William More.

I had a long, draining day on the trail of More's enthusiasms. I took the train to Worcester with my bicycle and – having visited the city's spanking new library, The Hive, to learn more about my subject – set off up the left bank of the Severn full of vim and investigative vigour.

I was aiming for the prior's home village of Grimley, which is on the other bank of the river four or five miles upstream from Worcester and about halfway to the next bridge. I had looked at the map – closely, I thought, but not closely enough – and had reasoned that I would be able to cross by means of the weir at Bevere Island. My reasoning was faulty; I could not even get to the weir, let alone cross it (which I wouldn't have been able to do anyway, it being a weir without a bridge).

The annoying consequence was that I had to keep pedalling

Worcester and its cathedral viewed from the Severn, 1829

find Grimley. The annoyance was intensified by my decision to forsake the noisy road for the riverside footpath, which was picturesque and afforded pleasing views of the river – including Grimley on the other side – but was very bumpy and liberally equipped with stiles that had to be surmounted by me and bike.

By the time I reached Grimley I had used up more of my day than I had allowed for, and had been forced to cycle much harder than I like to. I was hot and bothered and Grimley's charms were not of an order to soothe my savage breast – not immediately, anyway. It retains the name it had in Pilot More's day, but precious little else. It straggles pleasantly enough along a minor road off the A443, with the Severn curving its leisurely way beyond the fields to the east, but there is nothing at all distinctive about it. The church was restored beyond recognition in the nineteenth century, and the manor house on which More lavished so much attention and spending disappeared long ago.

As for his fishponds – his 'parke poole at grymley . . . ye mere at grymley . . . ye myddul poole in ye parke at grymley . . . ye stanke . . . ye fur poole at grymley . . . ye utter poole in grymley parke . . . ye stewe at grymley . . .' – they are not easy to locate and still harder to match to his references. According to the scheduling by Historic England, the three main ponds were elongated, narrow rectangles aligned north/south along the backs of what are now the gardens and paddocks of the houses on the east side of the road through Grimley. They are a lot easier to spot from Google Maps than they are from the ground, as they are concealed within thickets of alder and willow and undergrowth and behind barriers of reeds. But I did eventually fight my way through the vegetation and over a fence and was rewarded by glimpses of muddy banks and open water, although it was no more than a few inches deep. A definite pond, nonetheless.

When the ponds were being dug, the land around was organised in blocks of medieval ridge-and-furrow fields. Now it is all ploughed and made productive in the modern way, but the ponds and their immediate surroundings have been left to their own devices behind barbed wire, presumably because the ground is too marshy and clayey to be worth reclaiming. All that engineering – the dams and embankments, the leats, the sluices, the channels that fed the ponds from a spring to the north – has been taken back into the earth and swallowed up. But it is consoling that the whole intricate system and the mark it made have not been entirely erased.

Prior More was evidently an attentive son to his parents. When his father died at Grimley in February 1520, William ordered three hundred herrings, three salt fish and four salmon (two-and-sixpence on their own) for the funeral feast. His mother followed the next year, her passing marked by the singing of dirges in the cathedral (three-and-fourpence) and in Grimley church (one shilling). Her funeral breakfast included mutton, beef, pork and six geese, abundant bread and ale, and a great deal else. Fourpence was paid to 'Rd. Sawyer for dygging of ye pit in ye chauncel'.

Having found water in Grimley, it was time to head for another of Prior More's fishpond projects, at Battenhall on the southern fringe of Worcester. The complex is located in a shallow trough of agricultural land bounded to the east and south by the A4440 and on its other sides by the surburbs of Red Hill, Battenhall and St Peter's. As at Grimley, the manor house is no more, but its site – immediately to the north of the ponds – is occupied by Middle Battenhall Farm, a mainly seventeenth-century farmhouse with outbuildings now converted into very smart residences. The fishponds, three of them, are rough grazing although the layout and embankments and the old ridge-and-furrow fields around are fairly easy to discern.

Judging by the amount of time he spent there, Prior More seems to have preferred Battenhall to Grimley. He kept an 'ambling grey mare' there and recorded the arrival of her foals. He kept an eye on the swannery – 'upon seynt Dunstan's daye the swannes at Batnall browt forth four cynets in to ye poole'. He had the bedchambers hung with rich painted cloths, installed a new stained-glass window, hired bears for baiting and jugglers to provide amusement at dinner, and generally entertained in a manner befitting a country squire of exceptionally ample means.

Then there were the ponds – 'ye mot . . . ye nether poole . . . ye dey poole . . . ye over parke poole' and so on. He spent consistently and considerably on their construction and main- **tenance** – 'item ye clansynge of ye pool at Batnall with carige besides mete and drynke 102s 7d . . . item to John Kervar his man and 2 sawyers at batnal for making ye flud leat 3s 3d'. In summer the ponds were stocked with eels, presumably caught from the Severn where there were plenty. Tench were the next most popular species, with more modest numbers of bream, roach and small pike, which were stocked in winter.

Owing to more inept map-reading, it took me some time to locate Prior More's handiwork at Battenhall. By the time I had finished wandering around the somewhat unexciting mounds and dips and inspecting the overgrown trickle that fed the system, the afternoon was well advanced and I realised that I was not going to get to the prior's third country residence at Crowle, which is a few miles east of Worcester and would become the chosen place of his retirement.

Unlike me, William travelled in style, with a retinue of four gentlemen, ten yeomen, ten grooms, chaplain, steward and assorted lowly servants. Crowle was another moated manor house, originally built in the thirteenth century and substantially extended and refurbished for the comfort of the prior. His journal shows that over the years he spent heavily on it and its water features. The house – with its chapel, dining-hall, great kitchen and spacious chambers – was decorated with all manner of hanging cloths. The chambers were fitted with feather beds and the down pillows were covered in satin. Everything was itemised from the '18 platers . . . pottygers . . . sawcers' in the kitchen to the 'candilstycks and dashell'* in the chapel.

Outside, the moat was by 1533 'perfett made and fynyshed upon seynt Luke's day . . . whych mote cost in ye hoole charge £8 19s 3d'. The following spring it was stocked with '18 tenches' and '46 store breams', with more to follow. Everything – including the pigeon-house, the tithe barn and the smaller ponds – was made ready for Prior More's retirement from what had been a busy if not conspicuously holy working life.

But he nearly came unstuck. His success in life had not come without arousing envy, and he had made his enemies. Besides that, politics and the great divorce struggle between Henry VIII and Rome were sending waves out even as far away as Worcester. Complaints were made about More's lavish spending, favour-itism, accounting methods and ostentatious extravagance. He was accused of diverting alms intended for the poor to his own servants. There is a tantalising reference in a letter to Thomas

---

* A dashell is a brush for sprinkling holy water.

Cromwell from Hugh Latimer (appointed Bishop of Worcester in 1535 and later burned at the stake) to a 'great crime' of More's – that of permitting one of his monks 'to use treasonable language about the king's divorce and the character of Anne Boleyn'.

The downfall of Wolsey, the break with Rome, and finally the appointment of Cromwell as Visitor-General of religious houses, combined with the mutterings against him from within his own power base, persuaded the canny prior that it was time to slip away from the main stage. He took advantage of the lenient terms being offered to the 'heads of houses' who acquiesced in their own dissolution to negotiate favourable terms for his retirement.

More was given the use of Crowle for his lifetime with a pension of £50 a year, plus a lodging in Worcester 'with wood and fuel sufficient'. His debts of £100 were paid off and he was presented with silver cups, spoons and goblets as well as sheets, tablecloths, napkins and everything else he might require. In 1535 he took himself quietly off to Crowle, at which point his journal falls silent.

The destruction and upheaval that saw Prior More quit the scene and poor Abbot Whiting of Glastonbury hanged, disembowelled and dismembered were the cause of much satisfaction and advantage to others. Among them was that energetic henchman of Cromwell and instrument of Henry VIII's capricious will, Thomas Wriothesley, later Sir Thomas, later still the 1st Earl of Southampton.

As a reward for his assiduous work 'in the King's great business' and in the pulling down of shrines and images and in sundry other matters, Wriothesley received some of the choicest monastic estates available – including Quarr Abbey on the Isle of Wight, Hyde Abbey near Winchester, Beaulieu Abbey on the west side of the Solent, and Titchfield Abbey on the east side.

Thomas Wriothesley (1505–1550), 1st Earl of Southampton,
painted by Hans Holbein the Younger, c. 1535.

Titchfield was the choicest of them all. The Premonstratensian
abbey comprised a church, cloisters, chapter house, richly stocked
library and living quarters. The immediate surroundings consisted
of gardens, orchards, stables, a farm and a string of ancient fishponds in a natural hollow descending towards the River Meon.
Beyond were the estates: nine thousand acres of land, fifteen
manors, six dovecotes, six windmills and the rest. Wriothesley
had had his acquisitive eye on it for some time and did his utmost
to persuade the last abbot to hand it over voluntarily rather than

Titchfield Abbey

under compulsion. He succeeded, and in December 1537 secured possession. He sold off what he did not want – the marble, sculptures, altars and fittings from the church – and set about converting the buildings into a residence befitting the man who, before long, would be the king's Lord Chancellor.

A castellated gatehouse with four octagonal turrets became the entrance to Wriothesley's Place (a corruption of palace) House. Parts of the old church, including its tower, were demolished. The cloister became the central courtyard, the refectory grew into his great hall, and the rest of the abbey was converted into sumptuous apartments. There were four main fishponds, each feeding into the next one down; the three lower ones rectangular and the top one oblong. They were inspected by the new owner's project manager and found to be good – 'a mile in length . . . containing 100,000 carpes, tenches, breams and pike'.

The reference to carp is notable. The Letters and Papers of Henry VIII state: 'The bailey will give Wriothesley 500 carp . . . Mr Huttuft providing the freight, Mr Mylls tubs, Mr Wells conveyance of the carps so that in 3 or 4 years time he may sell £20 to £30 of them every year . . .'

Carp were imports from the Low Countries. The first authenticated mention of them comes from the household accounts of the 1st Duke of Norfolk, which state that on 15 May 1462 'my master putt into the mylle pond . . . gret carpes' as well as 'gret tenches . . . gret and smale bremes' along with roach and perch. The ponds seem to have been located near Layham in Suffolk, and there are several further references to 'my master' personally stocking his ponds. An entry for September 1465 refers to gifts of carp being made by the duke to 'my lady Waldegrave' and several others.

Originating from the lower Danube basin, probably in present-day Slovakia, carp had long been the domesticated freshwater fish of choice across continental Europe. Their virtues were manifold: they tolerated wide variations in temperature as well as low oxygen levels, grew fast and to a large size, were easy to breed and were catholic in their eating habits, and – compared with rivals such as bream and tench – made a tasty as well as substantial dinner.

It is strange that they should have taken so long to arrive in Britain. By the time the Duke of Norfolk was taking delivery of the first consignment for his ponds, there were 25,000 carp ponds and lakes in Bohemia, some of enormous size (and still producing big harvests of carp for the table today). It is the case that by then the heyday of pond construction in England had passed, but many of the existing ponds remained in use, and the manuals of the time show that the carp rapidly found favour with the discriminating pond owner.

It is not known if Thomas Wriothesley had a particular interest in the ponds at Titchfield Abbey. Given his other activities – diplomacy, intriguing against his former patron Cromwell, attempting to have Catherine Parr arrested, persecuting heretics and supervising the torture of the Protestant martyr, Anne Askew, and amassing a huge fortune – he may have lacked the time for more than the occasional stroll past their still waters. The later years of his shortish life – he died in 1550 aged forty-five – were largely devoted to his unavailing efforts to remain a power in the land in the immediate post-Henry period.

The mansion he had grafted onto the old abbey – 'a right stately house embattelid' in the words of the antiquary John Leland – survived him by a couple of centuries. Eventually much of it was dismantled by a subsequent owner, which had the effect of restoring to view a substantial portion of the original abbey, forming the romantic ruins still standing today.

The ponds, which preceded the arrival of Wriothesley and his minions by two hundred years, have fared even better. They must have been exceptionally well engineered, because they are still there – not as dips and lumps in the land or patches of reedy marsh, as with Prior More's ponds, but substantial sheets of water of the kind to get any angler's nose twitching. And the fish are there: tench, bream, roach and fine, fat common and mirror carp. Their welfare is attended to by the Portsmouth and District Angling Society (founded 1948) which obviously cherishes them and those who fish for them, judging from the sturdy platforms for anglers to sit in comfort, litter bins, notices and car park.

There was no one fishing the day I visited; it was October, when the best of the tench and carp fishing is over for the season. Autumn was in the air and the still, dark surfaces of the ponds were speckled with the first fallen leaves. I hoped to see the roll of a carp or a glimpse of the slab side of a bream, but it was very quiet. Extremely fishy, though, and marvellously secluded in a thick belt of trees that effectively muffled the snarl of the A27 half a mile away.

Carp became very popular as a luxury food item, and gave an extra incentive for some pond owners to look after their waters. Roger North in his *Discourse of Fish and Fish-Ponds*, published in 1713, wrote of the pleasure to be had from being able to 'gratify your family and friends that visit you with a Dish as acceptable as any you can purchase with Money; or you may oblige your friends and neighbours by making Presents of them'.

North, a son of Lord North, moved in elevated social circles and may well have discussed this matter of mutual interest with Lord Wharton, whose great estate at Winchendon near Aylesbury

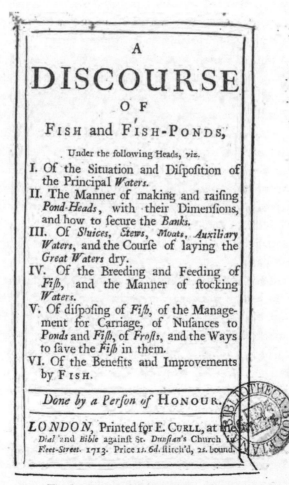

A

DISCOURSE

OF

FISH and FISH-PONDS,

Under the following Heads, *viz.*

I. Of the Situation and Disposition of the Principal *Waters*.

II. The Manner of making and raising *Pond-Heads*, with their Dimensions, and how to secure the *Banks*.

III. Of *Sluices*, *Stews*, *Moats*, *Auxiliary Waters*, and the Course of laying the *Great Waters* dry.

IV. Of the Breeding and Feeding of *Fish*, and the Manner of stocking *Waters*.

V. Of disposing of *Fish*, of the Management for Carriage, of Nusances to *Ponds* and *Fish*, of *Frosts*, and the Ways to save the *Fish* in them.

VI. Of the Benefits and Improvements by FISH.

Done by a Person of HONOUR.

LONDON, Printed for E. CURLL, at the Dial *and Bible against* St. *Dunstan's Church in* Fleet-Street. 1713. Price 1*s.* 6*d.* stitch'd, 2*s.* bound.

The frontispiece of the 1713 edition of
A Discourse of Fish and Fish-Ponds by Roger North.

included a number of ponds that he managed attentively. The records of the estate for 1686 reveal that the ponds were 'drawn' – presumably netted – between October and January: 'I did draw Sir William Stanhope's Pond and did leave and put into it since 254 Good big Carps . . . I did draw Spratlies Pond and I left in it and have into since 300 tench and 90 great Carps . . . the Horspond was drawn, I took 300 Great Carps out of it and put them in the pond next to it . . . in the Great Pond by the town there is 300 great Carp besides tench . . .'

Having earlier imagined Prior More walking through the cathedral precincts in Worcester planning the construction of his fishponds, I picture him now in his retirement in his manor house at Crowle surrounded by its moat.

It would hardly be apt to call his retirement well deserved, for he was a distinctly worldly prior even by the worldly standards of his time, conspicuous for rich living and prodigal spending of other people's money rather than piety or attention to his devotions. He was fortunate to have reached retirement at all – many of his kind paid with their lives for their dedication to comfort. William was shrewd as well as lucky, and he spent many years at Crowle before dying in 1552 in Alveston, a village in Warwickshire where his brother Richard – a Bristol wine merchant who had profited well on orders from Worcester – had made his home.

I see William emerging from the front door of the manor house on another summer's day in, say, 1546. Far away in London the king who visited such turbulence on the monks of Worcester is dying, gout-wrecked, ulcerated, obese. The vultures are gathering around him. But in Worcestershire peace reigns. The sun is lighting up the gables of the old house and the gardens and orchards beyond. The prior walks more slowly than when he was planning his great works. They are done now, and he approaches his favourite among them, the moat that encloses the house, with the tithe barn close by and the church reflected in the water.

He recalls the good times he has had here: William Smythe's wedding, for which William gave five shillings so his servants could feast and carouse; the village bonfire on St Thomas's Night, for which he supplied cakes, sack and 'a quarte of red wynne'; a St James's Day party at his neighbours the Winters, with minstrels, players and jugglers.

He reaches the bank of the moat and remembers that day in 1533 when he recorded in his journal that it was completed. He looks across its forty-foot width, and his eyes follow it as it curves around the garden's edge. It is well made, he says to himself. The sun goes behind a cloud, comes out again, and the surface glows. He sees a broad back, a great golden flank, a round rubbery mouth opening and closing, the slow ripple of disturbance.

He thinks of his dinner. A dish of carp, roasted, with rosemary, marjoram, thyme and parsley folded into its belly.

CHAPTER FOUR

An Angle on Fishing

By seven o'clock on a mid-June weekday morning Tottenham Hale had come to noisy life. Overground and underground trains clattered into the station every minute, exhaling commuters in regular breaths to swarm up and down the staircases and onto the pavements. Traffic juddered along the A10, dispersing towards Walthamstow, Haringey, Wood Green or on towards the centre of London. Everyone else seemed to know where they were going, moving purposefully towards their destinations. I drove hesitantly, causing irritation around me, then saw a sign: Ferry Lane.

Where there's a ferry lane, I thought, there must have been a ferry, and where there was a ferry there must have been water to cross. I turned left onto it, then left again onto Mill Mead Lane, which also sounded promisingly watery. I passed a cluster of new apartment blocks with names like Egret Heights and Lapwing Heights, collectively calling itself Hale Village but certainly not my idea of a village. Thus I came to the Weighbridge Café where I fortified myself with a major fry-up before getting my bike out of the back of the car and setting off past the allotments in search of the river.

Old Izaak Walton would have fortified himself, not at the Weighbridge Café, but at the Swan, just across from Tottenham High Cross. To get there from his home in Chancery Lane would have required a dawn start, as it is a good ten-mile walk. But they thought nothing of such exertions four hundred years ago; he and his friend, the chef Thomas Barker, would have worked up a keen appetite, getting keener all the way up Tottenham Hill.

An engraving of Tottenham High Cross, published in 1840.

An engraving of Tottenham Mills on the River Lea, published in 1840.

If it was a fine warm morning they might have cooled off in the arbour in front of the inn, where woodbine, jasmine, sweet-briar and myrtle interwove to shade the perspiring traveller. They might have shared a bottle of sack, milk, oranges and sugar, 'a drink like nectar'. Then, carrying their wicker creels, sixteen-foot rods, ale-stained horsehair lines, and other accessories all supplied by John Margrave at the Sign of the Three Trouts in St Paul's Churchyard, they would have set off for the river.

Not past Kwik Fit Tyres, Currys, Halfords, the Golden Buffet and BP Express Shopping, obviously. Tottenham was a true village then, strung out along its High Road, bounded to the north and east by the soggy wilderness of the marshes. The River Lea, the destination of the two anglers, wound its way through the marshes and on towards the Thames. But even then the extended process of taming the river and making it useful had already begun. Thanks mainly to the visionary energy of a Welsh-born entrepreneur, Sir

Hugh Myddleton, a twenty-mile artificial waterway known as the New River had been engineered along the Lea valley between Ware and Hertford in Hertfordshire to Islington to bring drinking water from springs along its course to thirsty Londoners.

Myddleton's New River was completed in 1613, when Walton was twenty. A year later Walton was the owner of 'half a shop' in Fleet Street, close to the junction with Chancery Lane. Within a few more years he was accepted into the Ironmongers' Company. He was in trade, but social divisions were not so rigid then. Although he was the son of a Stafford innkeeper, he was educated in the classics; he knew the poet and divine John Donne who preached at St Dunstan's in Fleet Street, and he moved in educated, literary circles.

It is pointless to try to date precisely the famous walk along the Lea from Tottenham to Ware and back, around which Walton shaped his *The Compleat Angler*. There was no such walk, no one expedition. This is a literary device, deployed to create an appearance of a narrative structure while concealing the true purpose, which was to collect between the covers of one book everything Walton had ever learned about the recreation of angling, everything he had read, and everything that other anglers who were his friends or acquaintances had told him.

To anchor the device of the journey, Walton provided a smattering of specific locations: Tottenham Hill, Tottenham High Cross, the Thatched House at Hoddesdon where Venator the huntsman declares his intention to 'drink my morning's draught'; Amwell Hill, where Mr Sadler has organised an otter hunt; Theobald's House, a royal palace just north of what is now the M25 near Cheshunt, the sight of which interrupts Piscator's lengthy lecture on the properties of water and the beauties of classical antiquity; the George at Ware, whose landlord 'host Rickarbie' displays a drawing of a very large trout.

However, the sequence of events is impossible to follow because there is no sequence. At the end we find ourselves back at

Tottenham High Cross, without actually ever having been in
Ware, and with no more than the haziest idea of where the
protagonists' footsteps have taken them or where they laid their
heads at night.

The flaws and faults of Walton's classic are very obvious. He
is incoherent, discursive, disorganised, obscure. He is childishly
credulous, ready to throw in any absurd myth about the prop-
agation of eels or the savagery of pike. His section on fly fishing
is borrowed entirely from his friend Thomas Barker's *The Art
of Angling*, and the tedious section comparing the respective
merits of hunting, hawking and angling was largely lifted from
the anonymous *The Gentleman's Recreation*, which came out
between the fourth and fifth editions of *The Compleat Angler*.
In fact Walton lifted other people's work left, right and centre,
including the dialogue form, usually without troubling to
acknowledge the debt.

So why bother with him? And how do we account for the
immortality of his book? More than four hundred editions
since its first appearance in 1653 testify to an appeal unmatched
by any prose work of its time and precious few since. Yet my
friend Jeremy Paxman called Walton 'unreadable . . . cumbersome, arch and dropsically embroidered'. Paxman's case is that
the man who should get the credit for *The Compleat Angler* is
not Walton at all, but his much younger friend (and, in effect,
adopted son) Charles Cotton. For the fifth edition, published
in 1676, Walton commissioned Cotton to provide a Part Two,
'Instructions How to Angle for a Trout or Grayling in a Clear
Stream'.

It is true that Cotton's advice is sound, very much more so
than the tips randomly scattered by Walton. But as prose,
Cotton's work is as inferior to the older man's as it is superior
in usefulness. He apes the dialogue form, but there is no spark,
no voice, no charm. Walton is often pious, tedious and prolix.
But there are many moments when the 'blithe and genial spirit'

– as the great American journalist and scholar of angling, Arnold Gingrich, called him – speaks with an unmatched simple eloquence about the joy to be found in the outdoors, in the fields and woods, 'beside the silver streams', in a fish caught and eaten.

Gingrich quotes this, on a big trout prepared for supper: 'the belly looked, some parts of it, as yellow as a marigold and some parts of it as white as a lily, yet methinks it looks better in this good sauce'. The passage about his friend and fishing companion, Sir Henry Wotton, is very touching: 'This man whose very approbation of Angling were sufficient to convince any modest censurer of it . . . was a most clear lover and frequent practiser of the Art of Angling, of which he would say 'twas an employment of his idle time which was not then idly spent . . . a rest to his mind, a cheerer of his spirits, a diverter of sadness, a calmer of unquiet thoughts, a moderator of passions, a procurer of contentedness . . .' And I love the way Walton presents his favourite species – chub, 'the fearfullest of fishes'; pike, 'the Tyrant of the fresh waters'; carp, 'a stately, a good and very subtle fish'; perch, 'a good and very bold-biting fish'; eel, 'a most dainty fish . . . the queen of palate pleasure'.

The timing of that first edition of *The Compleat Angler*, 1653, was no accident. Walton was a fervent royalist who viewed the convulsion of the Civil War and the execution of Charles I with horror and disgust. He kept his head down during those dark days, very likely removing himself from London to his native Stafford to avoid drawing attention to himself. It may well be that he went back to fish the river of his boyhood, the Sow, to remind himself that there was another side to life, one free from violence and vengeance. His book was designed to capture that other side. It succeeded in giving expression to the magic of this sport of angling for all time. No subsequent writer on the subject has supplanted Walton; the best (a tiny minority) have merely added to him.

Being a Discourse of

FISH and FISHING,

Not unworthy the perusal of most *Anglers*.

Simon Peter *said, I go a* fishing : *and they said, We also wil go with thee*. John 21.3.

London. Printed by *T. Maxey* for RICH. MARRIOT, in S. *Dunstans* Church-yard Fleetstreet, 1653.

The frontispiece of the 1653 first edition of
The Compleat Angler by Izaak Walton.

The subtitle, *The Contemplative Man's Recreation*, distilled the reason why anglers angle. It suggests consolation and a refreshment of the spirits. Fishing is an escape, but also a means to nourish, even heal, the inner self. It reminds us that this other side of life – the one that includes water, trees, flowers, meadows, moorland, birds, fish – is available to us at almost any time, accessible if we just reach out for it.

Charles Cotton called Walton 'Father', and subsequently the whole sport adopted him as its patron saint, sanctifying him and giving his book the status of holy writ. Pilgrimages were made to the places he fished. Angling clubs were named after him and his name was toasted at annual dinners. He gave birth to what the social historian of angling, John Lowerson, referred to as a 'persistent rural Arcadianism', permeated with tiresome bucolic sentimentality frequently expressed in song and painful doggerel.

But that should not detract from his achievement. He was the first to give expression in words to the pleasure of the sport of angling. It's worth remembering, though, that he was very far from being the first to experience it.

Who was? We have no idea, of course. Nor when. How did fishing – hunting fish by various means to eat them or trade them as part of an overall strategy for survival – evolve into angling, in which the pursuit acquired the extra dimension of pleasure? We know it happened and we can deduce how it happened, but we cannot tell who made it happen and when.

The sports of hunting animals and using birds of prey to catch them must have followed the same evolutionary path, and are immensely ancient. There are images of falconry from the Middle East, China and Japan dating back centuries before the birth of Christ; and it was a popular pastime for the elite in western Europe and England well before the Norman Conquest. The Old English poem, 'The Battle of Maldon', describing the defeat of the English by a Viking force in 991 CE refers to the English leader Byrhtnoth 'letting his tame hawk fly from his hand to the wood' before battle was joined. The Bayeux Tapestry shows Harold of England with a hawk before the Battle of Hastings in 1066. Hunting with or without dogs, on horseback or on foot with bow and arrow, is similarly referenced in image and word from the dawn of civilisation.

But of angling there is scarcely a word, beyond a fleeting and obscure mention in some lines of the Spanish-born Roman poet Martial in the first century CE, and the passage from *Natural History* by Claudius Aelianus (around 200 CE) describing how Macedonians used an artificial fly with red wool and fibres from a cock's feathers wound round a hook to catch their speckle-skinned fish. Moreover, the notion that Aelianus's Macedonians employed this method primarily for their amusement is clearly absurd. They had observed the speckled fish scoffing hatched insects, but the insect – whatever it was, and there has been much intense academic discussion – was too fragile to be used in its natural state, so they imitated it. They used a rod and line because there was no other way to propel the fly to where the fish could get it. They probably enjoyed themselves, just as earlier Stone Agers must have enjoyed themselves when they slaughtered a mammoth, but it did not lead to the formation of the River Astraeus Fly Fishing Club.

Hunting and hawking were amusements for kings and princes, the rich and the powerful, something to do between wars and pilgrimages. They were formalised activities requiring planning, staff, expertise and space. They lent themselves to rules and codes of conduct that reflected the organisation of society itself, and thus became outward and visible signs of the elite's status and grip on power – hence the impetus to record them in words and pictures.

Angling, although clearly a country sport, was very different. It is and was the opposite of formalised. It does not require planning or staff or much space – only a river or lake with fish in it. It can be entirely spontaneous and solitary. You don't need a hawk or a horse or a servant, just a rod, line, hook and bait or lure. It is quiet – no need for horns to sound, or whistles, or the cries of beaters.

This is not to argue that the elite did not go fishing, because they surely did. It is merely that neither they nor anyone else considered it worthwhile to record the event. Once more we are up against the tyrannical bias of the written word, or lack of it.

For a long time it was taken for granted by the English-speaking world that because golf, cricket, rugby, football and many of the other best things in life could be claimed to have originated in these islands, the same was true of angling. The assumption was based on the text known as *A Treatyse of Fysshynge with an Angle* which was printed in 1496 by William Caxton's assistant Wynkyn de Worde in a sporting compendium called *The Boke of St Albans* (although almost certainly written much earlier in the century).

Thanks mainly to Professor Richard Hoffmann's tireless ferreting through dusty medieval European archives, this assumption has been shown up as a fallacy derived from lazy cultural complacency. Hoffmann unearthed a number of references to angling that very considerably pre-dated *The Boke of St Albans*. The French cleric Guido (or Guy) of Bazoches (died 1203) wrote of the Archdeacon of León being pleased 'to fool fishes by various means' – those fishes including salmon, pike, eel and gudgeon. In Chrétien de Troyes's *Le Conte du Graal*, composed around 1180, Perceval comes across two men fishing in a boat on a river using live-bait – one of whom, a maiden at the castle tells him, is none other than the Fisher King, whose wounds in battle make it impossible for him to mount a horse, so he goes fishing instead. The Fisher King reappears in Wolfram von Eschenbach's *Parzival*, written in about 1220, this time fishing in a lake. And in the same shadowy knight/poet's *Titurel*, the young prince Schionatulander wades in a stream in the woods watched by his love and fishes for trout and grayling with a *vederangel*, translated as a feathered hook, otherwise known as an artificial fly or lure.

These snippets show that in continental Europe angling for pleasure had been embraced by society's top tier by the late Middle Ages. The very small number of people who would have read – or, more likely, heard – these chivalric poems would have been familiar with the references. The significance of the *Treatyse of Fysshynge with an Angle*, therefore, is not its date but the fact that it treated the subject in detail and was clearly intended by its unknown (if we ignore its improbable attribution to Dame Juliana Berners) author or authors as a textbook. It is short, concise and practical, and much of the general advice it contains is as sound now as it was then: 'The first and most important point in angling is always keep out of sight of the fish . . . kneel or else hide behind a bush . . . take care that you do not cast a shadow in the water . . . if a fish is frightened he will not bite for a long time afterwards.'

The *Treatyse* considered a question that must have been pertinent to its potential readership: which of the 'good and honest sports' – hunting, hawking, fowling and angling – was the best from the point of view of promoting health, happiness and peace of mind? The fact that it plumps for angling is irrelevant. It is significant because it shows that in the early fifteenth century – and probably long before that – angling for pleasure was included in the quartet of familiar and socially acceptable country sports. Nor was it a recent addition. The instructions on such matters as how to make a rod, how to twist and dye a horsehair line, how to forge, temper and sharpen hooks, and how to go about outwitting the different species were drawn from a substantial body of knowledge accumulated from many and varied sources over a considerable stretch of time.

How considerable is a matter of guesswork. The *Treatyse* pays most attention to the so-called 'coarse' fish – pike, chub, perch, eels and so on – and the likeliest baits for them: worms, maggots, grasshoppers, live fish and others. The section on fly fishing for trout and grayling is fairly short, suggesting a selection of twelve flies to be tied from wool and feathers. Andrew Herd, in his definitive *History of Fly Fishing*, astutely analyses the context: 'Rather than being the product of one person's experience, the text may represent a gradual crystallisation of many fishermen's ideas collated by a single author. If this is true, then the *Treatyse* is a monument to an age-old process by which spoken knowledge was distilled into isolated recipes before those recipes were amalgamated into longer tracts.'

The crucial point is that this was fishing for the fun of it rather than as a way to obtain food to stay alive. It was angling as opposed to fishing, although of course the two terms became and remain interchangeable. William Radcliffe, in his immensely scholarly *Fishing from the Earliest Times*, considered the thorny question of whether catching fish with a line and hook but no rod could be defined as angling rather than fishing, and decided it could not: 'I adopt as the definition of Angling the action, or art, of fishing with a rod.'

It is a convenient distinction, but shaky. The fishing rod evolved because it represented a technological advance. Some fish – big specimens, therefore sizeable meals – cannot easily be caught with net, spear or trap because they are too wary, and their preferred habitat is not amenable to those methods. But a light, tapered pole with a line attached to the end enables a bait or lure to be delivered accurately and without much disturbance to an individual fish. Should that fish take the bait or lure, its struggle to escape can be countered and defeated by the play in the pole in a way impossible with a hand line. As with all technological advances, it was a solution to a problem arising from a need. It was not invented for sporting reasons; it just happened to meet that need as well.

I went to Stratford-upon-Avon to consider a key question – was Shakespeare an angler? – and cycled upstream and down in search of answers.

The Avon as it passes through the town is dull, more munici-
pal boating lake than river. The stretch upstream from the
fourteen arches of Clopton Bridge is also quite dull where the
mansions along Teddington Road and their long, leafy gardens
allow the passer-by to see it at all.

Once beyond the golf club and the caravan and mobile home
parks, the river assumes a more properly rural character. Past
Teddington it executes a great loop to the north, then turns back
around Alveston. There is pleasant river frontage there, but it is
reserved for the owners of the fancy houses along The Rookery
and River Reach to enjoy behind their high brick walls.

Clopton Bridge in Stratford-upon-Avon, where William Shakespeare was born.

Beyond Alveston the road gives the humble cyclist occasional
snatches of river view as the Avon winds through green meadows.
I came to the edge of the deer park that extends south from the
glorious redbrick walls and soaring chimneys of Charlecote Park,
where I did something quite wrong. A footpath cuts away from
the road and through the park, affording lovely views of the

house. I had a short-lived wrestle with my conscience, at the end of which I had convinced myself that my need to address this important question about the Bard trumped National Trust anti-cycling regulations. I manipulated my bike around the high gate and past the NO CYCLING sign and pedalled on until I reached a dead straight track leading north towards the house over a most lovely old stone bridge. I propped the bike up against a tree stump and sauntered over to the bridge, which crosses a tributary of the Avon, the Dene. In the pool below the bridge four fat chub, one of them a good five pounds, were cruising around in leisurely style, opening and closing their pale, rubbery lips on invisible morsels.

Of all our freshwater fish, the chub is, I think, the most congenial. The game-fishing snobs scorn it, as they would, on the grounds that it is pretty much inedible and does not fight much when hooked. Both statements are true, and it is also true that – viewed from a narrow aesthetic perspective – the chub lacks refinement of looks. With its broad head and back, fat lips and silver flanks mailed with large scales, it is a solid, reliable, handsome citizen. It was the first fish of significant size that I had any success in catching, and I loved it for that; and there were plenty of them, and I liked them for that as well.

They are great eaters, chub, and they may be caught in any month of the angling season, whatever the conditions. Hugh Falkus and Fred Buller, in their masterly *Freshwater Fishing* (1975), listed more than fifty tried and tested chub baits, including bullock's brains, rabbit guts, and the pith from an ox's backbone as well as the more familiar worms and cheese. They are always on the lookout for juicy titbits such as caterpillars and beetles dropping off overhanging branches, and provide great sport on a dry fly, if the angler will put aside the supposed moral superiority of trout for a moment.

But chub are no mugs. They will take a bait or fly boldly, if they feel unthreatened. But any disturbance or sudden movement in their window of vision will cause them to sink out of sight – hence Walton's label 'the fearfullest of fish'. These chub at Charlecote were evidently accustomed to the company of watchers from the bridge and went about their morning perambulations unaffected, gliding from the shadows into the sunlight and back without a care.

A short distance away the Dene tumbled over a little weir to be subsumed into a lovely stretch of the Avon. The flow was steady but forceful enough to bend the midstream clumps of reed forward. Beds of reeds and rushes lined the sides, with banks of shaggy grass and wildflowers beyond. The water was clear and weedy and silently shouted chub at me.

There is an old, discredited story about the juvenile Shakespeare being summoned before the owner of Charlecote, Sir Thomas Lucy, and accused of poaching a deer. All nonsense, of course – how much more likely, surely, that he might have plotted to dap a grasshopper or flick out a live frog to snare one of the portly chub.

They chose the site well for their mansion, those Lucys. No wonder the spot inspired the poetic muse – witness these well-turned lines from a minor eighteenth-century versifier, the Reverend Richard Jago:

> Where Avon's stream with many a sportive turn
> Exhilarates the Meads, and to his bed
> Hele's gentle current wooes, by Lucy's hand
> In every graceful Ornament attend,
> And worthier such to share his Liquid realms . . .

Another clergyman with literary leanings, the Reverend Henry Ellacombe, Vicar of Bitton in Gloucestershire, wrote two lengthy articles published in the *Antiquary* magazine in 1881 under the collective title 'Shakespeare as an Angler'. Mr Ellacombe laid his cards on the table at the outset: 'I think there is little doubt that he was a successful angler and had probably enjoyed many a day's fishing in the Warwickshire and Gloucestershire streams to which he looked back with pleasure and refreshing memories when he was in London . . .'

To support his case Mr Ellacombe presented a host of quotations from the plays. Among the species Shakespeare mentions are salmon, trout, eels, gudgeon, dace and pike, the last two figuring in one of Falstaff's reflections, in *Henry IV Part II* Act 3 Scene 2: 'if the young dace be a bait for the old pike / I see no reason, in the law of nature, but that I may snap at him.' Unfortunately for Mr Ellacombe, the general fog of obscurity shrouding all but a few details of Shakespeare's life extends over whatever sporting enthusiasms he may have had. In a memorial volume, a friend and admirer of Mr Ellacombe conceded that 'it can hardly be said that his main thesis is proved'.

Who cares? The question of whether Shakespeare was a keen angler, an occasional angler, or no angler at all does not matter. What we do know is that he was brought up beside this river, the Avon, and that when his career in London was over he returned to live near it again. As Dr Johnson said, 'He that will understand Shakespeare must not be content to study him in the closet, he must be looking for his meaning sometimes among the sports of the field.'

Shakespeare knew his Avon intimately. He walked it, sat beside it, learned about its plants and flowers and its fish. Maybe he swam in it on hot summers' days, maybe he fished it. He would have encountered anglers and seen them ply their rods, talked to them and understood their terms of reference. He would have stored this knowledge and dipped into it later on. As the poet and story-teller 'Q' – Sir Arthur Quiller-Couch – expressed it in a sweet book about a canoe trip down the Avon, 'somewhere along these banks the Stratford boy spied the Muse's naked feet moving . . . somewhere he came upon her and coaxed the secret of her woodland music'.

The point, surely, is that Shakespeare took a close interest and keen delight in the countryside available to him, including the river and extending to those who took their pleasure from it – whether or not he joined in. And when Ursula in *Much Ado about Nothing* gloats that 'The pleasantest angling is to see the fish / Cut with her golden oars the silver stream / And greedily devour the treacherous bait/So angle we for Beatrice', or Cleopatra calls 'Give me my angle – we'll to the river there/My music playing far off I will betray / Tawny-finned fishes . . .', the audience would have picked up on the references without difficulty. The sport and its language had been sufficiently absorbed into popular culture to be understood and enjoyed. That would have happened only if angling itself had become a familiar, popular pastime.

Roughly thirty-five years elapsed between Shakespeare's death and the publication of the first edition of *The Compleat Angler*. Four more editions appeared before Walton's death in 1683 – the fifth, in 1676, included Cotton's contribution and was definitive. Sales figures are unknown, but Walton's decision to take the trouble to expand and revise his text – and his publishers' decision to produce the new version – strongly suggests that the sport enjoyed a healthy popularity. This is also reflected in the publication and republication of other angling books – among them John Dennys's poem *The Secrets of Angling* (1613), Gervase Markham's *A Discourse of the General Art of Fishing with an Angle* (1614) and Walton's friend Thomas Barker's *The Art of Angling* (1651), all of them grossly inferior to *The Compleat Angler* but evidently able to secure a readership.

The appeal of angling endured and grew over the succeeding centuries, to the point at which, in my lifetime, a figure of three to four million anglers has been regularly quoted. There are indications now that the sport is declining, for reasons I shall look at later in this book. Certainly there was not much evidence of mass appeal when I cycled up the Lea two days after the opening of the coarse-fishing season on 16 June. It was not until I neared Enfield Lock, between the North Circular and the M25, that I came upon signs of angling life in the form of two rods and a bivvy (a carp angler's tent) with the lower legs of the carp man himself visible through the flap.

That first stretch of the Lea navigation, north from Tottenham, is a satisfying edgeland, furnished with security gates, spiked metal fencing, CCTV cameras, warnings about the danger of robberies and death by electrocution or drowning, and notice boards appealing for the tidy disposal of litter. To the right of the smooth cycle path, hidden behind sheep-grazed grassy banks, is the string of reservoirs dug between the middle of the nineteenth and twentieth centuries to supply London's drinking water. Spread along the west side is a sprawl of lorry parks, car parks, warehouses, retail parks, offices, rubbish tips, sewage-disposal works and commercial enterprises of one kind or another. Notable among them are the steaming vents and smoking chimneys of the London Energy waste-burning plant and the glass and steel and undulating red roof of the Camden Town Brewery.

Houseboats, barges and strange hybrid craft lined one side of the navigation or the other. Their smartness perceptibly increased with the distance from London; those at the Tottenham end tended to the shabby, not to say derelict, supporting piles of timber and heaps of scrap metal and assorted rubbish. A significant proportion had clearly been abandoned for good to subside slowly into the mud – mute, rotting leftovers from dreams of an alternative, more liberated way of life.

The water was absolutely clear except when churned up by a passing boat, supporting beds of lilies and drifts of pale green duckweed. In places concrete banks and steel pilings asserted the artificiality of the channel. But elsewhere the shrubs, trees, nettles, brambles and other vegetation had been allowed to spill down and join the reeds and sedges to create a version of wild nature.

The cycle path followed the navigation so I had to as well.

The history of its construction is long and complicated and beside my point. Suffice to say that there are stretches where the 'old' Lea is incorporated into it and others where the 'old' Lea has been left to pursue its old wandering ways. The mapping of the navigation, the 'old' Lea and the multitude of connecting streams and channels was bewildering to me, and I was generally grateful for being steered in the right direction by the navigation, even though it was a bit soulless at times and very far removed from the spirit of old Izaak.

But every now and then I got a glimpse of a living stream. Not far upstream from Tottenham Lock a footbridge invited me to cross the navigation and see what was beyond its rigid confinement. Between it and Lockwood Reservoir was a narrow ribbon of a brook squeezed between unkempt banks, flowing urgently, its surface braided by competing threads of water. Strands of emerald ranunculus, the good, life-giving weed, waved in the current. It was tiny but I thought there must be fish there even if I couldn't see them, maybe a chub on the bend below where the 'old' Lea – which it was – headed out of sight around the back of what used to be part of the mighty Harris Lebus furniture empire, now another industrial yard.

Beyond the M25 and the A121 extends the Lea Valley Park – officially and annoyingly spelled Lee Valley Park – where old gravel workings, wetland, meadowland and woodland have been moulded into a great green lung for London through which the Lea and its various partners and offshoots thread their way around a complicated web of water. Cycle paths abound, and I took one that followed the sinuous course of the Flood Relief Channel, with island-dotted Seventy Acre Lake to my left. I spotted a carp man standing guard over his four rods beside a little bay on the lake. Fish as fat as Henry VIII are rumoured to cruise on their food paths between the islands, but – according to the angling forums – it is not given to ordinary mortals to catch them.

The path went around the side of a ghostly electricity substation and brought me to a bridge where I stopped, entranced.
A clear stream ran in lively style over clear gravel and pale sand,
partly clothed in waving bands of ribbon-weed. Clusters of reed
broke the surface, bending forward in obedience to the current.
Willow hugged the banks, competing for space with loosestrife
and valerian. Above the bridge was an exciting pool, at the
head of which the flow thrust itself between the reeds and out
towards the willows on the far bank. The water on the near
side was still, part-covered in lily pads. It looked fabulously
fishy – just the spot where Izaak and Thomas Barker would
have laid down their creels, unwound their lines from their
hazel and blackthorn rods and set to work dibbling a fat grasshopper for a fatter chub.

Alas I had no rod or line or grasshopper. I pushed on and
very soon met my friend the navigation running straight as a
ruler towards Broxbourne and Hoddesdon. The ride became tame
and suburban, the water confined by concrete, the narrowboats
neat and shiny in bottle green and burgundy liveries and burnished
brass fittings. I passed a pub, the Crown, and came to another,
the quirkily named Fish and Eels, but it was too early for pubs.
The Fish and Eels sits across from Dobbs Weir, an intricate set
of gates and sluices where the one-time British record chub of
eight pounds thirteen ounces was caught in 2003.

For the first time I passed several anglers, but none had any
action to report. A little way on, though, I came upon a bloke
sitting peaceably on his stool with a pole many metres long
poking out over the greenish, murky water, who said he had
had decent numbers of small roach and perch. Someone was
happy.

One of the Lea's main tributaries, the Stort, joins it quietly
from the east opposite the Rye House power station. Further
on I left the navigation for good, and took the road through
the village of Stanstead Abbotts, turning left onto the minor

Ware road with the 'old' Lea a meadow away to the left, invisible in a belt of trees. Beyond the river and the navigation and the old quarry, now a nature reserve, is Amwell – and Amwell Hill, where Venator had his rendezvous with Mr Sadler's otterhounds.

According to *The Compleat Angler* Piscator was here too, and they did some chubbing together. This stretch is well known as the home of the Amwell Magna Fishery, a fly-fishing club with very antique roots. The first 150 years from its founding in 1831 were chronicled in a little booklet by a past chairman, Kenneth Robson (a headmaster in Broxbourne and editor of the *Flyfishers' Club Journal*), with a foreword by the noted thespian angler, Michael Hordern. Later, more detailed – very detailed – research into the club's past was undertaken by another member who achieved celebrity in a very different arena, the retired Northern Irish punk rocker Feargal Sharkey.

It is pretty remarkable that there should be a stretch of chalkstream trout fishing within fifteen miles of central London at all. But it would be idle to pretend that Amwell Magna is some kind of prelapsarian throwback to a pristine past. Historically the members concentrated on the chub, perch and particularly pike; it was transformed into a trout fishery towards the end of the nineteenth century by consistent stocking of artificially reared fish from trout farms, and that is how it has functioned ever since. An analysis carried out in 2015 by the Wild Trout Trust found that there was a smattering of small, native trout, but that there was very little viable habitat available to enable that population to increase, and that stocking would continue to be necessary to 'satisfy the aspirations of the membership'.

The Lea faces many intractable problems. A glance at one of the old photographs on the Amwell Magna club's website illustrates one of them. Dating from 1888, it shows a wide stream brimming with water and thick with ranunculus (with someone fishing, but evidently not fly fishing, from a punt anchored across the flow). Greatly reduced water flows resulting from abstraction and the diversion of water to feed the navigation have shrunk much of the fishery to a narrow, slow, silty glide.

The Shoot at Amwell Magna Fishery in 1888.

All along the ten miles of the Lea that Walton covered, the river is under multiple attack: from abstraction, pollution, urban development and suburban sprawl, the annexation of the river bed by American signal crayfish and the banks by invasive knotweed and hogweed and – most destructive of all, from the angling perspective – predation by cormorants.

Twenty years ago, when I was the *Financial Times* fishing correspondent, I was invited by the Walthamstow Fly Fishers Club to witness the scale of their cormorant plague. At the time I was aware of the issue theoretically, but until I went to north London I had no idea of what it meant. Four hundred of the birds were roosting on one island on the reservoir. The leafless trees on it were bone white from their droppings, and in the evening the sky was darkened as they returned from their hunting. The club's policy was to stock only trout of three pounds or more, which are too heavy for a cormorant to lift. I noticed then that sections of the Lea nearby had been netted to keep them off.

It's most unlikely that Izaak Walton saw a single cormorant in his whole life, unless he paid an unadvertised visit to the coast to which they used to be confined. It is the modern development of fisheries and fish farms that has drawn them inland to find easy pickings. He certainly never saw that insatiable destroyer of aquatic invertebrate life, the signal crayfish, which was introduced here in the past half century. He would have known drought, but the concept of engineered water abstraction would have been unknown to him. In Walton's time the Lea and all the rivers still functioned pretty much as Nature made them; it is very hard for us, confronted by our intensely exploited, congested and engineered landscape, to picture how that was.

I went down to the gate into the Amwell Magna Fishery in the hope of finding someone to ask about its state of health, but it was locked up and there was no sign of anyone around so I pedalled on to Ware. Had the old George pub still been there, I would have stopped off for a pint and to pay my respects to the memory of 'mine host Rickarbie' and the great trout 'that is near an ell long' whose drawing Walton referred to. But the site is now occupied by Hairizon Hairdressers and TSB, so I didn't bother and instead took the train back to Tottenham.

CHAPTER FIVE

Fur and Feather

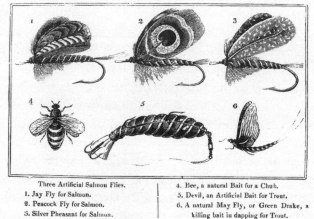

Three Artificial Salmon Flies.
1. Jay Fly for Salmon.
2. Peacock Fly for Salmon.
3. Silver Pheasant for Salmon.

4. Bee, a natural Bait for a Chub.
5. Devil, an Artificial Bait for Trout.
6. A natural May Fly, or Green Drake, a
killing bait in dapping for Trout.

Fine houses rise and decay and fall, while the rivers beside them keep on flowing. Judging from the old illustrations, Beresford Hall, where Charles Cotton was brought up and which he inherited, was fine enough, a handsome stone mansion set on high ground overlooking the steep, wooded gash in the landscape known as Beresford Dale. The River Dove flows down the dale. On the west bank is Staffordshire, on the east Derbyshire. The geology of the Staffordshire side is acid millstone grit, but the Derbyshire bank marks the start of a carboniferous limestone plateau, and the stream takes its character from both.

Charles Cotton was an only child and grew up accustomed to a life of gentlemanly ease. But as sometimes happened, the resources required to sustain the life of ease were deficient. His father, also Charles, was an obsessive and unsuccessful litigant and as a consequence of his many and expensive lawsuits the estate was heavily burdened with debt by the time the son inherited in 1658. The younger Cotton's cheerfully improvident ways compounded his financial problems, and at various times he was compelled to sell off portions of his estates. Towards the end of his life he sold Beresford itself, although he continued to live there; by the early nineteenth century it was in ruins, and in 1858 it was demolished.

Charles Cotton

Beresford Hall, a view from the back, as it appeared in Charles Cotton's time.

But Cotton left his mark, in more ways than one. In 1674 he had built on part of a meadow beside the Dove the uniquely charming Fishing House, his celebration of his friendship with Izaak Walton. 'My poor fishing house, my seat's best grace,' Cotton called it: a square stone room with pyramidal roof surmounted by sundial and ball, and the keystone over the door with his and Walton's initials intertwined and the immortal inscription *Piscatoribus Sacrum**. Although the black and white marble paving, painted wainscotting and other fittings subsequently disappeared, the building was solid and survives intact on its grassy peninsula with the stream flowing around.

His other mark, of course, was his contribution to *The Compleat Angler*. Cotton was a highly cultured man, an admired poet, translator of Montaigne from the French, widely travelled in Europe. But he was also a true countryman. He hunted and

* 'Sacred to fishermen'.

The Fishing House, built by Charles Cotton in 1674.

hawked and rode the moorland and dales of Staffordshire and Derbyshire. And he fished, passionately and consistently from boyhood. The twelve short chapters he wrote for Walton are steeped in knowledge and experience. He didn't leave any detailed record of his exploits so we cannot know how often he fished or what he caught. We can assume that he concentrated on the Dove, but there are other good trout streams within half a day's ride of Beresford: the Manifold, just to the west, the Wye and the Derwent to the east, not to mention the many miles of the Dove downstream from his fine house.

It is evident from his text that Cotton was a genuinely expert fly fisherman and fly tyer. He provides clear, detailed instructions on how to make a fly which any tyer would be able to follow today. He described sixty-five separate patterns, far more than had been itemised in all previous angling books in English combined. He used a wide range of materials, among them ostrich feathers and hairs from a hog's head, a weasel's tail, bear, camel, the tail of a black water-dog, as well as the sheep's wool, squirrel fur and partridge feathers that he would have found outside his back door. Cotton also devised a classification, dividing his patterns into categories: Browns, Drakes and Duns, corresponding roughly to the stoneflies, mayflies and smaller upwinged flies familiar to entomologists today.

At the end of the section on fly tying Cotton acknowledges that 'this way of making a Flie . . . was taught to me by a Kinsman of mine, one Captain Henry Jackson, a near neighbour . . . by many degrees the best Flie maker that I ever met with'. But we can be sure that Captain Jackson did not invent the method, that someone showed him and that that someone was shown by someone else. The same with the flies. Different tyers would have refined the patterns they had been shown, tweaked them, improved upon them – Cotton probably among them.

The point is that they were all operating within a single tradition, a comprehensive strategy for catching trout and grayling from moorland and upland streams that had evolved over many generations. We happen to know Cotton's name, but his distinction was not as a pioneer, but as a historian. It so happened that – anxious to win the approval of his 'Father Walton' – he sat down and over ten days (if he is to be believed) put down on paper his summary of the knowledge accumulated by his anonymous predecessors: knowledge handed down from father to son to grandson, from uncle to nephew, from old man to young boy, likely enough over centuries.

The Dove that emerges from beneath Hartington Bridge half a mile or so upstream from where Beresford Hall once stood is a very modest stream. I visited at the end of the very hot and dry summer of 2018, and was unsurprised to find it not looking its best. Its volume was meagre and its colour somewhat murky. The flattish gradient causes it to meander considerably through the meadows above the Fishing House – the bottom silty, the flow slack.

Around the Fishing House itself the flow came almost to a standstill. Cotton lovingly described it as 'a clear, delicate stream' but times have changed and it was dark, still and lifeless, hemmed in by overbearing clumps of snowberry and dogwood. Below the Fishing House the Dove enters the steepest section of Beresford Dale, more like a canyon. On the Staffordshire side the light is blocked out by walls of pale stone, thick with trees, and the Derbyshire side is also heavily wooded. It is shady, damp and somewhat claustrophobic. Although the pace of the water picks up here and there, it is emphatically not a bouncing, babbling mountain stream. I registered an occasional dart as a little trout or grayling dashed for safety, but it did not feel properly fishy to me, and I did not regret not being there to fish.

The heavily tramped footpath crosses from left to right bank above the most painted, sketched and generally gawped-at spot on the whole river – Pike Pool, where a single outsize column of limestone, cloaked in creepers and with sapling beeches sprouting from its base, rises like a stained molar from an oblong of dark water. When I was there the water was unmoving, although with normal spring flow there is a good ripply push between the rock and the high, tree-thick far bank, creating a tempting riffle towards the tail of the pool.

Below Pike Pool the woodland thins and the land flattens somewhat, allowing the margins to be grazed by sheep. The footpath continues to keep the river company, making fishing a somewhat public activity. The banks are close-cropped and eroded, the stream shallow and open and lacking both variety and cover. To be honest I would say that it was a lovely place to walk and – because of the history – fascinating to investigate. If I were Charles Cotton reborn and I lived beside it, I would certainly fish it, carefully choosing my moments (when the booted brigade are somewhere else). But I would not come a long way for the fishing; the water is not interesting enough, and much too public.

This stretch of the Dove is a victim of its own history. The immediate and enduring popularity of *The Compleat Angler* placed Beresford Dale on the itinerary for a new breed of angler/tourist. It also inspired, if that's the word, an outpouring in prose and verse imbued with that peculiarly arch and tiresome cod-Arcadian sentimentality so eagerly embraced in the first age of leisure tourism. No Derbyshire travelogue was complete without the obligatory jaunt to the Fishing House, a stroll by Pike Pool and a splurge of reflection on the contribution made by the two angler friends to the myth of good old England.

Cotton's own insipid lines

> Oh my beloved nymph, fair Dove
> Princess of rivers, how I love
> Upon the flowery banks to lie
> And view the silver stream . . .

acquire the status of immortal masterpiece compared with what came later. How about this, from John Edwards's *The Tour of the Dove* (1821)?

> How fair the limpid Dove! Whole ripples greet
> Each islet-stone or bush that intervenes
> Spring from hoary crags in contrast meet
> Full-blossom'd thorns and glossy evergreens . . .

Or this, the Reverend Samuel Bentley's view of the limestone column that rears from Pike Pool, taken from his *The River Dove: A Lyric Pastoral*?

> . . . placed just in the middle of yon pool
> Enormous it seems to be grown
> And nearly proportion'd by rule,
> And fashioned from one single stone . . .

Or this, a song from an abysmal pastiche in dialogue form, *The River Dove, with some Quiet Thoughts on the Happy Practice of Angling*, by John Lavicount Anderdon?

> Oh! The gallant fisher's life
> It is the best of any
> 'Tis full of pleasure, void of strife
> And 'tis beloved by many.

Enough?

They came, they stayed at the Charles Cotton inn in Hartington, they tramped the banks and peered into the Fishing House, then penned their odes and panegyrics to the Father of Angling and his adopted son. The effect, combined with the popularity of *The Compleat Angler*, was to make this short stretch of stream a place of pilgrimage. Many of those pilgrims, naturally enough, wanted to cast where Cotton and Walton's horsehair lines had landed. The fishing acquired commercial value, and the wealthier devotees bought it up. The problem was that the Dove in its natural state – a small stream with a limited population of mainly smallish trout and grayling that were not at all easy to catch unless you were accomplished in the Derbyshire method – could not satisfy those expectations.

Unlike us, the Victorians had no problem with the concept of improving on Nature's deficiencies. The riparian owners on the

Dove set about turning it into a viable fishery. They installed stone weirs at frequent intervals to provide shelter and refuge. They reinforced the banks with stone revetments to restrain erosion. And they addressed what they saw as the inadequate stock of edible-sized fish in the obvious way, by recourse to the fish farm. The novel technology of rearing trout in stews made it possible on the Dove, as elsewhere, to introduce fish that were a lot bigger than the natives, in whatever numbers the proprietor wished. They were also a great deal easier to catch than the natives; they were genetically short on caution, and would grab anything suggestive of food, in the absence of the minced horse-meat they were used to. By the standards of those days, this simply meant doing better than Nature.

Walter Gallichan's little book *Fishing in Derbyshire and Around* (1905) gives a good idea of how the river was managed at the turn of the nineteenth century. He describes the stretch below Hartington as 'strictly preserved . . . abounding with trout and grayling'. The right bank belonged to Sir Vauncey Crewe, the left to the Challoner family, 'who let the water to Mr Frank Green . . . this gentleman has repeatedly stocked with rainbow and other kinds of trout'. Below Beresford Dale the fishing belonged to Sir Thomas Wardle who 'has a stock pool in which he successfully breeds rainbow, Loch Leven and Fontinalis trout'.*

They were not to know it, but the combined effect of the engineering and the stocking degraded the character of the fishery beyond recognition. Had they returned a couple of centuries after their time, Cotton and Walton would have known where they were. But instead of the unimpeded natural stream they were used to, with its native population of small and tricky trout and grayling, they would have been looking at a succession of

---

* Sir Thomas made a fortune from silk dyeing and fancied himself something of a composer, publishing 'A Fishing Song' which begins 'We came to Dove one hot July and hoped for splendid angling / But with us disappointment came to give our hopes a mangling'.

impoundments, each holding a bunch of artificially reared outsize trout of various kinds engaged in a desperate hunt for something to eat. The fact that many of them were rainbows, a non-native strain, would have compounded the sense of unreality.

Within the past few years, under the guidance of the Wild Trout Trust, the owner at Beresford and other owners and clubs along the Dove have begun to reverse that degradation. The stocking of farmed trout, which persisted until the fairly recent past, has been ended. A number of the weirs have been removed or breached to allow a freer flow, although many remain in place. Other measures in hand or under consideration include fencing margins to keep livestock from trampling the banks and to promote plant and tree growth, allowing fallen trees and branches to remain in place to provide cover and vary flow patterns, encouraging lateral movement of the channel by removing revetments, and allowing coarse sediment from hillside screes to reach the river to provide spawning gravel.

A lot that could be done is being done. But it would be idle to pretend that – given the pressures on it – the Dove will ever return to that state of pristine wildness that Cotton and Walton took for granted.

Walton was a comparatively old man – well into his sixties – when he first visited Beresford Hall and fished the Dove. It is not known how many times he came in all. Cotton refers to him seeing the keystone for the Fishing House but 'never in the posture it now stands . . . and I am afraid he will not see it yet; for he has lately writ me word he doubts his coming down this summer'. That was probably in 1675, when Walton was eighty-two.

Walton was essentially a coarse fisherman. When he fished with Sir Henry Wotton on the Thames at Eton, or with Thomas Barker on the Lea, or on his native Sow, he would have mostly sat on the bank or his basket waiting for a fish that generally was not a trout or a grayling to take his bait. He would have found the Dove a considerable culture shock. It is quite likely that, at his age and with his sedentary inclinations, he never became much of a fly fisherman. He may have dapped a live mayfly in much the same way that he would have done a cater-pillar or grasshopper for a chub. But I picture him happily seated beside the placid glide around the Fishing House or opposite the rock in Pike Pool, with a worm or grub out, waiting for the knock-knock at the tip of his rod; or using a dead minnow or bullhead mounted on hooks and fished slowly in mid-water.

Izaak Walton goes fishing - a romanticised imagining.

Cotton's method required agility and extreme caution. His maxim was 'fine and far off' – he urged the angler to 'keep well out of sight, either by kneeling or the interposition of a bank or bush'. This would have been tricky for the ageing Izaak, as would the necessary technique of using the wind to place the fly lightly above the fish so that it drifted down without drag. Nor would Cotton have stayed in one spot for long. With his servant to carry his fishing tackle and bag of fly-tying materials, he would have expected to cover plenty of ground, moving upstream or down in obedience to the direction of the wind.

The instructions Cotton gives for fishing with bait as opposed to the artificial fly are cursory to the point of being useless. He clearly was not interested; he would have watched his elderly friend working his dead bait or worm through the slower pools and found it dull and pointless. Who can blame him? On a river such as the Dove, it is patently an inferior method.

Cotton was a fly fisherman as a result of geographical accident. He happened to grow up and live in a part of the country where using the artificial fly was by far the most efficient way of catching the native fish. Had he been raised by the Thames or Trent or Ouse he would have been a coarse fisherman like Walton. It was a happy accident that these two men – so disparate in age, temperament and experience – should have become such close friends that each wished to introduce the other to his favourite method, and that together they were able to pool their knowledge in a form that would last as long as angling itself.

I see Izaak as being entranced by the Derbyshire way of fly fishing, but also somewhat intimidated by its difficulty. He may have wished himself younger, so that he would have more time to learn it, or that he lived closer, because he would have known that to master it would require hard practice. As for Cotton, I doubt if he envied the older man his chub and pike, his worms and maggots. In the first paragraph of his very short chapter on worming, he dismissed it as 'not so easy, so cleanly, nor, as 'tis said, so genteel a way of fishing as with a fly . . .'

The clear implication is that he regarded fly fishing as superior both in efficiency and elegance, and Walton may well have agreed. One can certainly picture the two of them in the parlour at Beresford Hall, in a fog of smoke from Cotton's pipe, discussing the matter. The glory of *The Compleat Angler* is that it brought the two distinct traditions together. But it also defined that distinction. Cotton evidently preferred his way, but equally evidently he did not regard himself as a better person than Walton – quite the reverse.

The traditions walked hand in hand for a long time. Many anglers grew up in one or the other and stuck with it, but many others crossed happily between the two. It was not until much later that each began to acquire a social dimension, which over time caused them to pull apart in a way that neither Walton nor Cotton could have envisaged or would have approved.

CHAPTER SIX

The Ascendancy of the Laird

There is a sturdy, handsome sandstone viaduct that spans the Tweed between two Borders towns – historic and lovely Melrose, and distinctly unlovely Galashiels. It was built in the middle of the nineteenth century to take the Edinburgh–Carlisle railway line over the river, a function it continued to perform until the service was axed in 1969. After nearly half a century of quiet neglect it came to useful life again in 2016 with the opening of the Borders Railway between Galashiels and Edinburgh – a modest affair compared with the old line, but not cheap and not uncontroversial.

The passenger who gets on at the terminus at Tweedbank and takes a window seat on the left side of the train will, if paying attention, be rewarded with a fleeting view up the Tweed within a minute or so of departure. If the passenger is paying very close attention, he or she may glimpse broken water on the bend upstream. And if he or she should be a salmon angler, their heart will quicken, for they will suspect that it is the tail of a salmon pool, and they will be right.

I have fished Carryweil a couple of times and caught nothing. But each time I have walked up to it from the viaduct through the thick belt of trees that hugs the bank, and seen it reveal itself, I have felt that peculiar tugging in the heart region and tightening of the senses that every salmon angler knows. It is a perfect pool.

At its head the flow is squeezed at a pinch-point and responds by racing furiously over a wide shelf of boulders. The current is forced towards the far side, beyond which the pale, Soviet-style apartment blocks of Galashiels show above the trees. The fierceness of the flow subsides as it gathers itself into a long tongue of water that licks along the edge. The surface is restless, broken, serrated, ridged, roughened. There is depth here and there are good holding places for the fish behind the big boulders where they may rest for a moment before continuing to push on up. In good water there is ample force to work the fly, so that it lands near the far side and comes down and back across the current, darting and fluttering. A fish can take anywhere.

The problem with Carryweil is that it is a devil to wade. The current is comparatively slack where you get in at the top, but not negligible. The boulders are distributed haphazardly and most inconveniently, and they are big and very slippery with narrow, slippery channels between. You have to edge out to the limit of the tree canopy to get a line out at all. You slip and slide and sway and stumble, cursing the while, searching with your boots for a precious square foot of stable gravel where you will at last be able to focus on fishing instead of staying upright, while the water swirls around your thighs threatening to tip you over at any moment.

The hazards of Carryweil have not diminished over time.

This was it two hundred years ago – 'The wet stones were slippery and treacherous beyond endurance . . . my untutored feet took no hold and I floundered about in the superlative degree . . . I could not keep my footing . . . I swayed like a pendulum only more unevenly until down I went from a stone which jogged under my step and tipped me in about middle deep . . .'

The only significant differences between me fishing Carryweil and the man who wrote those words were that I had waterproof waders on and he was in 'light, flimsy walking shoes without nails', that he broke his rod and I did not, that he actually fell in and I did not, and that he had a salmon on (which he lost) and I never did.

He was an Englishman, William Scrope (pronounced Scroop), and his book, *Days and Nights of Salmon Fishing on the Tweed*, became the first classic of Scottish salmon fishing. The Scropes were Wiltshire landed gentry, from Castle Combe. William inherited at the age of fifteen, and a few years later inherited the estate of another branch of the family at Cockington in Lincolnshire. The notion of working for a living can never have crossed his mind. He became an accomplished amateur painter, exhibiting occasionally at the Royal Academy and being elected a member of the Accademia di San Luca in Rome, and – with the silver spoon firmly held in his mouth – devoted himself to art and the classics and later to his twin passions for stalking red deer and pursuing salmon.

At around 2.30pm in the afternoon of a late October day in 1868 a clergyman, George Forrest Browne, hooked an enormous fish where the River Earn meets the tidal River Tay near Perth. The fish took an artificial bait known as a Blue Phantom which was being trolled from a boat by Mr Browne, accompanied by his boatman Jimmy. After pulling hard in various directions while Jimmy pulled equally hard to keep up with it, the fish headed

The title page of the 1843 edition of
*Days and Nights of Salmon Fishing on the
Tweed* by William Scrope.

out with the ebbing tide along the north side of Mugdrum Island and out into the open estuary. At half past three the tide turned, and the fish with it. Sandwiches of potted grouse were gratefully consumed by Jimmy and Mr Browne (later a professor of archaeology at Cambridge University, and later still Bishop of Stepney and then Bristol).

By now the line – made up of two trout lines spliced together – was visibly fraying under the strain. Darkness fell, and the lights of Inchyra came on. A boat came out with whisky, cakes, cheese and a lantern. While the fish sulked on the bottom, Jimmy managed to splice on a new, stronger line. At ten o'clock, in pitch darkness, the tide turned again. The fish took off and came up to the surface – 'We can hear the huge splashes he makes as he rolls and beats the water.' The line went slack. For a moment Mr Browne thought the fish was running towards the boat and he reeled in like a man possessed. Then he lifted the bait from the water, minus its tail hook. After ten hours the fish had gone. A year later a giant salmon was taken in the nets at Newburgh, close to Mugdrum Island, with the mark of a hook near its nose. It weighed seventy-four pounds.

Size is one reason why salmon can inspire such fierce passion. The record, also from the Tay, was a fish of sixty-four pounds caught in 1922 by Georgina Ballantyne. Fish of forty pounds upwards are very unusual, and there are plenty of dedicated salmon anglers who have never caught a thirty-pounder. But they do occur, and any salmon of ten pounds or more will likely display when hooked a power and strength that no other fresh-water fish can come close to matching. When it feels the hook, a fish fresh from the sea, burnished silver in colour, muscled, its tissue packed with fat stored from its ocean feeding, behaves like an artillery shell leaving the barrel of a gun. The line flickers and twitches as the fly is taken, tightens, plunges down. The reel hums or screeches according to its engineering, the rod bends in an arc. There is nothing in angling that can compare with the battle with a salmon, and I speak as one who has flirted with salmon fishing for a long time without ever falling in love.

That is why Sir Walter Scott called it 'the king of fish' and declared that salmon fishing 'is to all other kinds of fishing as is buck-shooting to shooting of meaner description'; why Patrick Chalmers in his *Where the Spring Salmon Run* saw it as 'a sahib, a sportsman, and the most magnificent fighter that ever took a

A 1922 magazine spread on the record salmon taken
on the River Tay in Scotland, by Georgina Ballantyne.

fly'; why a contemporary writer, Michael Wigan, has referred to
it felicitously as 'natural royalty'.

Royalty is appropriate, but salmon are visiting royalty, making
them even more alluring. Born from eggs deposited and fertilised
in a scoop in the gravel on an often nameless upland stream or
burn, they hatch into blobs of life feeding from their yolk sacs,
turn into fry foraging around the birthplace, then into parr with

a station and territory to defend, then – after a couple of years or so – into smolts that run down their rivers and congregate in packs to head out to sea. They are gone, and all but a few of them will never return. But those that make it back – after a year or two or more feeding somewhere beyond Iceland – will do so as royalty.

It is impossible to know when angling for salmon as a sport developed, because there are no records. An incredibly tedious book by a former captain in Cromwell's army, Richard Franck – known as *Northern Memoirs* although its full title occupies a whole page – does include some instructions on how to tie a salmon fly. It was published in 1694 but describes a journey to Scotland that took place more than thirty years before and manages not to include even a shadow of an account of how the fly was fished or where or with what results. The limitations of the fishing tackle of those days would have made it very difficult to land a fresh-run salmon, even though a primitive prototype reel was in existence. Better far to try to spear it, lasso it or net it.

But over the course of the eighteenth century the notion of fishing for salmon for fun began to take root. The references are very sketchy, but there is a valuable letter reproduced in William Yarrell's *A History of British Fishes* (1841) from the Earl of Home about fishing the Tweed at the family's estate, The Hirsel, near Coldstream. The earl refers almost in passing to his uncle (presumably the 8th Earl) catching a salmon of sixty-nine and three-quarter pounds on rod and line in the 1740s. He himself records catching thirty-six fish in one day in April 1795, and twenty-six the next.

At that time it was a purely local affair. The Earls of Home lived on the Tweed and amused themselves with the salmon when the opportunity presented itself. Most of the fishing on the Tweed and elsewhere was controlled by the tacksmen who rented the rights from the landowners. They concentrated almost exclusively on commercial netting, but the abundance of fish was such that enough escaped the nets to make themselves available for sport – and there were a few local experts on hand to take advantage.

One such was John Younger, who was born in 1785 into a life of considerable hardship in a small village near St Boswells on the southern bank of the Tweed. His father was a shoemaker and he followed the same path, setting up a workshop where he made and mended shoes until shortly before his death in 1860. As a boy he learned to make flies, and with a hazel rod, in his words, 'fished for trout as much for my dinner as amusement'. He became an expert fly tyer and naturalist, and educated himself to read and love poetry and to write it. Younger became something a local celebrity, sometimes referred to as the Tweedside Gnostic because of his dissenting views and radical politics.

Late in life he wrote his autobiography, but his lasting memorial is his *River Angling for Salmon and Trout*, first published in 1840. A subsequent edition was accompanied by an anonymous 'Sketch of the Author's Life' in which Younger's austere but appealing character is vividly conveyed. 'The shoemaker's shop was a house of call for all the Waltonian brotherhood: dukes, lords, Galashiels weavers, escaped Parliament men, squires, cotton lords and a whole medley whose boot heels had crunched the pebbly shores of the glorious river or its tributaries came at times to hear John Younger discourse on the theme which ahead of rivals he had so well mastered.'

The span of his life saw a transformation in Tweed angling that was mirrored all over Scotland. In his boyhood and young manhood it was a poor man's river. As Younger recalled, 'individuals were employed by the tacksmen to fish for one-half of what they could kill'. One of these tacksmen was John Haliburton of Craigover, who rented the Mertoun water for £15 a year; when he passed Younger's shop he would call out to him to put down his apron and hammer and nails and come and fish.

John Younger, author of
River Angling for Salmon and Trout.

Then onto the scene strode William Scrope from distant
Wiltshire, who could have bought John Younger's shop without
noticing a dent in his income stream. Scrope nurtured a passion
for salmon angling and did not care what it might cost to
indulge it. He rented a fine house belonging to Lord Somerville
that overlooked the river at Melrose and set about securing all
the fishing he wanted. Younger looked back at his intervention
with a degree of bitterness: 'There were no gentlemen fishers
in those days as now come three hundred miles in cold spring
snows . . . it was years after this ere Scrope came round and
succeeded old John Wight and Geordie Sanderson by trebling

the rents of the Mertoun water, commencing what we may call the gentle epidemical mania for salmon fishing which has had the effect of these great lordly pikes driving us smaller fry out of the water . . .'

Younger regarded the coming of Scrope and those that followed him as a colonisation of his river by wealthy outsiders. The natives – the tacksmen and the local craftsmen such as himself – had generally coexisted on easy terms because there were no great social divisions between them. Now they were, in a sense, dispossessed by the power of money. But they were not driven away, because they were too useful. The lords and squires were tyros. They had the money and the leisure, and they were in love with the notion of salmon fishing. But they had little or no clue as to how to go about doing it. They needed the expertise of the likes of John Younger to tie the flies, to show them where the fish might take, to land the salmon when hooked. So they employed them, conferring on them the status of servant class.

Thus John Haliburton, who had had the Mertoun water for himself, was retained by Scrope as 'my fisherman' – doubtless on friendly terms, but each knew who was the boss. Scrope refers elsewhere to William Purdie who 'at that time rented the Bole-side water which runs by Abbotsford' and his son who 'came into my service as fisherman some seasons afterwards . . . he is a capital fly maker and boatman'.

In his classic book Scrope splices accounts of his piscatorial triumphs and disasters with quite detailed instructions on tackle and flies. There is a colour plate showing his six favourite flies – named Kinmont Willie, the Lady of Mertoun, Toppy, Michael Scott, Meg with the Muckle Mouth and Meg in her Brawns. The examples were, he says, 'tied by my fisherman, Charlie Purdie'. He alludes somewhere to a fly tied by himself, but in general he relied on the expertise of his retainers.

While Scrope dined with Sir Walter Scott at Abbotsford, or

with his landlord, Lord Somerville, various Purdies in their cottages busied themselves tying flies, making and mending rods, drying lines and preparing for the next day's fishing. If he had any qualms about the social gulf between him and the menials who made his sport possible, he held his tongue. The hierarchy that took control of the fishing on the Tweed in Scrope's time has stayed largely intact to the present day. There are the proprietors who own and let the beats (in some cases retaining the cream of the fishing themselves). There are the lessees (the latterday Scropes) who pay the rents and catch the fish. And there are the boatmen (ghillies elsewhere, but not on the Tweed) who attend the anglers and facilitate their sport.

That structure has never been seriously challenged, although aspects of it have been modified with the passing of time. Relations between the different tiers are generally amiable, as they evidently were two centuries ago. They are all bound together in a shared concern for the river's wellbeing. That concern may be derived from self-interest – the owners for their rents, the anglers for their enjoyment, the boatmen for their continued employment – but nonetheless it generally works for the good of the river.

However, it is hardly surprising that there should have been and should remain a lingering, often subliminal resentment against those who, by exercising the power of their wealth, took command of these natural resources. The so called 'anti land prejudice' has been attacked by commentators such as Sir Max Hastings. These critics point to the unchallengeable fact that angling makes a crucial and irreplaceable contribution to the local economies of the Borders and other regions, and that this contribution is possible only because of the spending power of owners and visiting anglers.

All true, and those whose livelihoods depend on those economies – boatmen, ghillies, tackle dealers, agents, hotel and B-and-B proprietors and so forth – would not get rid of the system if they could. But that does not mean that, deep down, they like it. And those further away, not dependent on the system and largely ignorant of how it works – land-rights campaigners and SNP members of the Scottish Parliament – exploit the blatant inequity for all they are worth by raising the emotive question Who Owns Scotland?

'It is to be thus: I stepping out of the boat at Loch Muick, Albert in his Highland dress assisting me out and I am looking at a stag which he is presumed to have just killed. In the water, holding the boat, are several of the men in their kilts – salmon are also lying on the ground . . . the picture is intended to represent me meeting Albert who has been stalking while I have been fishing, and the whole is quite consonant with the truth.'

These instructions from Queen Victoria to her favourite painter, Sir Edwin Landseer, were given in 1850, two years after she and her husband first leased the Balmoral estate on Deeside and two years before they bought it. The resulting canvas, *Royal Sports on Hill and Loch*, represents a remarkable exercise in myth-making.

An engraving based on Landseer's Royal Sports on Hill and Loch.

The stylised romantic scene is bathed in a watery, ethereal sunlight, which softens the rugged outlines of the peaks and takes away the harshness of the moorland. The figures are indistinct, their expressions unreadable. The Prince Consort, a German without a drop of Scottish blood in his veins, stands tall and erect in grey tartan coat and deerstalker hat like a Highland version of a medieval knight, his hand leading down his Guinevere, Victoria in white, plaid draped over her head. Tending one of the boats are two of the faithful retainers in kilts, waistcoats, boots and puff-sleeved shirts. The royal couple's son Bertie – in a kilt of different tartan, velvet coat and Glengarry cap – sits on a white pony, the animal's sad eyes fixed on the recumbent, dead-eyed stag. Behind Albert's stockings and brogues lies the salmon.

The picture has a strange, drugged quality, as if everyone and everything in it had quietly had their lifeblood drained away. It is saturated in an extreme and sentimentalised distillation of the Romantic ideal – appointed, as it were, by Royal Warrant – derived from an earlier and less mythologised model shaped in the novels and poems of Landseer's friend, Sir Walter Scott. There was no place in it for any of the uncomfortable realities of Highland life: the clearances, the imposition of sheep farming, the desperate poverty of crofting communities, emigration, feuding, nastiness of any kind. The landscape, though undeniably wild, is emasculated by the romantic glow. The retainers are permitted to keep a ruggedness of their own, but their whole attitude is one of submissive loyalty. They are no more than pieces of human scenery in the mythic stage set.

By erasing or literally painting over the real business of daily life, Victoria and Albert – aided and abetted by helpers such as Landseer – engineered a paradisial vision of the Highlands worthy of the Soviet propaganda machine. It is not surprising that subsequent Scottish social commentators viewed it with disdain. The Edinburgh novelist and poet George Scott-Moncrieff coined the term Balmorality for this exercise in imperial cultural colonialism – 'a glutinous compound of hypocrisy, false sentiment, industrialism, ugliness and clammy pseudo-Calvinism', he called it, 'in which all the treacheries and sordidness of the clan life of Scottish history were forgotten; a tartan patchwork quilt was laid over them.'

Landseer tinkered with *Royal Sports on Hill and Loch* for many years, and it was only delivered to the Royal Collection a year or so before his death in 1873. By then the colonisation it idealised had been matched by an actual annexation of Highland Scotland. In his masterly account, *Clanship to Crofters' War* (2013), the leading Scottish social historian Professor Sir Tom Devine charted this process. Between 1820 and 1880 almost three-quarters of Highland estates changed hands. The sellers were generally the chiefs of the historic clans, mauled and impoverished by taxes, death duties and collapsing incomes. The buyers were almost all English or Lowland Scots who had either made fortunes in industry or trade or inherited them. They did not buy these vast tracts of land with a view to making money, but to spending it. They wanted to ape the Highland dream promoted by their queen and her consort. They wanted their own Balmoral.

At the heart of the vision was the sporting estate, if possible accompanied by an existing baronial mansion, but to be fitted with one if need be. Improved transport – better roads, paddle-steamers, later the railways – made it possible for these new lairds to reach these previously inaccessible regions with comparative ease. As early as 1836 a guide to Scotland was able to state with confidence that 'a person might now dine in Edinburgh one day and breakfast in Inverness the next'.

Some of the new lodges were very splendid. Lochrosque Castle in Wester Ross, for example, boasted a newfangled water closet, 'superior dog kennel', coach house, vegetable garden and pony paddock in addition to six two-bed apartments. Others

Balmoral Castle, 1870.

were more basic, such as the one at Grimersta on the Isle of Lewis, which was described as late as 1871 as 'low, narrow, the walls only six feet high', with a combined dining and sitting room no more than twelve feet square and no running water.

The primary function of the lodge was to support access to the pleasures of the sporting estate, enabling owners and guests to 'enjoy the sport I love so well, the noblest sport of all, deer stalking', in the words of Duncan Darroch, a Lowland Scot landowner who bought the Torridon estate in Wester Ross in 1872. Huge tracts of land were fenced, provided with tracks for the removal of deer carcasses, and managed on behalf of what the land-rights campaigner Andy Wightman has characterised as 'this nouveau riche class of emergent landed proprietors'. By the end of the nineteenth century there were as many as 150 deer forests in Scotland, covering 2.5 million acres, establishing a pattern of ownership that persists to this day.

* * *

For the past fifteen years or so I have been a grateful guest during a week in July at a handsome but not overbearing example of the Victorian sporting lodge craze, a few miles inland from the coastal village of Bettyhill in Sutherland. It is quite modest in design, with no baronial or castellated pretensions, double-fronted in weathered grey stone with a short wing to one side and an annex with a corrugated-iron roof which was tacked on much later. The rooms are warm and spacious, the plumbing antique but serviceable. The whole interior is redolent of a distant time of ease: panelled walls, wooden floors, stone-flagged kitchen, huge cast-iron baths resting on legs, with a weighted adjustable column instead of a plug. The armchairs and sofas are deep and soft, the fireplace wide enough for a considerable blaze. A set of golf clubs leans against the wall in the downstairs loo, croquet mallets gather dust in a horizontal cabinet. Massive trees – Scots pines, sycamores, an elm and a wych elm, limes – look down on the house, but a wide gap to the front draws the eye over an idiosyncratic golf course in the foreground towards low, bare hills with rising peaks beyond.

A track leads from the house to the road that runs from Bettyhill on the sea along the valley to Loch Naver, Altnaharra and beyond. Where the track crosses the river there is a gauge which tells you at a glance the height of the water. Its level either quickens the heart with hope or deadens it with disappointment. Two feet is exciting, one foot is possible, at nought you start thinking about the beach, at three feet you are looking at flood and thoughts turn to books by the fire and those deep armchairs.

I am not really a salmon angler, but the Naver has been kinder to me than any other river I have fished. It is very lovely, winding along its mostly open valley in a classic sequence of riffle, pool and glide; big enough to have a touch of grandeur about it but offering a sweet intimacy as well, and wonderful wading and casting on its sweeping bends. When the water is right – high enough to bring the fish in from Torrisdale Bay on every tide, not so high as to be unfishable or to send them racing through to the loch – it can be magically productive. It is now in multiple ownership but a century ago it was owned by the Duke of Sutherland – one tiny part of a kingdom of more than a million acres that stretched from the Moray Firth far down the east coast up and across to the north and north-west coasts of the mainland.

George Leveson-Gower, 1st Duke of Sutherland, came from a Yorkshire landowning family. In 1785, when he was still plain Lord Trentham, he married Elizabeth, Countess of Sutherland, who had inherited a sizeable portion of northern Scotland from her father. In 1803 his already lavish fortune was swelled to an almost unimaginable size when he inherited from his bachelor uncle, the Duke of Bridgewater, coal mines that produced an income of £80,000 a year. He and his countess – who, by a legal quirk, retained control of her estates but not ownership – set about expanding their Scottish presence by snapping up smaller properties from financially hard-pressed owners at every opportunity. He died in 1833, six months after the dukedom was created; the land holdings were largely retained by his descendants until the turn of the century, when the 4th Duke decided it was all too much and instigated a disposal which was then continued by his son, the 5th Duke.

The family had other estates and grand houses in Yorkshire, Shropshire and Staffordshire as well as their mansion in St James's, London, now called Lancaster House. Their Scottish seat was Dunrobin, a baronial extravaganza designed by Sir Charles Barry and situated near Golspie in the far south of the Sutherland domain. The whole mighty enterprise was managed by a considerable bureaucracy and much time and effort were expended on sheep farming, forestry, mining, commercial fishing and farming. Much of the less productive land was divided into sporting estates which were leased to wealthy sportsmen keen to embrace the Balmoral model without actually having to own a part of it. Deer stalking and game shooting were the principal attractions, but the Sutherland empire included a sizeable share of northern Scotland's finest salmon rivers – including the Naver, the Helmsdale, the Brora and half the Shin.

For much of the nineteenth century the management focus with regard to these rivers was on commercial netting, some of it undertaken directly but most leased to third parties. Netting provided useful income, but increasingly the rentals from sporting tenants became more valuable – and those tenants began to nag the duke's men to restrict the netting on the estuaries so that more fish got upriver to put a bend in the anglers' rods.

In 1871 the Commissioner of Salmon Fisheries for Scotland, Archibald Young, urged the duke's factor that: 'No fixed nets should be placed within a limit of half a mile from either side of any of the Sutherland rivers, and that no net should be used within the rivers themselves, which should be kept entirely for angling which is yearly becoming more sought after and more valuable.' In 1900 the Sutherland Estates office in Tongue, on the north coast west of Bettyhill, received £2,100 in rents from the nets, and almost £12,000 from the sporting tenants.

Two years later, in 1902, Augustus Grimble published a one-volume condensed version of his *The Salmon Rivers of Scotland*. Despite being somewhat flawed in some its detail, Grimble's survey remains valuable in assessing the state of the rivers and of salmon angling at the turn of the century. At that time the Tweed was mercilessly hammered by commercial netting, and the worthwhile angling – and rents – were restricted to the autumn, when the nets came off. Grimble describes the thirty miles from Melrose to Coldstream as 'the cream of the Tweed fishing', and lists the proprietors and principal lessees. His workaday paragraphs bristle with names from *Burke's Peerage* and *Landed Gentry*: Lord Romney, the Dowager Lady Orr Ewing, Lord Polwarth, Sir

Henry Fairfax Lucy, Sir Edmund Antrobus, the Duke of Roxburghe, the Earl of Home, the Earl of Haddington and so on. The three miles of the Pavilion water that Scrope had leased from the 15th Lord Somerville was now owned by Mrs Henry, daughter of the 19th and last.

Today it is divided into three beats, Upper, Middle and Lower Pavilion, with Carryweil pool towards the top of Upper. I got on my bicycle beneath the viaduct and took the path that runs along the right bank to Melrose and beyond. Immediately downstream from the viaduct there is a long bend in the river. The far side is steepish, cloaked in ash, oak and sycamore. Scrope's rented house, Pavilion, a square, white Georgian villa with numerous additions, stands in a clearing commanding views up and down the river. From the footpath side it is a long, easy wade around the curve of the bend, an easy cast if the wind is not buffeting upstream, but I never even hooked a fish there.

Around the bend there is a grassy bank on the far side between the trees and the water. There is a good lie for a salmon there, but to fish it you have to cross over, which – before the railway reopened – meant a stiff walk across the viaduct. I was there on my own one afternoon when the biggest salmon I have ever had anything to do with put a head the size of a small dog's out of the water to take my fly. It roared downstream with irresistible force and broke me in the fast water above the next pool. The episode lasted no more than twenty seconds, just long enough for me to wonder how and where I might be able to land this fish, and left me feeling slightly shaky and not really able to believe the power I had felt at the end of my line.

That was some years ago. On the day of my cycle ride I was generally glad to be pedalling and not fishing. It was mid-September and the water was at a nice height. It should have been prime time, the start of the Tweed's fabled autumn run. But that year it failed utterly, causing much head-shaking and heart-searching along the whole river. There were plenty of anglers out on Middle and Lower Pavilion, casting away with dutiful persistence but no visible reward. I did not see more than a couple of fish swirl or jump, when the river should have been alive with them.

It was delightful, though, to be out in the soft sunshine with the leaves turning yellow and gold but not yet falling. I passed one pool after another: Kingswell Lees, where Scrope hooked his biggest fish, which he claims to have followed for a mile and three-quarters downstream before it was landed below Melrose Church; The Whirls, where – if Scrope is to be believed – he and his man Charlie Purdie were engaged in leistering, spearing salmon with a kind of trident, one night by torchlight when Purdie impaled an otter instead; Meg's Hole, where Black Meg of Darnwick, a witch, was chased into the river and drowned.

At The Generals, a normally productive pool towards the top end of Lower Pavilion, a couple were casting energetically under the eye of their boatman. She, younger and more receptive to instruction, was getting her line out nicely. He, quite a bit older and powerfully built, was expending much more effort to conspicuously less effect. From my side I could see that he was failing to load the rod properly, as a result of which the line kept collapsing on itself instead of rolling out across the water. He was audibly cross, his emotion doubtless compounded by the awareness that he was paying a great deal of money to fish a river where – even if his casting had been better – he was not going to catch anything. The boatman approached to offer some quiet words of advice only to be sent away with a flea in his ear. It could have been Scrope with Charlie Purdie.

Below Melrose Church is a cauld, a rough stone weir set at an angle across the stream. The river ran boisterously over it, then divided around an island of pale gravel with a good-looking run for a salmon along the far side. In the long, still flat above the cauld goosanders were diving for smolts, doing their bit to thin out the stock and further inflame the feelings of already aggrieved anglers. A cormorant perched motionless on a rock. It raised its wings as if about to join the goosanders in the hunt, then reconsidered the proposition and resumed its vigil. The amber stream ran on, very pleasant to behold but strangely and disconcertingly fishless.

CHAPTER SEVEN

For the Masses

This is the scene.

It is a Monday evening in late March 1880, in Sheffield. The venue for the monthly committee meeting of the Sheffield Anglers Association is in the Crown in Scotland Street, as it has been for the past few years. A shroud of sulphurous smoke from the innumerable chimneys of the innumerable factories, foundries and workshops that have made Sheffield the steel and cutlery capital of Europe covers the city. The light from the street lamps is filtered through the haze as if it were a muslin cloth, and the cobbles shine greasily with chemical residue even when there has been no rain.

The smoke inside the Crown is even thicker. At least half the men inside are smoking pipes, and a few are puffing on newfangled home-made cigarettes. The place is packed, all men and most of them fishermen. Because it is Monday, and Sheffield does not work on a Monday, they are at leisure, and the volume

SHEFFIELD SMOKE.
From a Drawing by A. MORROW.

The 'Sheffield Smoke' of the 1880s.

of noise indicates that a fair few have been there longer than is good for them. At this time of year there is no angling because two years ago Parliament passed an Act promoted by one of the city's MPs, A.J. Mundella, to prohibit it for coarse fish between mid March and mid June so they could have a chance to spawn in peace. So the fishermen in the Crown are restricted to looking back at the season just finished, ahead to the one that seems so infinitely distant to the passionate devotee of the sport, and discussing the burning issues of the day.

The committee members force their way through the crowd in the main bar towards the clubroom on the left. The landlord, a noted piscatorian himself, has a jovial but respectful greeting for each of them; they are noted men in these parts and the work they do for the Association has helped turn Sheffield into a hotbed of angling enthusiasm – as well as stimulating good trade for the pub. Ten years ago there was a handful of clubs and a scattering of anglers – now the Association includes more than two hundred clubs and counts more than eight thousand members, one in forty of the city's male population.

A fire blazes in the clubroom and the reflections of the flames dance on the sanded floor and nicotine-yellowed ceiling. It is a kind of angling museum. Old rods and nets are displayed on the walls. There are framed paintings and prints in a distinctly Waltonian style, and photographs of notable Sheffield men with notable catches. In one glass case resides Captain Taite's 25lb 12oz pike caught in the Keadby Canal in Lincolnshire in December 1872. In another is John Young's bronze-scaled, broad-shouldered 12lb 8oz barbel from the Idle, which flows into the Trent at Stockwith, facing a 6lb 11oz bream from the same river and just along the wall from a brace of thumping chub scaling 11lb 2oz together.

Here the talk is on the same subject as in the public bar, although quieter. The smoke is just as thick. The chairman consults his pocket-watch and thumps the gavel on the table. The first substantive item on the agenda is to review the agreement concluded last year with the Lincolnshire Association giving Sheffield access, under reciprocal terms, to forty miles of new water. There is general approval of the arrangement, as there is of the lease on four miles of the Trent at Torksey – although being tidal, with a powerful current flowing both downstream and upstream, it presents a challenge to Sheffield anglers generally more at home on canals and very slow rivers.

The secretary reports further correspondence from London expressing unhappiness with the length of the close season for coarse fishing. The London clubs say it's too long and is affecting membership and the tackle trade. But the Sheffield anglers are proud of their MP and his Act, and of the part they have played in protecting a precious resource. There is agreement around the table that no changes should be countenanced.

The secretary then reports on dissent closer to home. Most of the Sheffield clubs were formed in pubs and retain close links with them. But the growing temperance movement takes a dim view of those links, and an even dimmer view of angling on a Sunday. The views of the Association, firmly expressed to the accompaniment of some banging of tankards on the table, is that if the working man chooses to spend his Sunday on river bank or canal side rather than listening to sermonising, that is his business. As for the suggestion periodically urged by certain chiselling employers that Saint Monday, that sacred institution, should become another working day – well, the very idea is enough to provoke a crescendo of angry protest.

The meeting moves on to more parochial administrative matters. The chairman reports with satisfaction the successful conclusion of negotiations with the Manchester, Sheffield and Lincolnshire Railway Company for the provision of special angling trains to coincide with the major competitions on the Association's waters. The previous year eighty such trains ran from and back to Victoria Station, carrying 20,000 anglers who paid the equivalent of a day's wages for their concessionary tickets. This year, owing to rising demand, the company will be laying on at least one hundred. The secretary intervenes to say that guarantees had been given for both the volume of business and the behaviour of the fishermen. Anyone who stepped out of line risked being banned.

Membership is up again and subscriptions are coming in nicely. Several local tackle shops have donated rods, reels and baskets as prizes for the matches, welcome additions to the familiar kettles, sacks of coal and provisions. The committee agrees that 100 guineas from club funds should be used for cash prizes at the annual Gala at Kirkstead on the Witham near Lincoln. A motion is approved to maintain the annual contribution to the Benevolent Fund at five shillings per member. Hardship payments had been made over the winter to several widows and two members no longer able to work because of accidents in grinders' workshops. Another application had been rejected for falling foul of the rule that injuries resulting from 'fighting, wrestling, drunkenness or other manifest evil course' did not qualify.

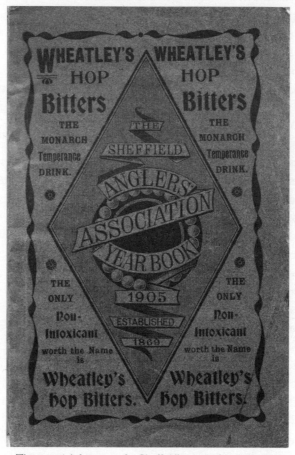

The essential document for Sheffield's army of anglers, 1905.

The fog of smoke grows denser and the voices more assertive as more tobacco and ale are consumed. Any other business is concluded and the chairman declares the meeting over. The committee members disperse – some to return home, some to join one or other of the conversations elsewhere in the pub. Everyone knows everyone and a stranger coming in would feel very much a stranger. Many of the customers came together to form the first clubs; some of the old-timers can even reminisce about the days when Sheffield's own rivers – the Don, the Sheaf, the Rother – had fish in them, before they were converted into open sewers.

Most of the talk centres on the shared interest – the season past, the season to come – and even when it drifts away to other subjects, it eventually returns to angling. You can see why they call the Crown in Scotland Street, Sheffield, 'the Anglers' Parliament'.

The scene shifts to the city's Victoria Station, and forward to the ungodly hour of 2.30 on a Monday morning in the second half of June. As always in Sheffield there is more smoke in the air than oxygen – factory smoke, locomotive smoke, tobacco smoke. The train for Torksey is jam-packed with anglers in caps and outdoor clothes, rods and nets and baskets, buckets containing maggots dyed in various colours, worms, and bags of bread ground to powder which they will mix with water to form balls of groundbait to attract the fish.

Everyone is smoking, everyone is male. There is a hubbub of broad Sheffield accents. The talk is liberally spiced with swear words. But hardly anyone is drunk, although the same will probably not be true when they all return many hours hence. Despite the hour there is an air of keen excitement. Good fellowship prevails. The insults hurled at latecomers hurrying along the platform encumbered by their gear is coarse but good-humoured. It is Saint Monday and the fishing season opened the week before.

An hour and a half later the train rumbles over the new iron bridge across the Trent at Torksey, slowing on its approach to the little station there. Those still awake get a glimpse of the river flowing broad and strong. Some are acquainted with it already and explain to those who aren't how it differs from the waters they are used to, such as the Keadby Canal or the sluggish Witham in the heart of Lincolnshire. The Trent here is tidal, which means that twice a day it flows upstream instead of down, and strongly.

The normal Sheffield method of angling, proudly proclaimed by Sheffielders as superior to all others, involves the use of a stiffish rod of ten feet or so with a highly flexible tip of whale-bone or lancewood, lines of undressed plaited silk and a length of gossamer-thin gut, a tiny crow-quill float, a tiny hook sufficient to hold two maggots at most and a few minuscule lead weights to make the float stand upright. It has evolved in order to catch generally small fish – roach, dace, gudgeon and the like – on canals and slow water. There are stretches of the Trent where it can be employed to good effect, but others – as those with the experience explain to the novices – where the current is too powerful and the fish run bigger. On these stretches it may be necessary to switch to the Nottingham method: stronger gut, bigger floats, more weight, bigger baits. The experts carry two rods and two sets of tackle to cover the eventualities.

The clatter of the train over Torksey Bridge alerts the locals to the imminent invasion. Anyone able to sleep through that is likely to be awakened soon afterwards as the train disgorges four hundred Sheffield men onto the platform with their gear and they head for the river. The first bands of light from the breaking dawn finger the eastern sky behind them as they march down the lane. Like a regiment on manoeuvres, they cross the Gainsborough–Newark road and reach what could pass for an army camp that has been set up beside the river.

They dump their equipment somewhere on the ground and form themselves into a queue which shuffles forward as the daylight strengthens.

Assorted poles and rods from
Practical Fishing for the So-called Coarse Fishes, 1906.

At the front, officials from the Sheffield Anglers Association are organising the draw. The four miles of river bank have been divided into stretches of ten yards or so known as pegs, each numbered from one to however many anglers have registered for the match. The low numbers are closest to the camp, the highest may be two miles away. Each man looks at the number he has drawn, assesses its location, retrieves his gear and sets off to find his peg. There are groans of dismay from those who pick the high numbers, which are greeted with more rough banter; it may take them a couple of hours across the fields and along the dew-soaked banks to reach their peg. For those closer to the base camp there will be time to investigate the lunch pack prepared by wife or mother, to assess the swim and assemble tackle at leisure, to have a smoke and a wander and exchange views with neighbours on the prospects for the day.

By nine o'clock it is assumed that everyone is ready. A bugle is sounded by one of the Sheffield AA officers, and the word is passed along the length of the match water. Four hundred pairs of arms swing four hundred rods through the air, the attached floats and

THE DRAW - *SHEFFIELD & DISTRICT GALA MATCH* - SUN 16TH SEPT. 1945

Sheffield anglers wait to find out where they'll be fishing, 1945.

baits hit the water. Four hundred hands sling balls of bread ground-bait into the swim, the consistency and target area carefully judged to draw fish within casting distance. The match is on.

The appeal of angling – the desire to escape into the countryside and be a free spirit in a natural, unspoiled world – was felt by all classes of society. But as that society became ever more class-divided, it was inevitable that the response to that appeal became increasingly dictated by opportunity, which itself was dictated by wealth and social position. By the middle of the nineteenth century the upper tiers were well on their way to securing for themselves the trout and grayling fishing that was conveniently accessible from major centres of population. That kind of fishing – the kind Charles Cotton preferred – was a very limited resource, and the laws of supply and demand meant that it was quickly removed from the reach of ordinary working people. Around

London, for instance, there were trout streams in Hertfordshire, Berkshire and Hampshire where the fishing rights were snapped up by clubs of gentlemen or moneyed middle-class professionals eager to fish the artificial fly.

At the same time that the fly-fishing rivers were being reserved for the benefit of those with the money, the industrialisation of Britain was having a devastating impact on the rivers that ran through or near the great mining and manufacturing centres. The Thames in London, the Trent in Stoke, the Tyne in Newcastle, the Mersey and Irwell in Manchester, the Don and its tributaries in Sheffield – all were degraded to the status of conduits to receive and remove industrial waste and the filth from the slums. Within a generation the industrial towns and cities of England, South Wales and Lowland Scotland had wiped out the fish populations on their doorsteps.

But the workers toiling amid the smoke and the grime and the din still yearned for the Waltonian vision of Arcadian England. They dreamed of open fields, flowery meadows, birdsong, trees in blossom, the silver streams. They wanted to go fishing.*

In Sheffield the first fishing clubs were formed in the 1860s. They were intimately associated with particular pubs and arose from what another historian, Richard Holt, termed 'the essentially street-based milieu of most working-class sports'. It was natural that the grinders, cutlers, furnacemen and foundry workers talked fishing in the workplace, continued the talk when they spilled into the pubs in the evening, and in time organised themselves into a club – all under the benevolent eye of a landlord who rightly regarded anglers as more likely to behave themselves than football supporters or dog-fighting enthusiasts.

---

* At this point I would like to pay a heartfelt tribute to the social historian and authority on sport and leisure, John Lowerson, on whose work this whole section is based. Lowerson, who died in 2009, wrote a series of scholarly, literate and witty studies of the place of angling in English society, and without his exhaustive investigation of the available resources – chiefly old angling journals – I would have had very little to say on this rich subject.

The demands of the working man's working week made his free time very precious. Sheffield clung fiercely to Saint Monday, but elsewhere it was more common for Sunday to be the one day of leisure (the half-day on Saturday, when it came in, was of little use to anglers). In time angling became associated with the anti-Sabbatarianism that took hold in the second half of the nineteenth century for diverse reasons. In 1860 the Friendly Society of Shoreditch in London became the first angling club to do its angling on a Sunday, and the example was soon followed by other London clubs, as well as those in Sheffield, Birmingham and Manchester.

One of these London clubs was the Brothers Well-Met, who gathered on Sunday and Thursday evenings at the Berkeley Castle in Raherne Street, in the City. The landlord, Mr Clout – 'an old London angler' in the words of the *Fishing Gazette* – saw an opportunity to combine business with pleasure and made a deal with the London, Brighton and South Coast Railway Company to run a special 'Cockney anglers' service every Sunday during the fishing season to and from the quiet Sussex village of Amberley, from whose station the jolly excursionists made their way to the River Arun to fish and have fun.

Mr Clout's enterprise flourished. The Berkeley Castle became as much ticket office as pub, to the extent that by 1877 he was selling four thousand tickets a season for the weekly Amberley outing. The charge was two-and-sixpence return, third-class only, half-price for 'children under 12 providing they are not more than 5ft in their stockings'. The big club day of the year was in August, when, according to the *Fishing Gazette*, the gathering contained 'a fair sprinkling of the wives and sweethearts' anxious to partake of Mr Clout's 'regular good feed'. Moreover the Brothers Well-Met also staged a Ladies' Match in which 'the fair creatures stuck to their rods like glue and displayed an amount of skill that would have frightened a nervous fisherman'.

The growth of angling and angling clubs followed much the same path in all the great industrial cities of England. The collective purchasing power of the associations made it possible for their officers to bargain from a position of strength with the railway companies, and with the riparian owners whose waters were brought within reach by the spread of the rail network. Despite the progressive example set by Mr Clout and the Brothers Well-Met, working-class angling continued to be overwhelmingly male. However, it was also seen – not least by employers – as a force for good. Clubs had to be able to assure the railway companies and the owners of waters that their members would behave themselves. In general the assurances were fulfilled; the threat of expulsion was an effective one, and instances of drunkenness, cheating and anti-social behaviour were severely punished. On the other hand, betting on the outcome of matches, although against the rules, was widely condoned.

The progress towards social respectability was closely observed by one of the most delightful and individual writers on the sport, J.W. Martin, known throughout the angling world by his nom de plume, 'The Trent Otter'. Martin was born in the Fens in the middle of the nineteenth century into a life of poverty and hardship. He left school at the age of ten to help his widowed mother, working at various times as a canal-boat boy, a bricklayer's labourer and a blacksmith's assistant. As a young man Martin moved to Newark, where he helped run a fishing-tackle shop and got to know the local Trent experts and their methods. He wrote a little book, *The Nottingham Style of Float Fishing and Spinning*, which brought him to the attention of the founder and editor of the *Fishing Gazette*, R.B. Marston. Marston became his mentor, sent him books to open his mind, and encouraged him to write more himself. Several more books followed – my favourites are *Days Among the Pike and Perch* and *My Fishing Days and Fishing Ways* – written in an earthy, good-humoured style all his own.

Martin eventually prospered enough to have his own tackle business in London. As a young man he had encountered the Sheffield angler at a competition and was appalled – 'the very

The 'Trent Otter' with a young disciple.

scum of the Sheffield dregs . . . the very lowest of the low grinders whose every word was an oath . . . they consumed more beer and tobacco than was good for them and conducted themselves in such a manner that any respectable angler felt ashamed of himself and the company he found himself in'. Over time Martin witnessed the 'dregs' being uplifted by the sport that was his life's passion, so that he was able to write in his *Coarse Fish Angling* (1908) that 'it is a pleasure to engage in one of these contests, no ungentlemanly conduct being tolerated'.

Working-class fishing was focused on the match. With such great numbers of anglers taking up the sport it was clearly unfeasible to allow free movement on club waters. The only way was to allocate each man his peg, his ten yards, and it was inevitable that the competitive spirit was unleashed. On a single day in 1893 twenty-three of the Sheffield clubs ran separate

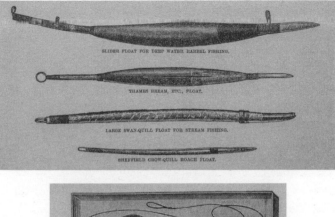

SLIDER FLOAT FOR DEEP WATER BARBEL FISHING.

THAMES BREAM, ETC., FLOAT.

LARGE SWAN-QUILL FLOAT FOR STREAM FISHING.

SHEFFIELD CROW-QUILL ROACH FLOAT.

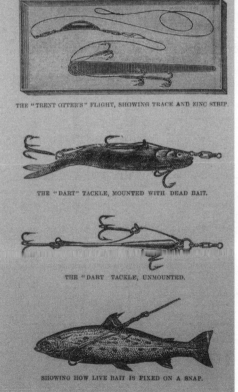

THE "TRENT OTTER'S" FLIGHT, SHOWING TRACE AND ZINC STRIP.

THE "DART" TACKLE, MOUNTED WITH DEAD BAIT.

THE "DART" TACKLE, UNMOUNTED.

SHOWING HOW LIVE BAIT IS FIXED ON A SNAP.

Assorted items of tackle from
The 'Trent Otter's' Little Angling Book, 1910.

competitions. Generally the prizes were basic – kettles, clogs, coal and the like – but for the bigger matches the promoters pushed the boat out with valuable cash prizes which pulled in vast numbers of entries. A match staged by the Queens Head, Furnace Hill, Sheffield on the Witham in Boston attracted 1,300 participants.

A by-product of the rapid growth of competitive fishing was a new tenderness towards the resource that made the exercise possible – the fish. Historically anglers killed their catch, whether it was a trout or a chub, and ate them or gave them away or sometimes left the corpses on the bank. The officials of the new angling clubs swiftly worked out that if everyone killed the fish they caught there would very soon be no fish left to catch. As one, they brought in a rule that all fish caught had to be kept alive in a keep-net tethered to the bank so they could be returned to the water after the weigh-in. The fact that most of the target species were tasteless and bony probably made it easier to enforce the rule. The practice of catch-and-release – as it is known today – swiftly became entrenched in the ethos of the sport and has remained so ever since.

The Sheffield match angler was not too particular about what species of fish he caught – gudgeon, bleak, dace, ruffe, they would all take a maggot and they all counted at the weigh-in. But there were two species – roach and bream – that were regarded with particular affection and were courted with particular attention. This was partly because they were bigger – it would take half a dozen gudgeon to match a single decent roach for weight, and twice as many to equal an average bream. But it was also because of their sociable inclinations. They go about in shoals, and if you could seduce a shoal of either into your patch of water and keep them there and keep them interested – well, you could fill a net and win the match.

Of the two, the roach is by some distance the more handsome. With its small, delicate mouth, golden-red eye, silvery sides and belly, it is a distinctly elegant, even pretty fish, and its red-tinged fins give it a dash of colourful vivacity. I have caught a few in my time but not one over a pound, and have never come close to a red-letter day such as that described by the great pioneer of sports broadcasting, Howard Marshall, in a piece entitled 'The Day the Roach Went Mad', when – in a mere two hours on the Hampshire Avon – he caught sixty pounds of them, with five fish going over two pounds each. Another top-class angling writer, H.T. Sheringham, loved the roach dearly, both float-fishing for them in the conventional style and – ahead of his time – with a fly rod.

In his marvellous book, *Coarse Fishing*, Sheringham declared that he had respect for the bream – before admitting that many did not share his sentiment. I'm afraid I am one of those who do not, although I freely confess that my experience of them has not been extensive enough to allow any other feeling to develop. Seen from the side, the bream appears imposing with its tall, bronzed flanks, but from above its is slender and even meagre, like a house with a broad double front which is only one room deep. Its small head and small eye suggest limited intelligence, while its sliminess – Sheringham blamed this for its low reputation and suggested wearing an apron to fish for it – makes it somewhat unpleasant to handle.

But I am not a roach-fisher or a bream-fisher, and those that are like nothing better than to get stuck into a shoal of either. A good catch of bream is measured in stones rather than pounds, and the fact that they offer no more resistance than a similar-sized piece of wet sacking is easily forgiven when they are on the feed. As for roach, Sheringham correctly identified them as the most important freshwater fish of all – measured by popularity. Nine out of ten of the anglers to be seen at a London railway station on a Saturday or Sunday heading for the Thames or the Lea were, he judged, equipped for roach fishing – 'and nine out of ten of them set little store by any other kind of fish'.

* * *

In time the competitive urge promoted by the angling clubs in the great industrial cities began to spread wings nationally. The Sheffield AA had begun staging what it called All England matches in the 1880s on its waters in Lincolnshire, but in practice it came down to Sheffield men against Lincolnshire men. Dialogue and co-operation between the various city associations on such matters as resisting a proposed rod tax led to the formation of the National Federation of Anglers in 1903. In October 1906 the first National Championship, sponsored by the *Daily Mirror*, was held on the Thames at Pangbourne, near Reading. In advance there was much trumpeting of the merits of the differing regional styles – Sheffield for fishing fine and light, Nottingham for heavier tackle and bigger baits, London for a long pole with no reel and a fixed line. The clear winners were the Boston Angling Association, deploying the Sheffield method, with the Sheffield AA second and London well back in fourth place.

Once established, the working-class enthusiasm for match angling never waned. Post-1918 the Sheffield angler was compelled by market forces to bid farewell to his beloved Saint Monday, but the special trains continued to run out of Victoria Station on Sundays throughout the season. As late as 1955 the *Sunday Chronicle* ran a feature under the headline 'Sheffield – the City of Angling Widows' describing the 'excited, determined, chattering exodus' of 35,000 anglers in the early hours of Sunday morning on trains and coaches heading for the Trent, the Witham, and the canals and dykes of Lincolnshire.

According to the newspaper, many went straight from a thirteen-hour shift in the blast furnaces, and returned from their fishing to begin their next shift. Why this passion? the writer wondered. The answer came from the secretary of the Sheffield and District Anglers Association, Mr J.W. Taylor: 'When fishing they feel they get everything they need – air and sun, rest and quiet. Any local doctor will tell you that fishing is the foundation on which the steel industry continues to progress.'

But alas for Sheffield! It has long since lost its place as a city of angling and as the steel capital of Europe, the decline of each mirroring the other. The collapse of heavy industry in the 1970s and 80s and the steep rise in unemployment inevitably impacted on the membership of the angling clubs. Falling income made it impossible for the Sheffield AA to hold onto its waters, and the downhill spiral fed itself even after the worst of the economic slump was over. The loss of waters and support was compounded by a shift in the coarse-fishing world away from river fishing and matches to the specialised pursuit of huge, artificially reared carp stocked in syndicate-run stillwaters. At the last annual meeting of the Sheffield Anglers Association in 2011, four members showed up. Later that year the association and its few remaining waters were taken over by the Scunthorpe Pisces (previously the Scunthorpe Police Angling Club).

The city that once had two hundred angling clubs now has none. Nor is there a single tackle shop, where half a century ago there were dozens. The Crown in Scotland Street, the Anglers' Parliament, is a cheap hotel called Sleep.

It is a curious chain of events that has left Sheffield devoid of organised angling, yet the city's river, the Don – whose toxic, fishless filthiness drove the Waltonians of a century and a half ago in search of clean waters far away – has been reborn in a remarkable way. The disappearance of the industry that made the city great has allowed its river to breathe again in a way that the old committee members of the Sheffield AA would have found inconceivable.

Salmon now run through the city on their way to spawn upstream. Populations of wild brown trout and grayling are expanding on the Don and on tributaries like the Sheaf and the Rivelin that historically were no more than sewers and waste channels. Sheffield has become a destination for a new breed of urban fly fisher. The fishing is free so they have no need of a club to organise it. There is, however, a branch of the Wild Trout Trust called SPRITE – Sheffield Partnership for Rivers in Town Environments – which brings volunteers together to clear rubbish, monitor fish and invertebrates, carry out habitat work and spread the message among schools and community groups.

At Torksey, Sir John Fowler's Grade-2-listed tubular box-girder bridge still spans the Trent. But no train has crossed it for sixty years, and it now carries a cycle path that heads west from Torksey towards the steaming towers of Cottam power station. Torksey Station, where the angling specials discharged their eager passengers, has been entirely erased from the map, although the route of the line to Lincoln is discernible on Google Maps. Station Road, down which the angling army marched in the breaking dawn, runs through a golf course, and the station site is covered by a bijou development of six- and seven-bedroom mansions called The Fairways.

The bridge was built across the northern tip of a thickly wooded river island. I stood on it looking upstream. The cooling towers and chimneys of the next power station, West Burton, were etched against the skyline. The river banks were delineated by broken lines of scrub willows, with flat farmland beyond. The tide was running strongly upstream, pushing urgently either side of the island. The water was cocoa brown, the surface roughened by the breeze. A sign declared that the fishing was rented to the Scunthorpe Pisces, but there was not an angler to be seen and the water is no longer listed on the club's website.

An angler myself, I would not have known where to start on water like this, so intimidatingly big and powerful and hard to read. I very much wanted to find someone who did. I cycled a little way south along Church Lane, where there is a succession of bungalows with gardens stretching down to the river. At the bottom of one of them I spotted a white-haired old boy in a cap and wellington boots standing guard beside two fishing rods and a long-handled landing net.

Waiting for a bite on the Trent.

He was, he informed me, hoping for a bream or two, although he'd only just cast out and was waiting for the tide to slacken. He'd spent most of his working life at Cottam power station and as a member of the fishing club there had fished the lower Trent with extreme keenness, thinking nothing of getting to the prime spot above Cromwell weir in the middle of the night to bag a swim, even though you weren't allowed to fish until dawn. You could get a hundred pounds of chub in a session there, he said, nostalgically recalling his younger, more energetic self. Now he had the fishing at his back door he fished much less, although when the granddaughters came over they liked to catch something. And this morning – well, he'd just felt like some bank time. Maybe the bream would oblige.

The thing about the Trent, he said – the river now at the top of the tide and still, the water over the bank and sloshing around his boots – is knowing where the fish are and when they feed. That takes some doing – a sentiment that doubtless would have been echoed by those grinders and cutlers and furnacemen of long ago. The river is much cleaner now and the nature of the fishing has changed beyond recognition. There are species in the Trent that J.W. Martin and the old Sheffield men would not have known because they weren't there – alien zander and catfish, even the occasional golden orfe. The chairman of the Scunthorpe Pisces told me they had had several reports of sturgeon being caught.

In his wonderful memoir *My Fishing Days and Fishing Ways*, Martin recalled a tackle dealer in Newark, Owen by name, whom he knew in the 1870s, by which time he was too ancient and decrepit to fish any more. Owen showed the young Trent Otter his barbel-fishing gear: a solid timber rod weighing more than three pounds, line of hempen cord and a weight 'to brain the first barbel it dropped on'. The old man pointed at an entry in his fishing diary recording the best day he ever had – 'thirty-two barbel had been slain . . . they weighed more than two hundredweight, largest nearly fifteen pounds, an average of seven'.

It would gladden the hearts of the veterans of those days to know that the Trent – and particularly the tidal stretch below Cromwell weir – is now regarded as perhaps the prime destination for big barbel in the country. The growth rates assessed by the Environment Agency are phenomenal, and specimens of fifteen pounds plus are recorded on a regular basis.* The tackle has advanced light years beyond the greenheart and whalebone of yesteryear. Martin recommended using a big lobworm as bait, having chopped up and thrown in a couple of thousand to get the barbel interested, or a chunk of the fat and animal fragments left at the bottom of the tallow chandler's copper melting vat,

---

*   The Trent record was broken in July 2020 by a fish of twenty pounds six ounces.

while the experts of today use fish-oil pellets or bigger balls called boilies, made of semolina and soya flour flavoured with fish oils, blood and more exotic ingredients.

The world has moved on. The Sheffield Anglers Association and the special trains have gone the way of the blast furnaces. But the river keeps flowing, and the anglers keep coming.

CHAPTER EIGHT

Salmon on Ice

For a mere fishmonger's residence, Pitfour Castle is impressive. Built in 1784 in the overblown castellated style pioneered by Robert Adam – and possibly designed by Adam himself – the three-storey pile with towers and central dome stands on the edge of the village of St Madoes a few miles east of Perth and looks out over the waters of the Firth of Tay. It was those waters and the salmon that ran through them that nourished the very considerable fortune accumulated by the man who commissioned the castle, the Great Fishmonger of the Tay, John Richardson.

For almost thirty years Richardson controlled the commercial exploitation of the salmon of the Tay – with the Tweed, the most productive river in Scotland. That period saw a complete transformation in the trade in salmon; Richardson was the driving force behind the first stage of that transformation, and a helpless observer of the second.

Richardson was born in 1760, and his father was a partner in

Pitfour Castle

an enterprise called the Perth Fishing Company. As a young man Richardson took control of what became Richardson and Co. It is recorded that by the early 1770s the family controlled most of the tacks on the Tay, which was fished by net and coble from the mouth of the Isla about twelve miles above Perth down to the mouth, three miles below Perth.

At that time the Firth of Tay – which extends twenty miles or so from the mouth of the river to the sea – was hardly fished at all, because it was too wide and shallow for the net-and-coble method. The money was made from the river and its mouth. In 1795 John Richardson stated that he was paying £7,000 a year in rents for the tacks down to Newburgh, just below where it reaches the firth; from there to Tayport near the sea the rents were worth no more than £500. Although his business was concentrated on the Tay fishing, it was not restricted to it. To sustain exports he bought in fish from a host of other Scottish rivers – including the Tweed, Findhorn, Spey, Beauly and Oykel, and from as far away as Grimersta on Lewis in the Hebrides.

The old ways of preserving salmon for shipment were to salt them or pickle them. An important refinement of the second of these was known as kitting. It was developed in Newcastle in

Perth Bridge, crossing the River Tay. Illustration from 1850.

the 1740s, apparently using salmon brought by packhorse from the Tweed. The salmon had their backbones removed before being simmered for half an hour in a liquid composed of salted water and beer and then packed into barrels, known as kits, topped up with strong vinegar flavoured with cloves, ginger, mace, rosemary and lemon peel. The process was embraced with enthusiasm in Perth, where – according to George Penny's *Traditions of Perth* (1836) – the backbones were 'sold to the people for a trifle and supplied a good and cheap dinner for many a family' as well as being used to impart 'an excellent relish to a *pundie* of ale'. Penny described how cartloads of salmon were driven each morning to Richardson's boiling-house, so many that sometimes the coopers did not have enough kits ready for them. The leftovers, called roans, 'were thrown into the river which attracted vast numbers of large eels and this afforded fine eel fishing'.

Kitted salmon remained edible for several weeks, if not months. That made it possible for them to be supplied to London – by far the most important market – long after the fishing season finished at the end of August. But Richardson's trading network spread far further than that. The company records list many of Europe's biggest cities and ports as customers – among them Paris, Rouen, Marseilles, Bordeaux, Rotterdam, Bilbao, Venice and Livorno. A note dating from 1795 refers to several hundred barrels originating from Fort William on the west coast of Scotland and from Berwick at the mouth of the Tweed being delivered to Venice, 170 barrels going to Bilbao, and other consignments landed in Marseilles and Dunkirk.

Richardson was acutely aware that if he could get his premium-quality fish – the big silver protein-packed spring salmon arriving from the sea from January to the end of April – to his premium market, London, in decent condition, he would make premium profits. At that time of year the ambient temperature was generally low enough for a 'fresh' salmon to remain edible for a few days. As soon as possible after capture they were packed into baskets with straw for insulation and loaded onto one of Richardson's fast smacks. With a following wind these boats could make it to the Port of London in fifty hours, where a single fish would fetch as much as eleven shillings and five pence.

But this trade was always a gamble. If the smack lost time because of bad weather her cargo would go off fast. Richardson's skippers had standing orders that if this happened they should put into any port they could reach and sell the fish for whatever they could get. And in any event, by May it was generally too warm, and thereafter the fish were sent in kits.

This was a supply squeeze in urgent need of innovative thinking to loosen it. As so often, the breakthrough came through serendipity. John Richardson was acquainted with the Perth MP George Dempster, who came from a rich family of Dundee merchants and was a true Enlightenment figure – in his youth a friend of David Hume and James Boswell, a linguist and scholar, a pioneer of land improvement on his estate at Skibo in Sutherland, a fierce opponent of the war against the American colonials. Among his many posts, Dempster served as a director of the East

India Company until he resigned in protest at what he regarded as unwarranted territorial ambitions. It was at their offices in London in 1786 that he happened to meet one of the Company's more intriguing and exotic figures, Alexander Dalrymple.

Dalrymple was the East India Company's official hydrographer (as well as being a Fellow of the Royal Society, the originator of what became known as the Beaufort wind scale, and the first man to propose the existence of Australia). He had travelled widely around the islands and territories of the southern seas and had become familiar with the Chinese trading post at Canton. In the course of their conversation, Dalrymple told Dempster that, to keep their catches fresh for transport inland, Chinese traders packed them in ice which they had stored in ice houses located at strategic points on the trading routes.

Dempster, in a manner befitting a progressive freethinker, saw the possibilities at once. In his own words, 'I took pen and ink and on the spot wrote an account of this conversation to Mr Richardson.' Richardson was sceptical, as he later admitted – 'we made the experiment rather in consequence of Mr Dempster's earnest manner of writing than in expectation of any good'. But make the experiment he did, and it changed everything.

To begin with, the scale of the operation was limited by the difficulty of obtaining enough ice. But Richardson soon had a string of ice houses constructed between Perth and the mouth of the Tay. Salmon were taken to one or other of these as soon as possible after capture, then shipped to London six or seven to a box, packed between blocks of ice. In September 1788 Richardson reported that: 'The salmon fisheries on the Tay employ between two and three hundred fishers. Six vessels are employed during the season running to and from London which is the principal if not the only market – a considerable part are sent fresh in the spring season and for the past two years the greatest proportion of the fresh salmon have been packed in ice.'

Richardson had bought the Pitfour estate and built his castle before Dempster's intervention, so he must have been doing good business already. Now he did even better. His control of virtually the entire Tay salmon fishery and the transport route out of Perth enabled him to balance supply with demand precisely. It did not suit him to catch too many fish; that merely depressed the price. Between 1784 and 1799 the annual catch averaged between 36,000 and 46,000 fish a year. That was sufficient to sustain Richardson and Co. handsomely without depleting the stock unduly or threatening the sustainability of the salmon run.

It was, of course, a monopoly. With hindsight it is easy to see that it acted as a powerful conservation measure. Furthermore – unlike many conservation measures that would follow, derived from more altruistic motives – it was rigorously enforced. But in an age of competition it could not last. Serendipity took a hand once more, this time with very different results.

On the other side of the country, on the Scottish side of the Solway Firth, two fisherman brothers from Annan, William and James Irvine, had being trying out ways to increase their catches of salmon. On the Solway the ebbing tide left extensive pools between exposed sandbanks in which fish were inclined to hang around until they were filled again by the incoming tide. In 1788, near the mouth of the Annan, the brothers set up nets around one pool or another stretched between stakes that were driven into the sand, in such a way that the net opened with the flood tide and closed on the ebb, trapping the salmon that had strayed into it.

They were successful with their method, so much so that they looked around for somewhere else to try it. The Solway is a long, wide estuary that receives the waters of the Eden and Border Esk on the English side and those of the Annan, Nith and Cree on the Scottish. The ebbing tide exposes vast stretches of sand and mud, which are then covered to no great depth by the incoming tide. The Firth of Tay presented an east coast match

– they could almost have been the two stains left when a piece of paper is folded through an ink blot. The Irvine brothers travelled to Perth, but because the configuration of the firth meant that they did not find the standing pools as on the Solway, they did not persevere with the venture. But by then they had acquainted a kinsman of theirs, John Little, with their fixed net, and he was more persistent and ingenious.

In 1797 John Little set up a version of the Irvine brothers' stake net on the foreshore at Seaside, an estate on the north side of the Firth of Tay owned by James Hunter. That part of the firth had never been systematically fished, because it was too wide and shallow for the traditional net-and-coble method. But John Little immediately caught salmon in his stake net. He was not to know – no one knew then – that when returning from the sea to their birth rivers, salmon tend to hug the coast on their approach to their estuary and then the sides of the estuary itself as they seek and hold the scent that guides them upriver. Those whose business it was to catch them soon cottoned on.

At the end of that first season John Little negotiated a tack with Hunter on behalf of himself and his three brothers. In 1801 the Seaside stake net – by then adapted so it could take fish on both the ebb and flood tides – recorded a catch of almost three thousand fish. The following year it was over five thousand. Unsurprisingly the owners of previously unfished stretches of shore along the firth fell over themselves in the rush to make deals with Little & Co. Other tacksmen saw the opportunity, and the stake nets spread along both sides of the firth like bindweed.

John Richardson identified the threat at once. A year after the first net appeared at Seaside he wrote to the Perth Town Council to argue that stake nets were illegal. His argument was taken up by the Earl of Kinnoull, who owned the lower part of the Earn (which entered the firth opposite Pitfour Castle) and who brought a legal action against Hunter of Seaside. The essence of his case – a principle that would be argued and re-argued in countless lawsuits over the coming decades – was that John Little's stake net was catching fish that would otherwise have run up the Earn and were rightfully the earl's. Hunter's lawyers maintained, quite wrongly, that the salmon taken in the stake net never intended to go upriver at all, and that those that did have that intention swam straight up the middle of the firth and did not linger along the sides. It followed, they argued, that John Little's nets had not diminished the number of salmon available to the earl's tacksman – John Richardson.

In the event Hunter lost, and the Seaside net was suppressed in 1805. But by then the stake-net horse had bolted. Other land-owners along the firth who had let tacks for substantial rents on previously worthless stretches of sand and rock were not all inclined to sacrifice the income on the basis of one legal ruling. William Maule of Panmure, on the north side east of Dundee, was getting £2,700 a year for fishing previously let at £100. William Dalgleish of Scotscraig, on the opposite side near Tayport, saw the value of his fishing leap from a few pounds a year to £2,000.

The river proprietors were hit hard. The rents they were able to charge plummeted as the estuary ones soared. Several of them, led by the Duke of Atholl, brought an action against Maule of Panmure and a whole gang of co-defendants – including the Earl of Wemyss, Lord Kinnaird, Lord Dundas, and Dundee Town Council – all of them the owners of actual or prospective stake-net sites. The plaintiffs claimed, as had the Earl of Kinnoull, that their fish were being stolen by others in breach of their rights; and further, that the stake nets were causing an overall decrease in salmon abundance. Mr Maule and his friends maintained that, as their fishings were on the firth, they could not be regarded as governed by the ruling in the earlier case, which clearly applied only to the river, and accused the river owners of seeking to perpetuate a monopoly.

The case eventually reached the House of Lords, where, in

1812, their lordships ruled that the defendants had 'no right either by themselves or by those employed by them to erect or use yairs, stake nets or other machinery of the same nature for the catching of salmon'. The ruling seemed unambiguous enough, but it changed nothing. The estuary owners were not going to let go of their new income stream lightly, and the river owners were not going to back down having gained the legal advantage. The stage was set for a lengthy and tedious succession of court wrangles which profited the lawyers but no one else.

In the meantime a virtual netting free-for-all continued and expanded on the Firth of Tay. In 1806 John Richardson of Pitfour, assessing accurately that there was no chance of his benign monopoly being restored, retreated to his castle, leaving the shrinking operations of his company in the hands of his son. The impact on the river rents was severe – the Duke of Atholl's fell by more than a half, General Graham's at Balgowan by two-thirds. In the aftermath of Richardson's departure, his tack of the fishings owned by Perth Town Council was taken over by John Stevenson from Berwick at £1,500 per annum. A year later he was desperately trying to unload it at half the price.

The massive shift from the river net-and-coble netting to the estuary stake nets is illustrated by the overall catch figures. In 1801 around 57,000 salmon were officially taken, a third by the estuary nets. In each of the years 1807 and 1808 the total exceeded 60,000 – four-fifths of them accounted for by the estuary nets. Broadly speaking, the shared catch went up in these years, but not drastically. But the effort put into catching those fish intensified considerably, which had the effect of disguising the impact on the stock, the basic resource. Most of those involved in the fishing shared an anxiety about its health and long-term prospects, but hardly anyone was prepared to voice it.

The pattern of events on the Tay was, in time, replicated all over Scotland where the geography of the estuaries was amenable to the installation of stake nets. The scale and value of the fishing varied a great deal, but a fairly constant theme was the outbreak of hostilities between long-standing holders of river netting rights and the estuary owners with their tacksmen stake netters. A vivid example was the war waged by Murdo Mackenzie of Ardross in Sutherland against various netting interests whom he accused of stealing his fish.

Having inherited the extensive but unproductive Ardross lands from his mother, Mackenzie borrowed heavily to buy the fishing rights on the River Shin and on the Kyle of Sutherland – into which the Shin, the Oykel, the Cassley and the Carron all debouched. But no land went with those rights, and he watched enraged and powerless as stake nets proliferated along the tidal approaches to his river. He instigated various lawsuits and even wrote a hefty book, *A View of the Salmon Fishery of Scotland* (1860), in which he set out his individual opinions on the state of the law and the behaviour of salmon as well as heaping abuse on anyone who disagreed with him.

Mackenzie was described in Evander MacIver's diverting *Memoirs of a Highland Gentleman* (1905) as 'a gentleman in manner but careless in his dress and habits . . . said to be an atheist, his social manners were loose . . . he was not married but a Highland woman, "Cursty", lived with him and was the mother of a large family of sons and daughters . . . he had a mania for litigation'. Mackenzie eventually precipitated a showdown with the de facto ruler of most of northern Scotland, the Duke of Sutherland, by hiring a gang of labourers to dig an entirely new channel to take the Shin into the Kyle of Sutherland, away from the accursed nets. Legal action by the Sutherland Estates ensued but was cut short when the duke – acting as only the super-rich can – ordered his men to buy Mackenzie out. Mackenzie cannily saw his chance and demanded that the duke purchase the whole of the Ardross estate, as well as the fishing rights, for £100,000. The duke paid up, then sold the land to Sir Alexander Matheson while retaining the fishing.

The stake nets that spread along the east and north coast estuaries caught significant numbers of salmon and grilse and contributed usefully to the incomes of tacksmen and owners. But the scale was small compared with that on the Tay and on the Tay's one serious rival in supplying the London market, the Tweed. The principal method on the Tweed was and continued to be net and coble – stake nets did not arrive until later, and then along the coast rather than in the estuary. But the antagonism between the proprietors of the different sections was quite as warm as it was between riparian and estuary owners on the Tay. It arose from the same cause – resentment on the part of those on the middle and upper Tweed at the scale of depredation on the lower Tweed. The crucial difference was that there could be no question of curtailing or suppressing that depredation by recourse to the law. It was legal; all anyone could do was to observe its impact and protest.

The almost fifteen miles of river between the mouth at Berwick and the bridge at Coldstream was swept by nets continually and persistently from the start of the season in January to its end in mid-September, except for the weekend 'slap' between 10pm on Saturday and 2am on Monday, and when floods made it unfishable. The Reverend Thomas Johnstone in his *History of Berwick* (1817) reported that the total rental on the seven miles from the mouth up to Norham had risen from £7,000 a year in 1799 to £25–30,000 at the time of writing. Seventy boats worked the nets, six men to a boat. The declared catches were phenomenal – in 1804 thirteen thousand boxes of salmon were shipped out of Berwick, each box containing six stone of fish. Between 1811 and 1815 an average of almost 100,000 fish a year were being taken – two-thirds of them grilse, the smaller salmon that have only been to sea for a year. Between 1815 and 1820 that average rose to 120,000.

Such a scale of slaughter could not last, and after 1820 the number of boxes sent to London never exceeded five thousand again. By the middle of the century, annual overall catches were down to just over 30,000 fish, and the rents followed the same downhill path. Overfishing was not the only factor – pollution from the textile mills of Hawick, Gala and other border towns became an acute problem – but it was the main one.

All over Scotland technological advances – in fishing methods, and equally significant, transport links – enabled fishermen to do what they will always do given the chance, overfish. Some of the new breed of tacksmen supervised empires of netting. William Hogarth, based in Aberdeen, rented tacks on the Tay, Dee, Don, Spey, Findhorn, Naver and Thurso, right the way round to the Lochy on the west coast – in 1836 he paid £20,000 (perhaps £1.5 million today) in rents. George Little, one of the Little brothers who started the stake-net ball rolling, had tacks on the Tay, Spey Forth, Nith and Annan in Scotland, the Border Esk, Eden and Lune in England, the Bush and the Bann in Northern Ireland, and on several Irish rivers including the Shannon. John Johnstone of Balmerino, the chief tacksman on the Firth of Tay, paid £7,000 a year in rents and employed one hundred fishermen, plus twenty women to clean the fish and six coopers to make the barrels.

The pattern of exploitation was general. For a time increased effort pushed catches and rents up, and prices down. Gradually the upward curve flattened, peaked and declined. Everyone involved knew what was happening but there was no power capable of restraining it. The nearest to an absolute ruler was the Duke of Sutherland; his netting manager was Andrew Young, who also leased netting stations from Sutherland Estates on the Kyle of Sutherland. Young contrasted His Grace's enlightened attitude in banning 'stake nets, bag nets and ruinous fixtures on all rivers and estuaries' with the plunder elsewhere which, he said, had rendered most other rivers 'fishless . . . almost worthless'. Alexander Russel, editor of *The Scotsman* and author of *The Salmon* (1864), wrote: 'Already it may be safely said that three quarters of the natural supply [of salmon] has been lost . . . a little more care and that loss may be repaired, a little less care and that loss may be made complete and irreparable.'

Parliamentary select committees sat and pondered the matter and accumulated hills and mountains of testimony. But the conflict between the competing interests went too deep; even when they could agree there was a problem, they blamed someone else for creating it and demanded that anyone but themselves should solve it. Predictably, the legislation resulting from these interminable exercises amounted to little more than some tinkering at the edges – alterations to the close season, new sanctions against poaching, more protection for fry and smolts and the like. In 1860 a select committee of the House of Lords recommended that 'all cruives and fixed engines' (i.e. stake nets) should be abolished – but by the time the Commons had finished with the bill the fatal words 'if practicable' had been added, rendering the legislation futile.

Meanwhile the theatre of operations gradually expanded. The discovery that salmon coming into estuaries from the sea tended to stick close to the shoreline as they sought their birth river suggested the same might be true on the approach to those estuaries. The first open-sea stake nets were installed near the mouth of the South Esk at Montrose as early as the 1820s. The gently shelving sandy Berwick coastline was ideal for stake nets, which crept north and south from the mouth of the Tweed.

Localised poaching – spearing fish on the gravel as they spawned, netting pools at night, targeting smolts and so on – was endemic on all rivers. But as the scale of commercial netting grew, so did large-scale illegal fishing by organised gangs. The development of other kinds of nets – particularly bag nets, large, arrow-shaped, weighted with anchors and supported by cork flats for use in deeper water, and hang nets, a type of drift net – made it possible to exploit all kinds of water at any time.

On the Tay the proprietors banded together to appoint a superintendent of fisheries to recruit watchers to patrol the estuary so as to crack down on illegal fishing. The gangs of poachers favoured the hang net, but they also used spirling nets – designed for sprats and smelts – to catch salmon. In 1882, in what was dubbed the Battle of Gutter Hole, the Tay watchers led by Alexander Lumsden followed and attempted to intercept two spirling smacks engaged in salmon fishing. In the ensuing fracas one of the watchers was badly injured and two of the poachers who tried to escape by swimming to Mugdrum Island at the mouth of the river were drowned.

The Tweed presented different and more intractable challenges. An Act of Parliament in 1807 – promoted by, among others, Sir Walter Scott and the Lord Somerville who had rented Pavilion to William Scrope – established a statutory body, the Tweed Commissioners, with powers to police the river and levy contributions from proprietors to pay for it. Over time, organised poaching became an increasing problem. A Tweed speciality was the use of the stell net, a semi-circular curtain of netting held by a rope at the shore and fixed by anchors to the bed of the river. It was clearly a fixed engine and it was deadly in its effectiveness. The proprietors on the lower river argued that it was sanctioned by ancient usage, but its destructiveness was apparent and it was eventually outlawed at the same time as another time-honoured method of slaughter, the leister or spear beloved by Scrope.

Despite the strictures of the law, the bailiffs employed by the Tweed Commissioners had their work cut out trying to keep the various kinds of illegal fishing under control. In 1861 a Royal Navy gunboat was called out against Burnemouth fishermen drift-netting at sea and the nets were seized and burned. Two years earlier on 15 October 1859, the *Berwick Journal*, under the headline 'Riots at Spittal', carried a dramatic report of a battle between bailiffs and fishermen at the mouth of the Tweed. Stormy weather had prevented the whitefish fleet putting to sea, while drawing into the river a huge influx of salmon ready to forge their way upriver. The season for salmon netting had closed, but the spectacle of the salmon was too tempting and the boats went after them – with the bailiffs in pursuit.

'Nearly the whole village [of Spittal, across the mouth from Berwick town] turned out, not merely to a man but a woman . . . eight boats supported by the populace on land armed with slings . . . they not only drove thirteen water bailiffs over the Berwick side, but gave chase, captured the bailiffs' boat and sunk her . . . the men were disguised in their wives' bedgowns and there is likely to be some difficulty in identification . . .'

No natural resource, however seemingly inexhaustible, could withstand such pressure indefinitely. All over Scotland reported catches were falling. Poaching was rife and the legal netsmen were driven to desperate straits by the fatal combination of fixed rents and falling incomes.

But the concept of overfishing – of actually putting the future of a resource in peril by exploiting it beyond its capacity to sustain itself – was at odds with orthodox Victorian thinking. During the wrangling over the impact of the stake nets, much was made of the doctrine of Linnaeus that 'the divine economy guarantees a full abundance to all, there are no scarcities in nature . . . the Creator arranges a system of differential reproduction rates by which the harmless and esculent animals will safely reproduce more than their predators thereby maintaining their own numbers while providing a livelihood for their neighbours . . . man must vigorously pursue his assigned work of utilising his fellow species to his own advantage'.

However, a new economic factor was making itself felt in the market. It derived from the growing popularity of angling as a sport and the willingness of wealthy sportsmen to pay well for their pleasure. The rampant netting of estuaries and the lower stretches of rivers obviously diminished, and in some cases pretty much wiped out, the supply of salmon upriver to where anglers and their rods might be waiting. Where a whole river system was in single ownership, it was in the owner's interests to limit the number of fish taken by the nets so that more were available to the anglers. As we have seen, that is what happened with the Duke of Sutherland's choicest rivers such as the Naver, Helmsdale, Oykel and Cassley.

Elsewhere it took longer for the logic of rebalancing netting and angling for economic benefit to dawn on jealous and greedy owners. Alexander Russel clearly identified the way ahead – 'we may state generally that the decline in Scottish rivers was universal . . . although in one or two cases, such as the Spey [much of it controlled by the Duke of Gordon] and the rivers of Sutherland, where the fisheries are in the hands of one great proprietor who has resorted to a wise moderation, a great difference for the better was observed'.

The problem on a river in multiple ownership such as the Tay was this where was wise moderation to come from, when foolish excess had prevailed for so long? The answer was, as it usually is, from enlightened self-interest. Towards the end of the century a consortium put together by the Perth tackle dealer Peter Malloch, a noted authority on the life cycle of the salmon, formed itself into the Tay Salmon Fisheries Company. Lavishly funded by members of the Paisley thread-manufacturing dynasty, the Coatses, the company rapidly accumulated tacks on the river and estuary by the simple expedient of outbidding competitors. It quickly established a virtual monopoly, and Malloch – the first managing director – implemented a management strategy in which hang nets were eliminated, the netting season was shortened and the number of fishing stations reduced, and the watchers were sent forth to kill as many seals and pike as they could. In 1905 Malloch reported with evident self-satisfaction that 'with one or two exceptions we control the netting and are working with the upper and lower proprietors, the Tay District Board and all concerned, and, I may add, are satisfied with our dividend'.

The effect was undoubtedly beneficial to the river – which

received significantly more salmon to migrate upstream to spawn – and to the owners who were able to negotiate longer leases with anglers at higher rents; but not so for the tacksmen, who were elbowed off the water. Malloch boasted that there were now twenty fish for each one when they started. He himself was a major beneficiary in his capacity as lessee of rods from Lord Ancaster, who owned the prime beat at Stobhall. W.L. Calderwood, in his commanding survey *The Salmon Rivers and Lochs of Scotland* (second edition, 1921), reported that the annual rent for Stobhall had risen from £80 a year to over £1,000.

The rebalancing between netting and angling interests occurred slowly and haphazardly around the north of Scotland. The records of the Sutherland Estates provide the fullest picture. For instance, Melvich Bay – where the Halladale reaches the sea between Bettyhill and Thurso – was intensively netted by successive tenants of the estate, who regularly and with impunity breached the terms of their leases by using more nets than they were entitled to. The second of these, Alexander Speedie – who had multiple tacks around the north and north-west coasts – paid £200 a year to fish Melvich Bay, while the angling on the Halladale was let for just £60.

Elsewhere, as we have already seen, the management of Sutherland Estates curtailed netting to enhance angling rents – the tenants on the Halladale's neighbour, the Naver, were paying £600 a year. By 1900 the angling rents from the four rivers flowing into the Kyle of Sutherland – the Shin, Oykel, Cassley and Carron – were the same as for the netting. A few years later all the fishing rights had been acquired by the proprietors, and from then on netting played second fiddle.

Contrast this happy (for some) situation with that prevailing on the Tweed. There, despite the existence of the Tweed Commission, the schism between the lower river and the middle and upper rivers persisted. Calderwood reported that there were thirty-nine netting stations between Berwick and Coldstream, deploying sixty-two nets. The rents were simply too valuable to be surrendered – particularly as the lowest part of the Tweed, from Norham to the sea, has very few attractions from the angling perspective because of the tides, the great width of the water and its general featurelessness.

Because the netted section was so long, the weekend 'slap' from Saturday evening to early Monday morning gave almost no protection to incoming salmon even where it was observed. Those that entered the river on the Sunday would merely be caught somewhere upriver on the Monday. In normal flows, very few salmon escaped the forest of nets to reach potential spawning areas above Kelso. That meant that the only spawning stock were the fish that arrived after the end of the netting season in mid-September; and these were pretty much the only fish available to the anglers as well.

To a dedicated salmon fisherman such as the historian, anti-quarian and long-serving Conservative MP Sir Herbert Maxwell (the grandfather of the naturalist and otter-lover Gavin Maxwell), the state of the Tweed was the source of sadness and futile anger. In his *Book of the Tweed* (1904) – otherwise a celebration of the river's history, heritage and beauty – Maxwell wrote:

It took a long time to impair the productiveness of this fine river but that has been accomplished at last. The modern improvement of netting, the sedulous removal from the channel of every obstacle to the sweep of the seine, combined with the long stretch of the river above the tide which is surrendered to netting, practically have put an end to spring and summer angling. The proprietors from Inverleithen [on the upper Tweed] upwards, chief guardians of the best spawning grounds, have been robbed of all chance of fair sport until a season when fish are in a condition when no fair sportsman would care to take them. It is no longer in their interest to check poaching and it is notorious that they have ceased to make any attempt to do so.

Maxwell's solution was essentially the same as had already happened on the Tay and on the Dee, where all nets on the non-tidal stretch were progressively bought off between 1873 and 1909. 'The day cannot be far distant', he wrote, 'when the riparian owners of Tweedside will follow the example on the Tay, the Dee and other northern rivers ... by buying up all netting rights above the tide. The regeneration of this fair river is merely a question of wise co-operation.' In fact it would be the best part of a century before the scourge of netting on the Tweed was lifted – and the spirit of 'wise co-operation' urged by Maxwell had very little to do with it.

From Pitfour Castle rich, cereal-growing fields stretch down to the northern shore of the Firth of Tay. A little way to the east is Mugdrum Island, a long, low, reedy glorified sandbank – the scene of many a tussle between the Tay watchers and the poaching gangs of old, now a peaceful, rustling nature reserve watched over by a local wildfowlers' club.

The Great Fishmonger of the Tay, John Richardson, would have known every inch of this shore and water in every season, in every weather, at every stage of the ceaseless tides. He would have known the name of every sandbank and mudbank – Kerwhip, Channelhead, Abernethy, Gilderoy, Peesweep, Sure As Death – and the course of every channel, where the salmon ran and where they rested.

He had fifteen years of retirement before his death in 1821. In that period most of what he predicted and feared came to pass, as his careful, highly profitable stewardship gave way to a reckless free-for-all which turned the estuary into a battleground. Doubtless he reflected on all this as he looked out from his bedroom window across the broad, restless, silt-laden water towards the netsmen's stronghold of Newburgh beyond Mugdrum Island. On a fine day he surely would have strolled down the track to the water's edge and up the shore a little way to Carnie pier, where the boats loaded and unloaded, past the various fishing stations – Carnie Lodge, Hen Lodge, Glove Lodge.

The Richardsons continued to go up in the world, and left fishmongering far behind. John Richardson's grandson, also John, inherited his maternal grandfather James Stewart's estate at Urrard on the River Garry near Pitlochry, added the Stewart to his surname and died Sir James Stewart-Richardson. He continued to use Pitfour Castle as his main residence, but subsequently it fell into disrepair and suffered various indignities, including a fire which badly damaged the east wing and later conversion into apartments. When I visited I was told forcibly by a lady living in the converted stable block that it was private and, no, I certainly could not go inside. Unbending a little, she disclosed that it was a bit of a mess and that dry rot was on the march.

Rather like the castle, the Tay looks much the same as long ago from the outside, but appearances are deceptive. More than twenty years after the last commercial nets ceased operations, it remains one of Scotland's premier salmon rivers and is fished persistently and consistently from January to October. These days they catch four to five thousand fish a year. In 1920 Calderwood estimated the rod catch at 14,500; the average caught by the nets between 1841 and 1846 was 71,000. The figures tell a story.

CHAPTER NINE

A Gentlemen's Club

On an April day in 1937 Arthur Severn, a long-standing member of the Flyfishers' Club, saw something that displeased him considerably – a fellow member walking along Piccadilly in a red tie and without a hat. On the 21st of that month – the day before Mussolini informed the Chancellor of Austria that Italy would not come to his aid if Hitler invaded – Severn wrote to the club secretary to protest at this outrage. A further letter on the same subject (it may be that there were two separate incidents, one of hatlessness and one involving the tie) followed on 26 April, the day the Luftwaffe and the Italian Aviazione Legionaria bombed the Basque town of Guernica.

Part of Europe was at war, and the rest was sliding that way. And a member of the Flyfishers' Club saw fit to lodge an official complaint about the way another member was dressed.

Nine months later the slide was accelerating into headlong descent. On 1 February Mussolini ordered the Italian army to adopt the goosestep when marching. Three days later Hitler took personal command of the German Wehrmacht. Nine days after that he summoned Austria's chancellor to the Berchtesgaden to tell him that Germany would invade if its just demands were not met. On 20 February Hitler delivered a three-hour speech in the Reichstag in which he vowed to protect German minorities wherever they were found. The next day Anthony Eden resigned as Britain's Foreign Secretary in protest at Chamberlain's policy of appeasement.

You might have thought that at such a time, against such a background, a dispute over whether or not it could be considered sporting to use an artificial fly sunk a little way below the surface of the water in order to catch a trout might have appeared somewhat beside the point, even trivial. Yet the committee of the Flyfishers' Club, educated men who were distinguished in their varied professional fields, saw fit to stage a debate on that subject on the evening of 10 February 1938. The membership filed into the club's premises at 36 Piccadilly, hung their hats, took their seats and put aside whatever dark thoughts they may have had about the crisis in Europe in order to listen to contrary views about the eating habits of brown trout on the handful of chalkstreams in Hampshire, Berkshire and Wiltshire.

To be fair to the committee – or at least some of the committee – the intention was to lance a boil that had seriously impaired the atmosphere in the clubroom. It was hoped that by airing the differences between those who considered that using a fly sunk below the surface was a legitimate tactic and those who did not, each side would recognise and respect the opinions of the other and the matter could then be closed. It is a sign of the distance that the sport of angling had travelled since the time of Walton and Cotton that such a deep and bitter dispute should have arisen at all. But it had; it would take more than a polite debate in a Piccadilly clubroom to settle it, and its ripples and echoes are still felt today.

The fly fished below the surface imitates one or other of the upwinged insects on which chalkstream trout feed in the stage before hatching out, and was and is known as a nymph. The floating fly, known as the dry fly, imitates the insect after it has hatched, when it rests briefly on the surface until its wings are dry enough for it to take flight and get down to mating.

The undisputed prophet of the difficult art of fishing the nymph was George Edward Mackenzie Skues, a dry-stick unmarried solicitor of exceptionally acute intelligence, with a sharp tongue and pen and an obsessive passion for chalkstream trout fishing. By the time the debate at the Flyfishers' Club took place, the undisputed prophet of the dry fly had actually been dead for almost a quarter of a century. Born Frederic Hyam, into a wealthy Jewish family of German extraction, he changed his surname to Halford and kept quiet about his Jewishness throughout his adult life. His approach to the supposedly relaxing pastime of angling was quite as obsessional as that of Skues.

G.E.M. Skues   Frederic Halford

The two men were once friends – Halford had proposed Skues for membership of the Flyfishers' Club. But men with obsessive temperaments who engage in the same pursuit and become pre-eminent in it are destined to fall out. Obsession breeds conviction which breeds certainty which breeds the vanity of rightness.

Skues knew from his intense study of the trout on the Abbots Barton stretch of the River Itchen just outside Winchester that they took most of their food in the nymphal, sub-surface stage. To be successful, he argued, the serious angler needed to be able to exploit that preference by using a sub-surface imitation. Halford, a less accomplished angler and less acute observer, compensated for these deficiencies by sheer dedication, spending countless hours squinting through a microscope at laboriously collected examples of insects in the fully hatched phase, and countless more hours tying or having others tie imitations of them in fur and feather that minutely mimicked their colouring and texture.

By the time Skues began to form his beliefs and theories and articulate them – mostly in articles for the journal of the Flyfishers' Club – Halford had already produced two books setting out his creed, *Floating Flies and How to Dress Them* (1886) and *Dry-Fly Fishing in Theory and Practice* (1889). No one before Halford had ever applied such forensic rigour to the sport. What had generally been regarded as a pleasantly absorbing way to spend a May day or an evening in June had been turned into a subject of scientific inquiry, with Halford – bent over his microscope or fly-tying vice, rarely seen fishing and never just for the fun of it – as chief scientist.

Having toiled for so long conducting and writing up his researches, Halford was understandably inclined to regard his word as the final word. Those who were his followers elevated him to the position of ultimate authority. Then onto the scene had crept this apostate, this heretic.

Skues did not publish his first book, *Minor Tactics of the Chalk Stream*, until 1910, twenty years after the formulation of the Halfordian creed of the dry fly. In an effort to be tactful, Skues touched only lightly on the matter of the nymph. But not tactfully enough. According to Skues's much later account – which his masterly biographer, Tony Hayter, considers too neat and epigrammatic to be entirely convincing – Halford confronted him: "'You know, Skues, what you say in that book can't be done. Mind, I'm not arguing, I'm telling you." I replied "Halford! What good do you think you're doing by telling me a thing can't be done which I have done scores of times." He got up and left me and never spoke to me again.'

Whether or not it actually happened – it seems equally likely that it was Skues who took mortal offence – is beside the point. There was a decisive breach between the two men that – in a curious example of life after death – continued and indeed widened long after Halford himself had quit the fly-fishing scene for good. In the absence of his rival, Skues became the dominant figure in the scientific or pseudo-scientific arena of trout fishing. But, although he had good friends in the Flyfishers' Club and through his legal expertise had made himself indispensable to the committee, he was too much the loner, too outside the norm to be popular. As time went on, he became increasingly confident of his position and increasingly strident in his disparagement of Halford. This process culminated in a piece for the 1937 winter number of the journal in which he took each of the basic tenets of Halford's teaching, assaulted them and sent them on their way with the capitalised 'HE WAS WRONG' appended to each.

The other problem Skues had with his fellow fly fishermen was that he was too damn good at catching trout. The Abbots Barton water on the Itchen, which he fished for half a century, was chalkstream fishing at its most testing. Unlike most other fisheries, it was not stocked, which meant the members of the syndicate that rented it were dependent on a limited and variable population of extremely wary and discriminating trout for their sport.

Skues's expertise with the nymph enabled him to catch and kill – in those days all sizeable fish were killed – what the other members came to regard as a disproportionate share of the decent trout. A groundswell of hostility developed towards him, which he became aware of but – being so sure of himself and something of a social misfit – he preferred to confront. On the last day of May 1936 the 77-year-old Skues, having caught a two-and-a-half pound trout on one of his nymphs, met one of the other syndicate members, Gavin Simonds, on the river bank. Simonds – a leading barrister, later a judge, Law Lord and eventually Lord Chancellor – told Skues that in his view the use of a nymph represented a breach of their lease because it was not an artificial fly any more than a caterpillar was a moth or butterfly.

This specimen of nonsensical sophism was supported by others in the syndicate who were envious of Skues's uncanny ability to catch fish when no else could, notably Neville Bostock, the boss of the Northampton shoemakers Lotus. Two years later poor old Skues was, in effect, forced out of the syndicate and off the Itchen.

In the meantime, the Flyfishers' Club nymph debate had taken place. It would be tedious for anyone not closely interested in the ethics of fly fishing to go through the arguments, which had been rehearsed in the pages of the club journal and elsewhere for several years. Skues, who was as poor a public speaker as he was a deft and witty writer, spent most of his allocated time laying into the ghost of Halford. That ghost – and this is the most bizarre aspect of a pretty bizarre episode – was represented by a formidable figure who, in his shadowy and devious way, was at that time playing a key role in the events that would, in eighteen months or so, see Britain at war.

The long and murky career of Joseph Ball (from 1936 Sir Joseph Ball) has long intrigued historians. Born in comparatively modest circumstances in Luton and educated at King's College, London, he became a Scotland Yard detective specialising in the identification and interrogation of aliens, suspected spies and assorted subversives. In 1915 he joined the newly established intelligence network known as MI5, where he became a senior officer and organised various 'dirty tricks'. The most notable of these was the forged Zinoviev letter setting out Soviet Russia's plans for mobilising the British working class into revolt, whose publication in the *Daily Mail* a few days before the general election of 1924 helped precipitate a Conservative landslide.

In 1927 he migrated to Conservative Central Office and took charge of publicity – becoming, in effect, a pioneer spin doctor. By then Ball had established a network of influential contacts – intelligence agents, police officers, businessmen, journalists and politicians – who shared his own right-wing, pro-German, anti-Semitic sentiments. Always working behind the scenes, he made himself indispensable to the party leadership – and in particular to Neville Chamberlain, who became Prime Minister in May 1937. Their friendship was made and cemented on the river bank. Chamberlain was a keen salmon fisherman but a chalkstream novice, whom Ball – an experienced and highly competent trout angler – took an obsequious pleasure in inviting to his house at Kimbridge on the Test and instructing in the rituals of the mayfly hatch.

Chamberlain relied on Ball to organise covert operations. Ball established a secret channel of communication with the Italian ambassador in London, Count Dino Grandi, to attempt to coax Mussolini into restraining Hitler. He dispatched the notorious Nazi sympathiser Henry Drummond-Wolff to Germany to ask Goering what terms the Führer would accept to avoid war. Even further in the shadows, Ball funded a toxic little publication called *Truth*, which was used to conduct a vicious campaign of vilification against Chamberlain's Jewish Secretary for War, Leslie Hore-Belisha. He was associated with the Nordic League, which described itself in its constitution as 'an association of race-conscious Britons' and was led by the rabidly anti-Semitic MP Archibald Ramsay.

How and why Joseph Ball got involved in the nymph debate at the Flyfishers' Club is as obscure as almost everything else about him. He was a very keen chalkstream fisherman and a stalwart of the club, and was friendly with Halford's son Ernest. Whatever his motives, he approached the job of leading the prosecution against Skues with his customary thoroughness. He closely studied all Halford's published work, consulted a range of authorities on the behaviour of nymphs and the feeding habits of trout, and wrote a seventeen-page indictment.

The debate itself seems to have been a bit of a damp squib. Skues spoke, badly, but had his supporters, among them J.W. Hills – John Waller Hills, a former MP and government minister, and author of the classic *A Summer on the Test*, who had previously referred to Skues as 'a great man' and to fishing the nymph as 'not only legitimate fly fishing but fly fishing of a high order, harder than the floating fly'. Ball presented his case, supported chiefly by Dr James Mottram, a leading oncologist and pioneer of radiotherapy, who had once been an enthusiastic nymph fisherman before seeing the Halfordian light.

The somewhat patchy report in the club journal suggests quite a few of the speakers from the floor knew very little about nymph fishing and were confused as to whether they were for it or against it. There was no vote at the end, no victory or defeat. This was a gentlemen's club, after all. Hands were shaken, warm if not wholly sincere professions of respect exchanged, and the members departed into the dark February night.

The most interesting aspect of the nymph debate was not the debate itself, but that it should have taken place at all. What had happened to the contemplative man's recreation, the brotherhood of the angle, that it should have fissured in such a way?

A century before, there were no such fissures. The styles of angling were dictated by location, not by social status or notions of purism. Those who loved the sport where the game fish – salmon, trout, to a lesser extent grayling – prevailed mainly fly-fished but were not above using a spinner or bait. The south country chalkstreams where the snobbery of the dry fly would be born and flourish were actually quite lightly fished then and were considered nothing special. In the mayfly season, usually the second half of May, sporting gents would gather on the Test and Itchen and fish with the natural insect in much the same way Cotton did 150 years before, and would catch a lot of trout. But the rest of the time they hardly bothered, because they knew nothing about matching an artificial fly to the various insects on which trout fed, and the fishing was simply too difficult.

Where the rivers ran slow and the dominant species were the coarse fish, anglers of all social classes fished for them using bait. Thomas Salter's *The Angler's Guide*, first published in 1814 and evidently intended primarily for the London market, gives useful insight into prevailing attitudes and preferences. Salter included a pretty basic section on the techniques of fly fishing, and recommended that anyone interested in that branch of the sport should avail himself of the facilities available on the Colne – where he may 'indulge himself in angling for trout by paying for board and lodging' at the Crown and Cushion or the White Horse in Uxbridge – or on the Wandle. But for London anglers the Thames and its tributaries were the obvious destinations, and coarse fish the target species.

Salter recommended various locations. At Staines, boats could be hired from the Bush 'and good sport met with near the bridge' where 'many barbel weighing near twenty pounds each have been caught'. At Chertsey the anglers' hostelry was the Cricketers,

'Dipping' or 'dapping' for chub, from
Thomas Salter's *The Angler's Guide*, 1841

where boats could be hired 'and tackle if a visitor should be deficient'. The Anchor and the Kings Arms at Shepperton both welcomed the brotherhood, while a mile away was the Duke of York's residence, Oatlands, where 'Her Royal Highness the Duchess sometimes takes the diversion of angling and one of the boatmen residing in the village named Dabler receives a salary for attending her.'

On the Lea, Salter reported, 'several miles are preserved for the angler's diversion for which he pays an annual sum of between ten-and-sixpence and twenty-one shillings'. At the Crown in Broxbourne could be found Mrs Scorer and her sons, with a stretch down to King's weir on which Mr Carruthers took a chub of six-and-a-quarter pounds dapping a bee. The Horse and Groom at Leabridge was served by hourly stages between 8am and 8pm, 'enabling the London angler to enjoy his favourite sport daily'; the pub even had lockers for storing tackle. Further down towards Stratford and West Ham there was fishing for roach, dace and flounders, but Salter warned that the banks were very slippery and the angler was likely to be annoyed by passers-by asking 'what sport . . . do the fish bite and other rude interrogations'.

Although there were trout in the Lea, and some big ones, the emphasis was firmly on the chub, roach, perch and particularly the pike. The records of the Amwell Magna club indicate the social profile of the membership; they were highly respectable middle-class professional men – engineers, booksellers, wine merchants and so forth – with a sprinkling of gentlemen of private means with addresses in Regent Street or Cavendish Square.

One of the most distinguished members of the club of a later era was Robert Bright Marston, who fitted well enough in that social bracket – his father, Edward, was a partner in the respected London publishing house of Sampson Low, Marston and Co. – and who, over half a century, had an immense influence over the sport he loved with a deep passion. Like his father, who wrote numerous sketches under the pseudonym The Amateur Angler, R.B. Marston was a true all-rounder, accomplished with a fly rod on the chalkstreams but just as content stalking a chub or spinning for pike. In 1878, at the age of twenty-five, he took over a languishing publication called the *Fishing Gazette* which he ran until his death in 1927, turning it into a dominant and indispensable feature of the angling landscape.

Thomas Salter recommended various angling hostelries in and around London – among them the Swan at Ditton.

R.B. Marston casting for a chalkstream trout.

'It will be the desire of the new proprietor,' Marston wrote in his first issue as editor of the *Fishing Gazette*, 'to make it generally acceptable to all classes of angler.' He was as good as his word. The paper reached out to the new legions of working-class anglers by inviting and publishing detailed reports from the clubs springing up in the great manufacturing cities. Its range was as wide as the angling world itself. A random volume collecting six months of weekly numbers in 1909 contained articles and shorter items with such headings as 'Bass at Bideford', 'Fishing in Austria', 'Good Sport with Carp', 'The Salmon Season on the Beauly', 'Cod Fishing at Scarborough', 'A Casting Pool in Chicago', 'Cheshire Trouting', 'Christmas Day on the Trent', 'A Grand Lot of Dace', 'How the Italian Organ-Grinder Caught the Grey Mullet', 'Huchen on the Fly', 'Hunting in Abyssinia', 'Mahseer in Central India', 'Mayfly on the Mole', 'Tuna at Catalina'.

Marston's eclecticism embraced all classes of fish, of angling and of angler. It was shared to a great degree by his fellow angling journalists: Francis Francis, who was the long-serving Angling Editor of *The Field*, and his successors there, William Senior and H.T. Sheringham – the last of these, in my opinion, the finest of all our fishing writers. What characterised all these men was their generosity of spirit and breadth of sympathy. They disliked the purism that grew from Halford's groundbreaking work and did their utmost to challenge it.

Yet paradoxically it was Marston and the ailing Francis Francis who unwittingly created the seedbed in which that purism and its accompanying intolerance were able to flourish. On 17 January 1885 Marston's *Fishing Gazette* carried a prospectus for a 'Club for Fly-Fishers . . . to bring together gentlemen devoted to fly-fishing generally, to afford a ready means of communication between those interested in this delightful art . . .' Apart from Marston himself, the committee included two other journalists, Henry Ffenell, editor of *Land and Water*, and William Senior of *The Field* (Francis Francis was by then terminally ill), and two other well-known angling writers, Alfred Jardine and Harry Cholmondeley-Pennell.

Socially and geographically the Flyfishers' Club – at least in the early days – cast its membership net quite wide. But being a London club where many if not most of the members necessarily did most of their fishing on the chalkstreams meant that, beneath the genuinely welcoming surface, there was a strong bias towards what was turning into a highly specialised branch of the sport. This bias was promoted, from perfectly honourable motives, by Halford who became the leader of what Peter Hayes, in his entertaining and illuminating monograph *Imitators of the Fly: A History*, characterised as 'a tightly-knit Jesuit-style seminary of dry-fly purism' – although Hayes makes the point that, at that time, it represented no more than a small clique within the club.

The dry fly had evolved from the general way of fly fishing going back to Cotton and beyond. Because they were so light, these imitations cast for feeding trout and grayling would have remained on the surface for a little while and then sunk, but not far, and were taken by fish at both stages. They were cast whichever way the wind made possible, although by the middle of the nineteenth century a distinct school had evolved advocating casting upstream on the grounds that this enabled the fly to be presented more naturally (without dragging across the current), that it made it easier to hook the fish, and – crucially – that it enabled the angler to stay out of sight.

The first references to a 'dry fly' date from around then. The difference was that this was an artificial fly specifically intended to imitate the fully hatched insect and designed to stay on the surface. When it began to sink, as it inevitably did after a while, it was whisked off the water and dried until ready to float again.

It was an effective method at a time when the hatches of the trout's favourite insects tended to be prolonged and abundant when they happened. Advances in fishing tackle – shorter rods of greenheart and later split cane, silk lines, gut casts, eyed hooks, engineered reels – made the management of the dry fly much easier. Aided by the appearance of a new generation of professional fly tyers, the technique spread steadily from the West Country and Derbyshire where it originated to the chalkstreams of Hampshire. There it was turned into a cult.

Halford and his associates devoted an incredible amount of time and energy to the study of chalkstream invertebrates – chiefly the *Ephemeridae*, or upwinged flies – and to an obsessive quest to devise exact imitations using feather fibres and wisps of animal fur. As these studies progressed and the fruits were published, there settled upon the leader and his disciples the conviction that, because what they were doing was so demanding, so consuming of effort and time, so very detailed and scientific, it must of itself be superior aesthetically and spiritually to other ways of fly fishing. It followed that the chalkstreams – on which this vast labour was exclusively conducted – represented a superior setting for fly fishing, and its trout a higher form of fish life.

A plate from Frederic Halford's *Floating Flies and How to Dress Them*, 1886.

The evolution of this doctrinal purism was reinforced by the general tendency of males moved by a shared keenness for a particular pursuit to organise themselves into clubs. Once they form the club, the next steps are to make rules, develop a common ethos, and restrict access to the location for the pursuit – river, grouse moor, golf course, tennis courts – to those with whom the founders feel comfortable. The premier chalkstreams of southern England – the Test, the Itchen, the Kennet, the Avon and a few others – amounted to a very limited angling resource which well before the end of the nineteenth century had been entirely taken over by the wealthy elite.

As he grew older and was ever more revered, Halford became increasingly intolerant of dissent – witness the breach with Skues. The assumption of superiority and its associated intolerance persisted after his death, as lesser men came onto the scene, maintaining control of the chalkstreams for themselves and their like. After 1918 the generation of those admirable all-rounders – Marston, Senior, Sheringham and the rest – died off or aged and lost their influence. The Flyfishers' Club became ever more focused on the chalkstreams and less of a broad church, its tone set by the likes of Joseph Ball, Neville Bostock and their tribe.

They feared and disdained poor old Skues because he was not one of them. He was too clever, too solitary, too odd – weird, it would be said today. At school (he was a Wyckhamist) they would have bullied him. In adulthood they ganged up on him and drove him – the most brilliant mind ever to be turned onto the great matter of the trout's eating habits – off the river he had fished since before some of them were born, away to a lonely old age in a hotel on a river, the Nadder, whose deficiencies only served to remind him of all he had lost. They did so because he dared to challenge an orthodoxy that was founded on ignorance, snobbery and prejudice, and was infinitely far removed from the contemplative man's recreation.

*   *   *

A landmine explosion in Piccadilly in 1941 damaged the premises of the Flyfishers' Club beyond repair, and it took refuge at the Garrick, never to return. After the war it occupied various spare corners of various London clubs before forging a link with the Savile Club and taking over the top floor of 69 Brook Street in Mayfair, where it remains in apparent contentment.

I was a member for a time in the 1980s when I was writing regularly about fishing for the *Financial Times* and other publications. I never really felt it was my natural milieu, and I resigned after receiving an officious letter from the extremely officious secretary rebuking me for breaking the prohibition on 'talking business' in the clubroom (I had been lunching with my friend Merlin Unwin, a well-known publisher of fishing and countryside books, and had – perhaps surprisingly to whichever nosy-parker eavesdropper reported me – been discussing books with him).

These days I am a very occasional guest. They have wonderful treasures there, and I like to pause to look at the photograph of Skues on one knee, staring keen-eyed upstream, searching for the dimple of a feeding trout; at the rod Halford gave to William Senior, at the flies donated by past masters such as the Test riverkeeper W.J. Lunn and the Americans George La Branche and Theodore Gordon, at the great stuffed fish and the shelves filled with volumes setting forth the studies, theories, reminiscences, tall tales, fantasies and furious prejudices inspired by our sport.

The old pre-war animosities are long buried; not forgotten, because the historians of angling love to reheat them, but not so much that they burst back into flame. They still have debates at the Flyfishers' Club, but the subjects are carefully chosen to stimulate amicable disagreement rather than discord and warfare. Not many members wear a hat these days, and no one raises an eyebrow at a red tie.

CHAPTER TEN

Wye Wizardry

As war clouds gathered over Europe and the Flyfishers' Club debated the life cycle of insects the size of a fingernail, down in Herefordshire the Wizard of the Wye was starting the salmon-fishing season in his meticulous way. In the event, 1938 would prove to be an unusually lean year for Robert Pashley; he was too unwell to fish for much of the summer, and had been compelled by health reasons to give up wading and fishing from the bank, and was restricted to sitting in a boat. Nevertheless he still managed 103 salmon for the season, which amounted to almost a tenth of the total caught by anglers on the river in what was generally a poor year.

Two years before, in 1936, the Wizard had enjoyed his *annus mirabilis*. Fishing mainly on the two beats he rented below Ross-on-Wye – Goodrich and Hill Court – he landed 678 salmon of an average weight of sixteen pounds. The majority were taken on a fly, which he fished with a ten-foot trout rod rather than a big salmon rod. His twenty-six best days produced 260 fish, the best of them sixteen. It was a productive year all round on the Wye, with a declared rod catch of 5,916. And this one man caught well over a tenth of them. No wonder they called him the Wizard of the Wye. Or sometimes the Napoleon of salmon fishing.

Robert Pashley plays a salmon.

Pashley's approach to his sport was, in its way, as obsessive as Halford's to his. The difference was he spent that time actually fishing. Pashley had firm ideas about how to catch salmon, which he communicated to his friends. But he never published a word on the subject, nor worked on any new theories or techniques. He just went fishing, seven days a week when the conditions were right.

One of those friends, H.A. (Humphrey Adam) Gilbert, described in his book *The Tale of a Wye Fisherman* (1953) how Pashley went about fishing the Vanstone, an incredibly productive pool on the Goodrich beat below Ross. He began by going down the near side, keeping well back from the bank, striking every fish at an angle to ensure that the hook found a hold in the side of the jaw. Only when he had made 'the maximum catch' on his side did he wade in and 'deal with those which lie further out in the stream'.

Gilbert described in awestruck tones a day in April 1929 on the Hom stream at Hill Court – 'the first time Pashley allowed me the privilege of watching and learning some of his methods'. Because the water was very low, the Wizard decided to fish a bait, a salted minnow on a mount with silver fans, cast from an old-fashioned Malloch reel and an ancient ten-foot split-cane spinning rod. He hooked and landed a salmon first cast, and having killed it, laid his rod on the grass and walked along it to straighten out the bends. Twelve casts later he had another five fish. He moved down to the Dog Hole and killed another three 'with a calm efficiency which seemed almost ruthless'. In all Pashley had eleven for the day – 'such is magic', gasped Gilbert, 'combined of course with superb fishing'.

Other anglers – non-wizards – might have been content with half a dozen. After all, hooking, playing and landing one salmon is very much like hooking, playing and landing another. But this was evidently a man in the grip of a serious hunger, not merely to catch salmon but to catch more than anyone else, to be the best. In an angling life that extended over the first half of the twentieth century, Pashley caught more than ten thousand salmon from the Wye at an average weight of sixteen pounds. These are mind-boggling figures.

It helped that he was born and brought up by the river and lived all his life in the family home, Kerne Lodge, which looked across (and still looks across) the Wye at the ruins of Goodrich Castle. It helped, too, that he was born into the comfortably upholstered life of a sporting gentleman of abundant private means. His friends emphasised that he did not just fish, that he gave generously of his time and money to worthy causes – as a

Goodrich Castle from across the Wye, 1839.

rural district councillor, county councillor, chairman of the parish council, chairman of the Wye Catchment Board, governor of several schools and much else.

But with the Wizard, fishing came first. He leased the two prime lower Wye beats for many years and had access to plenty of others – to have Robert Pashley fish your water was counted an honour. He had a boatman to row him whenever he needed, and men to trim the bushes, saw off inconvenient hanging branches, cut the grass and generally keep the place in order so that it could fulfil its principal function. He could look out of his window and decide there and then if it was worth his while going out. Not merely did he fish more days in a season than plenty of passionate salmon anglers manage in a decade, but he could select those days when his experience told him the chances were good. Pashley had the cream of it, all the time.

The biggest factor in his success, however, was one which had nothing to do with him – and that was the abundance of big

Wye salmon in those golden years. The credit for that belonged
to an earlier generation of campaigners. Had Pashley been born
half a century earlier he could never have enjoyed the triumphs
that were his. Who knows, he might have switched to his
secondary hobby, at which he also excelled – breeding Old English
game cocks and bantams.

In 1860, the government became sufficiently concerned at the
reports from all over the country of the plunder and destruction of salmon fishing to set up a Royal Commission to
investigate the issue. The commissioners looked closely at the
Wye, which should have been among the two or three most
productive rivers in England and Wales, and found a state of
anarchy in which whatever laws there were for the protection
of salmon were not so much broken on a regular basis as
ignored along its entire length.

H.A. Gilbert relates how in 1857 Edwin Partridge of Ross –
one of the Wye Conservators appointed to enforce the regulations
– took a large boat downriver in order to seize illegal nets. By
the time he reached Chepstow his craft was loaded to the
gunwales with the gear he had taken, and there was room for
no more. All along the Wye salmon were killed by net, gaff or
spear at any time of the year, with no regard for any close or
spawning season. Landowners and magistrates joined in the fun
with as much gusto as the lowest poacher. The parr, the infant
salmon in the stage before smolting, were netted in huge quan-
tities and eaten like whitebait. Much of the illegal as well as legal
fishing was carried out from coracles, little boats shaped like
half-walnut shells and made of hides or tarpaulins stretched over
a framework of laths, which were very cheap, light enough for
one man to carry, perfect for surreptitious launching at night.

The assumption of an unspoken right to take salmon at every
stage of their river cycle was deeply ingrained in all levels of
society, for whom the sport of angling counted for almost nothing.

The Rebecca Riots which broke out in rural mid-Wales in the late 1830s – so called because the participants dressed in items of women's clothing for their exploits – were mainly targeted at the tollgates installed on Welsh roads by the hated English government. But an important secondary outlet for resentment was the rivers, where some owners were trying to restrain the traditional help-yourself slaughter.

Rhayader, on the upper Wye in Radnorshire, was a hotbed of Rebecca-ism. Gilbert reproduces a report dated 1856 describing how eighty Rebeccaites with blackened faces and wearing long smocks and handkerchiefs around their heads marched one night around the marketplace brandishing guns, swords, cutlasses, spears and pitchforks before proceeding to the river. Under the light of torches they hunted salmon on the shallows with spears. They caught only six, because the local conservator had gone through the water before they arrived doing his best to scare the fish upstream. During the episode a gun was fired in the general direction of the steward of one of the local riparian owners, and another observer had three spears held to his chest.

The Royal Commission was followed by the 1861 Salmon Fisheries Act, which banned the more outrageous forms of destruction. But in rural Wales the provisions of the legislation were routinely flouted – at least partly because the sympathies of many local landowners, who served as magistrates when cases came to court, were with the poachers. Rhayader continued to be a centre of dissent, and there were periodic clashes between the new water bailiffs and organised gangs proclaiming their affiliations by dressing in petticoats and smocks. In 1877 the Wye Board of Conservators complained to the Chief Constable of Radnorshire about the destruction of fish by 'formidable gangs of armed men who patrolled the country by night with blackened faces'. Much of the poaching was utterly brazen; the Chief Constable reported crowds of up to four hundred gathering to watch the fun.

Over the course of 1880 there was a spate of incidents in the Rhayader area, thirteen in November alone, and the stories reached the ears of newspaper editors and Home Office ministers in London. The situation was complicated by the usual antagonism between the owners on different sections of the river. Those further down the river denounced those higher up for the indifference or active support given to 'the organised resistance of farmers and labourers to the law'. The upper owners were equally resentful of those towards the bottom of the river for deriving significant incomes from their netting rights. One told the public inquiry set up in response to the trouble, 'Rebecca had always taken and always would take fish out of the river. There was that trait of Rebecca which they could not get rid of.'

It was seen and accepted that the legislation designed to protect the salmon was having virtually no effect. Sparing salmon that otherwise would have been speared or gaffed merely made them available for someone else to take, so why not do it yourself? 'In this dismal era', Gilbert commented, 'everyone was more or less in the wrong. Selfishness ruled supreme.' In the nick of time a saviour appeared in the form of John Hotchkis, the chairman of both the Wye Fisheries Association and the Board of Conservators – a man, in Gilbert's words, of 'very tempestuous, masterful and original character'.

Between 1878 and 1908 Hotchkis steadily negotiated a takeover of the netting rights along the lower Wye above the tidal point, restraining their operation and eventually getting rid of them altogether. He was persuasive and influential and had some – though erratic – financial and moral support among the owners. But the most important factor in his eventual triumph was the determination of the netsmen to go on taking as many salmon as they could regardless of the consequences. Catches declined, then plummeted. Rather late in the day the owners woke up to the fact that had been under their noses for some time – that there was more money to be made from the likes of Robert Pashley than from scooping the salmon up and dispatching them to Billingsgate.

Hotchkis's great objective was to rid the whole of the non-tidal Wye of the nets so that its salmon would have unimpeded access upstream – either to be caught by anglers paying good money for the pleasure, or to reach the tributaries and the great web of spawning streams in the Welsh mountains so that the whole cycle could be sustained. The netting of the tidal section from Monmouth down to the Severn Estuary below Chepstow continued under licence from the Board of Conservators, which bought the rights from the Crown in 1924. The angling and the netting were the complementary components of a management policy that continued until towards the end of the century, when the decline in salmon abundance made netting no longer viable.

The catch returns show that, very broadly speaking, the rod and net catches on the Wye achieved and maintained an equilibrium. In some years the netsmen caught more, in others the anglers. In Pashley's great year of 1936, for instance, the rods took almost six thousand fish and the nets almost four thousand. Nineteen thirty-eight was a terrible year all round: 1,100 to the rods, fewer than a thousand for the nets.

The gentlemen proprietors and lessees such as Pashley, Gilbert and the other noted historian of Wye salmon fishing, J. Arthur Hutton, all believed unquestioningly that for the river to achieve its full potential for exploitation, commercial netting was as necessary as angling. Just as unquestioningly they would have regarded the control that they and their peers exercised over the river as right and proper. And from the perspective of conserving the salmon they were right.

But that assumption did not go unchallenged. For a time battle was joined between John Hotchkis on the one hand, and the political reformer and land-rights campaigner John Lloyd on the other. Lloyd came from a landowning family in Brecon and went to Oxford University, but nevertheless identified strongly with the cause of the Rebeccaites. He himself had operated nets on the middle Wye in Herefordshire in the 1870s, when he was also a member of the Board of Conservators and an assiduous enemy of illegal netting. But he changed his tune and by the end of the century was accusing the Conservators of persecuting the netsmen 'in the interests of mere sport' and called for 'the fishermen of the Wye to be freed from the bad, oppressive laws a tyrant's hand has imposed upon them'.

He was eloquent and passionate, but powerless. The interests of the ruling class prevailed and the rural working class were shunted off the rivers that they and their forebears had fished since time immemorial. The Rebeccaites were crushed and their voice was silenced.

All over England and Wales – and, to an extent, in Scotland – the same battle was fought, with the same result. In 1861 Charles Dickens wrote in his weekly paper, *All the Year Round*, 'the cry of "Salmon in Danger" is now resounding throughout the length and breadth of the land'. He called for an end to the 'wanton destruction' caused by poaching and pollution and reported in tones of outrage that on the Ribble and Hodder in Lancashire 'the young salmon are caught by the thousands on their way to the sea and sold to be eaten at eight pence a pound'.

The Salmon Fisheries Act of that year set a uniform close season over the winter months, and included measures intended to restrain the discharge of industrial waste and filth into rivers, to restrict the use of weirs as fish traps, and to limit the use of fixed nets. More legislation came later, setting up the Boards of Conservators to manage whole river systems, with the power to bring in bye-laws. Enforcement was, and remained for many years, the disabling flaw in the system. But at least the legislative machinery had been put in place that would, over time, enable the same class that ran the country to maintain control over the cream of its salmon fishing, and exclude those below them on the social ladder.

Thus, in that February of 1938, Robert Pashley was able to sit and check his rods and reels and lines, and pause to look out of the window at the river he knew so well and be confident that – whatever Herr Hitler might be cooking up in distant Berlin – at least here in Herefordshire there was nothing to cause him anxiety. He had seen enough of salmon fishing to know that there could be no certainty about the quality of sport to come. But he could be sure that whatever salmon did come back from the sea and make it up as far as his beats would be available to him. Poachers, Rebeccaites and other intruders would be kept at bay. Everything that could be done to facilitate his enjoyment had been done.

The nymph debate at the Flyfishers' Club was not covered in detail in the columns of the *Fishing Gazette* – unlike at the club's annual dinner a week or two later, where the speeches were reported as faithfully as if it had been a debate in the House of Commons, the laborious witticisms and hearty pleasantries sign-posted for the benefit of readers with bracketed references to *(Laughter)* and *(Applause)*.

The issue of Saturday 12 February – two days after the debate – carried the familiar wide range of articles: 'Good and Bad Days on the Onny' by E. Moore Darling, 'Amateur Rod and Tackle-Making (Part 1)', 'Looking Forward, Looking Back' by Basil Hall (about trout fishing in Australia where, according to the writer, 'riparian rights are unknown and Demos walks abroad'), 'A Shetland Loch', 'Pike Fishing in Ireland' by Dr K.C. Edwards. Angling reports from the Thames referred to the perch at Henley being 'on holiday' but Moulsford being 'alive with good roach'. At Teddington weir Mr W. McBride reported being out with his friend Mr Sydney Lewis and the two of them landing eighty-nine roach in the session.

From Lincolnshire came the story of a two-pound roach caught on the Glenny by Mr Julian which was subsequently identified by the 'skilled ichthyologist' Dr C.W. Pilcher as a carp. Mr Hinson had been 'among the bream' on the Witham and an unnamed Sheffield angler had had two stones of 'broadsides' (bream). The Nottingham and District Angling Association's report mentioned 'good bags of redfins' (roach) at Sawley on the Trent. The Birmingham and District AA reported that nine new clubs had applied for affiliation, and the total membership now exceeded 18,000. In the classified ads section J.T. Pickersgill of Whinney Hill Foot Farm at Oxenhope near Keighley was offering liver- and beef-fed maggots at one-and-sixpence a tin, or sixteen tins for ten-and-sixpence. An alternative source of this essential coarse-fishing bait was the Maggot King, located in Buckingham, 'the largest breeding factory in the world'.

On the Wye the *Fishing Gazette* reported 'excellent conditions' with a dozen fish of between sixteen and twenty-six pounds caught the previous weekend.

Nineteen thirty-eight was shaping up to be just another fishing year.

Eighty years on I made a singularly unsuccessful attempt to follow in Robert Pashley's wizardly footsteps. His class of well-to-do gentlemen of leisure are not in evidence as they used to be, and the Wye salmon fishing has become much more democratic as well as unproductive. Many of the beats are now controlled by the Wye and Usk Foundation, a pioneering environmental charity that has done heroic work to restore and enhance the spawning habitats, to improve access for fish, and generally to try to arrest and reverse the collapse in the salmon runs of the 1990s. The foundation's portfolio includes Goodrich Court and Hill Court, which can now be fished by anyone on payment of a fairly modest daily fee.

Goodrich Court, which includes the legendary Vanstone, the pool on which the Wizard did such slaughter, was solidly booked up, but Hill Court was available. It was a fine, warm May day and I went first to the upper section which includes Pashley's Crib, a sort of mini-weir that he had had built across part of the river to create holding water.

The remains of the crib are still there and the river still runs around and over it, but everything else has changed. There was certainly farming along the banks of the Wye then, and there is farming now – but I doubt if Pashley or anyone from that era would easily recognise it as such. E.C. Drummond (Agriculture) Ltd of Homme Farm own and lease a thousand hectares of land on which stands a city of polytunnels for growing strawberries and an immense shuttered poultry unit. The central yard resembles a medium-sized industrial estate, and great fields of wheat and potatoes stretch away into the distance. Fifty full-time staff are employed, with a seasonal workforce of up to four hundred.

The river flows around the edge of this enterprise, used as a source of water for thirsty plants but otherwise left to its own devices and to the anglers. I set up my fifteen-foot salmon rod and set off upstream in search of Pashley's Crib. The way down to the river was blocked by a dark thicket of willow, alder, elder, brambles, nettles, collapsed tree trunks and branches and a lot else. It was testing work, forcing my way through it in chest waders while trying not to snag my rod tip in the tree canopy. The bank dropped steeply down to where I presumed the water's edge to be. I slid down, floundered through clinging mud and emerged into daylight beyond the trailing willow branches.

The river was wide, the flow strong and even. There was not a soul to be seen anywhere. Lucky Pashley had sat in comfort at the end of a punt with a man on the oars and the anchor, and the banks were trimmed and orderly. I was already up to my waist and the current was tugging insistently at my legs. I tried to get out a line but the tangle of trees made it extremely difficult and my heart really wasn't in it. I kept wondering what would happen if I tipped over. There was no one to pull me out, and I had no idea if the water below me was shallow enough to reach the bank.

I cut my losses, battled back the way I had come and drove down to Kerne Bridge, past what had been Pashley's house perched above the road and the river. I crossed and followed the track up the right bank around a big bend below the noble and highly picturesque ruins of Goodrich Castle until a dense wood spilling down to the river's edge made further progress impossible. My instructions said this was the Ford stream, described as the best bit of fly water on the beat, and it was handsome: a long, restless, powerful run down the middle beyond the fractured remains of another, this time nameless, crib.

It was a steep descent but once I got in the wading was not too alarming. My line went out nicely beyond the main push of the current so that the fly came around working over the lies. By now it was distinctly warm, the sun blazing from a cloudless sky – pretty hopeless conditions even if there had been any salmon present, which there weren't. I never thought I was really in with a chance of a fish, but it was pleasant enough until I tripped over a rock and subsided full length in the water. I took this as a sign that the enterprise was futile. As I hauled myself on all fours up the bank, Wye water cascading from my clothes and from inside my waders, the end of the handle of my landing-net struck me a sharp blow on the end of my nose, and for a moment I wanted to cry.

This was not salmon fishing as Pashley had known it. But a lot about the river today would make him wring his hands in dismay. At weekends throughout the summer, fishing is almost impossible except early in the morning and late in the evening because of the armadas of canoes that float downstream on most stretches below Glasbury. The days when every beat had a ghillie and a boat and the banks were kept in order for the salmon angler have long gone. The economic balance of power has tilted decisively away from the salmon-fishing interests.

Coarse fish species – particularly barbel, chub and perch – have thrived and spread as the salmon runs have declined. Once-celebrated salmon beats – such as Moccas, between Hay-on-Wye and Hereford – are now mainly marketed for the coarse fishing. There is nothing particularly novel about this – Gilbert noted that 'the Wye is now the playground of the industrial areas from Wigan to Swansea . . . coarse fishing rights now equal in value over long lengths of the river the value of the salmon fishing rights'. But in 1951 – the last year for which Gilbert provides figures – the rods caught over four thousand salmon on the Wye, and nets almost 1,700. Over the years 2018 through 2020 the average annual catch has been below 500.

On 9 September 1939, six days after the declaration of war, the *Fishing Gazette* informed its readers that it was removing its offices from London to Beckenham in Kent.

The issue of 23 December carried a valedictory statement from Allcock and Co. of Redditch, the leading suppliers of tackle for coarse fishing and game fishing: 'We pray that when the doctrine of force has been discredited and evil things eliminated, the blessing of peace may be restored to us so that we may once again derive to the full the enjoyment that is offered by the "best and most innocent of all recreations".'

CHAPTER ELEVEN

While Life Lasts

In December 1945, nine months after the end of the war in Europe, a little book was published which represented an answer to the prayer from Allcocks of Redditch for the doctrine of force to be discredited and the best and most innocent of recreations to be enjoyed again. It was printed 'in complete conformity with the authorised economy standards' on very thin paper that rustles as you turn the pages. Although it is the size of my hand, it contained more than five hundred pages. It was small but very meaty, and it was seized upon eagerly by a readership hungry for the magic it distilled.

The Fisherman's Bedside Book was an anthology of writing about angling. Apart from some Walton and one extract from Scrope, it was drawn from the period between 1850 and the conflict that had just finished. It could have been subtitled 'An Antidote to the Horror of War' in the way it presented the sport of fishing as an alternative to the belligerence of the modern era.

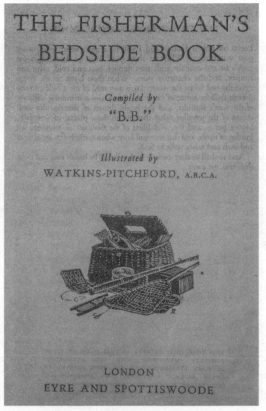

The title page of the first edition of
The Fisherman's Bedside Book, 1945.

Much of it was filleted from the books of the acknowledged masters: H.T. Sheringham, J.W. Hills, Lord Grey of Falloden, Arthur Ransome, Patrick Chalmers, Negley Farson, Halford, Skues, William Senior and others. It also extensively referenced a wider range of nature writers – principally Henry Thoreau, Richard Jefferies and W.H. Hudson – whose quests to find meaning and consolation in the natural world took them to the waterside and caused them to meditate on still and moving water.

The selections evince a comprehensive knowledge of the

available literature. But there is an extra dimension to *The Fisherman's Bedside Book* which lifts it from being just an exceptionally well-chosen miscellany of angling and countryside writing. The anthologist had the brainwave of placing advertisements in fishing and sporting journals and circulating angling clubs to invite anglers who had never dreamed of joining the throng of published authors to send him their accounts of their triumphs and disasters. 'Anglers in all walks of life have contributed,' he wrote in the introduction, 'and this is as it should be, for all belong to the Brotherhood, whether he be salmon fisher or humble angler for roach. There are not many books for the "poor man" fisher, which is a pity, for the latter are far in the majority.'

He also provided the illustrations. Post-war stringency did not allow for photographs, but did not preclude the reproduction of a score of full-page studies on scraperboard – and a host of smaller ones. These watery scenes, scratched with a blade on a blackened board, are extraordinarily evocative. A monk sits beside a monastic pond staring at his float. A Devon stream curls around the roots of a great tree. A millstream emerges from beneath an old stone bridge into a pool fringed with reeds and lily pads. A rock-strewn sea-trout river tumbles away through wild Highland scenery. The feel and atmosphere of water in a landscape are captured with a haunting truthfulness.

When *The Fisherman's Bedside Book* was published, its illustrator and compiler, Denys Watkins-Pitchford, was an art master at Rugby School. He was born in 1905 and his father was the rector of Lamport, a small village in the gentle green countryside between Market Harborough and Northampton. The family lived in the fine Georgian rectory opposite the even finer and older Lamport Hall, the ancestral home of the Ishams. The Watkins-Pitchfords belonged firmly in the upper social bracket, but Denys – one of twins – was considered too delicate to be subjected to the rigours of the normal boarding-school education. He was schooled at home and left to wander the fields and woods and

The legendary carp water, Redmire Pool (see page 206), depicted by Denys Watkins-Pitchford.

to teach himself the ways and rhythms of the natural world.

This was fox-hunting and shooting country, and he became a devotee of both (though quite quickly lost his enthusiasm for the hunt). But it was emphatically not trout-fishing country. The rivers and brooks, exemplified by the Nene, were generally sluggish and murky. They were complemented by an abundance of ponds and lakes whose character suited only the coarse fish. By default, the lad became a coarse fisherman.

Thus he had a natural affinity with 'the "poor man" fisher', far apart though they were in class and circumstances. In selecting contributions – as opposed to extracts from published books – for his anthology, Watkins-Pitchford spanned that same divide. Sir Harold Gillies wrote thrillingly of 'The Mammoth Sea Trout of the Laerdal' (in Norway), General Sir Charles Grant KCB, KCVO, DSO described catching a thirty-pound salmon on the Severn, Mrs Victor Hurst recounted battles with the salmon of the Shiel in the western Highlands of Scotland. They found themselves rubbing shoulders with the likes of Albert Buckley, who sent in his account of catching the then record carp of twenty-six pounds from Mapperley Lake in Derbyshire, H. Green (a record perch from Stradsett Lake in Norfolk) and J.H. Grief (a twenty-five-and-a-half pound pike caught on 21 December 1941).

Of particular interest to me when I first came upon *The Fisherman's Bedside Book* many years after its publication was the story entitled 'A Midnight Battle with a Monster Barbel' submitted by Mr J.L. Webb of Reading. This epic encounter took place on a September night in 1943, 'opposite the fourth meadow below the French Horn at Sonning'. The French Horn was and still is a celebrated Thames hotel close to Sonning Mill, which was a favourite venue for me and my two angling brothers in my boyhood days when the passion for fishing burned so fiercely inside me that for lengthy periods each day I could think of nothing else.

The Fisherman's Bedside Book covered a great range of coarse and game angling at home and abroad (plus a nod at sea fishing at the end). To distinguish between his writing and illustrating roles, Watkins-Pitchford had adopted the pseudonym 'BB' – the calibre of shot he used – for his writing. As 'BB' he wove a gentle commentary around the extracts, written in his highly distinctive, simple, straightforward style. He also included several more substantial pieces of his own taken from an unpublished and possibly non-existent volume which he called *Fisherman's Folly*.

In them he mused on random matters under titles such as 'The Fisherman's Inn', 'The Valley of Enchantment', 'The Philosopher Defines the Honest Fisherman' and 'Don't Forget'. One, 'The Abbey Moat', is a potent and characteristic portrait of a long-abandoned monastic stewpond, the home of huge carp – 'those fish were, I firmly believe, uncatchable . . . only one did I see on the bank and it was dead . . . it lay like a stranded barque, its ribs like ship's timbers and a skull as big as my two fists . . .'

In all 'BB' wrote fifty-odd books, many of them for children, two of which – *The Little Grey Men* and *Brendon Chase* – can be regarded as classics. He illustrated all his own books and many other people's work, and by artfully balancing his dual roles maintained a long and successful, if not hugely lucrative, career. Together with fishing, rough shooting and wildfowling were his passions (he did not care for organised pheasant and partridge slaughter), and he provided a weekly column for the *Shooting Times* until shortly before his death.

By his own account and that of others, 'BB' was something of a bungler as a fisherman. His stories regularly recount self-inflicted disasters – fish lost through incompetence, nets left behind, tackle not checked properly and so on. His influence came, not from his expertise, which was limited, but from the manner in which his fishing books fired the imaginations of a generation that had come through the war and was now ready to embrace the old sport of angling in a new way.

A few months after its publication, a copy of *The Fisherman's Bedside Book* was given as a present to a younger man with a very different approach to the passion he shared with 'BB'. Richard Walker was an engineer, Cambridge-educated, with an outstandingly keen, analytical mind. Born and brought up in Hertfordshire, he, like 'BB', had haunted streams and stillwaters as a boy. But quite unlike 'BB', Walker had the kind of mind that rejoiced in the solving of problems – and the problem that preoccupied him was how to outwit large, wary fish.

He and his boyhood friend Peter Thomas concentrated particular attention on carp. At that time only a handful of carp of over twenty pounds had ever been landed, and the received wisdom among the coarse-fishing community was that they were too big and powerful and cunning to be worth targeting specifically. 'BB' indulged his own fascination with the species at length in *The Fisherman's Bedside Book*, and in 1947 Walker and Thomas invited him to come and fish with them.

'From this joint operation', Walker wrote many years later, 'grew what we call specimen-hunting today.' Carp enthusiasts from various parts of the country became aware of each other and exchanged letters about experiences and tactics. 'While we were fishing at Mapperley', Walker recalled, 'someone came up with the idea of forming a club with a regular rotary letter. I said "let's call it the Carpfishers' Club." BB said "we're doing more than fishing for carp, we're catching 'em. Call it The Carpcatchers' Club." We did.'

In that year, 1951, one of the founding members, Bob Richards, broke the carp record with a fish of thirty-one and a quarter pounds from a three-acre pond hidden deep in the Herefordshire countryside. It was close to a fine old manor house, Bernithan Court, but was called Redmire to disguise its whereabouts. Twenty years earlier, it had been stocked with a mixture of mirror and common carp from strains originating from a fish farm in Holland and imported by a man called Don Leney, who worked for the Surrey Trout Farm in Haslemere. Leney was responsible for providing his so-called 'Galician' carp for stocking into hundreds of ponds, lakes, rivers and canals all over southern England. Where the conditions were favourable – as at Redmire – they grew steadily to a great size and age.

Walker studied the Redmire carp closely. He knew there were specimens there bigger than the record fish caught by Bob

Richards. He designed a ten-foot split cane rod specifically for big carp – the prototype of what became the Mark IV model – and a reel to go with it. In the early morning of 13 September 1952 he caught a common carp – one of the few commons from the original stocking of Redmire – which reshaped the emerging world of specimen hunting. Highly conscious of the value of publicity, Walker arranged for the fish to be collected and taken to London Zoo, where it was weighed by an Inspector of Weights and Measures and brought the scales down to exactly forty-four pounds. The carp, by then named Clarissa, was placed in a tank which became a place of pilgrimage for countless anglers including my youthful self, until she died in 1971 at a considerably reduced weight.

The capture of Clarissa was one of the triggers for a tremendous upsurge in the popularity of coarse fishing. Another was the appointment by the mass-circulation *Daily Mirror* of a writer/artist called Bernard Venables as its first Angling Editor. Venables produced a weekly strip cartoon recounting the year-round experiences of Everyman Angler, Mr Crabtree – with hat, tie, tweed jacket and pipe – and his fresh-faced son Peter. This subsequently became a phenomenally popular book, *Mr Crabtree Goes Fishing*, which sold more than two million copies and made the *Daily Mirror* (but not its creator, because he was an employee) a considerable pile of money.

In 1953 a new weekly publication, *Angling Times*, was launched with Venables as editor and Walker as star columnist. It rapidly surpassed the fading *Fishing Gazette* (which quietly expired a few years later) and established itself as essential reading for anyone who aspired to catch a fish worth taking a picture of.

I aspired. So did my two fishing brothers. We had saved up for and bought our Mark IV Avon rods (a lighter and more versatile version of the carp rod). We had Intrepid Elite fixed-spool reels, later graduating to the Mitchell 300 or Young's Ambidex. We hung around the tackle shops of Reading – first

Bernard Venables fishing for barbel on the Avon.

Perry and Cox in Kings Road, where there was a glass case of golden tench set up by the master taxidermists J. Cooper and Sons which mesmerised me, later T. Turner and Sons in Market Place. We bought maggots by the bucketful and roamed our lawn on damp nights in summer harvesting lobworms which then lived – and sometimes, with unpleasant results, died – in our wormery until needed. We read *Angling Times* closely, except the coverage of match fishing which we despised, despite knowing nothing about it. We studied Richard Walker's column as if it were a weekly revelation of divine truth.

The man was all-knowing. He had caught the record carp. He had fished head-to-head against the captain of England's champion match-fishing team and trounced him by catching an eleven-pound barbel. Name a species – carp, chub, barbel, perch, roach, rudd – and Walker had landed a specimen. And he told you how to do it. He had no secrets, except the location of the waters he fished, which was fair enough. His style was simple, direct, no frills, no nonsense. He was like the best kind of schoolmaster, because he took the trouble to talk your language and got his hands dirty.

My brothers and I tried to follow the Word of Walker. We discovered that in fishing, as in all walks of life, there is a gap between the expert and the average practitioner that no amount of youthful keenness can bridge. We tended to see our problem as being the waters we had access to. Our carp water, a moat in the grounds of a big house owned by family friends, had no carp in it bigger than seven pounds or so – we knew that because it was only three feet deep and you could see all the fish clearly. Our tench pond never produced anything bigger than three pounds. We caught plenty of chub and perch on the local river, but they never exceeded a size that the great Walker would have curled his lip at.

We went after the fabled trout of the Thames on weirpools near and far and never caught one. We spent hours on the millstream at Sonning. On one memorably awful occasion one brother and I borrowed a punt and paddled and poled it down our river to its confluence with the Thames and then up to Sonning so we could emulate the great J.L. 'Wormy' Webb by fishing through the night. One very small silver bream between us was the result.

The truth was that we were average, and Walker and his fellow experts were exceptional. Walker would never have bothered with our carp moat, nor with our tench pond; he would have located other waters with bigger fish in them, which we never had the wit to do. He would have caught the Thames trout, the five-pound chub and ten-pound barbel that we could only dream of.

What actually mattered was that he kindled the fire of enthusiasm that drew us repeatedly to the waterside, where we learned about nature and beauty and the inexhaustible fascination of still and moving water. He fed those flames, week in, week out. He was the spokesman for a movement that recruited legions like us, that nurtured a burgeoning fishing-tackle industry, that promoted an awareness of the preciousness of the aquatic environment and a corresponding fervour in defending it against polluters and government-licensed vandals.

It is no coincidence that over the thirty years that Richard Walker produced his columns for *Angling Times* – all of them written in longhand, with never a word crossed out – fishing for pleasure became, after gardening, the nation's favourite pastime. His style was didactic and severely practical; he rarely wrote in lyrical fashion about the spiritual side of the sport, although he has far from immune to it. He was content to leave that to his friend 'BB', who never caught a real specimen but with his pen and scraperboard blade captured the inner dimension more faithfully than anyone else of his generation.

'BB's one angling classic, *Confessions of a Carp Fisher*, was published in 1951. Two years before that he had produced an engaging collection of fishing stories with the regrettable title *Be Quiet and Go A-Angling* under the pseudonym Michael Traherne (assumed because of an obscure copyright dispute). Later he concentrated increasingly on children's books and shooting journalism. But in 1958 he published a very short book clumsily entitled *A Carp Water (Wood Pool) and How to Fish It*, best shortened to *The Wood Pool*. In it he told how he took charge of a neglected, weed-choked pond in the Northamptonshire countryside near Kettering, cleaned it up and stocked it with one hundred of Donald Leney's mirror and common carp, and what became of the pool and the fish.

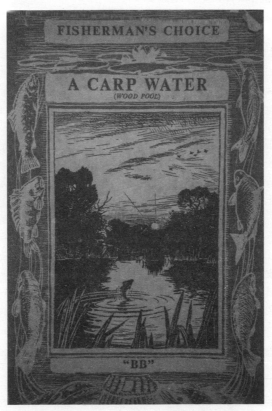

The first edition cover of *The Wood Pool*, 1958.

The opening of the book is pure 'BB', no fuss, no fanfare – 'The way to the water is hot walking for I begin this portrait of the pool in June.' He describes the path through the rough meadows, the flight of purple hairstreak butterflies, the palisade of alders that signals the nearness of water, the smell – 'a hint of rotting leaves in it, a half-sweet, half-rotten perfume which is very pleasing' – the boathouse with its tarred timbers, the channel through the reedmace leading to open water. Opposite the first page is his map, showing a pond shaped liked a gourd or a fat tadpole. At the narrow end is the boathouse, from which the channel – whimsically named Congo Channel – winds through reed beds to reach the plump, rounded body of the pool, passing the Island and Frog Channel, with Open Water and Deep Water extending towards the Spillway at the end.

The narrative is shaped by his work on the pool and the boat-house, the introduction and subsequent monitoring of the fish, and the fishing; but 'BB' meanders here and there as reflections and memories occur to him. There are digressions on night fishing, cooking eels, the destructiveness of otters, the history of carp fishing and the like. He owns up to having caught nothing at Redmire despite repeated attempts, his one run from one of the giants having coincided with the distracting arrival of a noisy farm boy just as the bait was picked up – 'shocking bad luck' is how 'BB' characterises the episode, but it would never have happened to Walker.

The Wood Pool is an extended meditation on the beauty and magic of still water. Its climax, insofar as it has one, is the chapter describing how 'BB' caught his biggest carp, 14lbs 10oz, after a 'ding-dong battle of pully-hauly'; and how he lost one of the patriarchs by leaving his rod propped up on the gunwale of the boat so that it snapped in two when the fish made its bid for freedom.

Opposite the title page is the one full-page scraperboard illustration. It shows the sun setting over the trees, geese flighting, the water framed by the reeds, a carp leaping in the dying light – a scaled crescent suspended above concentric ripples. It is formalised, but incredibly atmospheric.

My copy has a quavery signature inside the front cover – 'D.J. Watkins-Pitchford M.B.E. "BB"', with a line underneath. I went to visit him not long before his death in 1990 to write something about him for the *Financial Times*, and I had the presence of mind to take my copies of his books to sign. He had remained loyal to the county of his birth, and had by then lived for many years in a curious old round tollhouse in the garden of which he had dug three small ponds whose tench would take worms from his fingers.

By then he had suffered kidney failure and was on dialysis, but he was still hoping to make a last wildfowling foray to Scotland if someone would lend him a Land Rover and if he could arrange treatment for his kidney at a hospital in Aberdeen. Just before I left, he showed me a rod and reel propped up against a wall. He said Dick Walker had made them for him and that a man from Sotheby's had told him they might be worth three or four hundred pounds if he sent them to auction. I told him I thought they might be worth a good deal more than that and advised him to advertise them in the angling press. A month or so later I had a letter from him thanking me – he had got £3,000 for them by placing an ad in *Angling Times*.

Walker died two years before 'BB', in 1988. By then his carp record had been broken by a fish of fifty-one pounds, another Redmire giant. It was caught on sweetcorn by Chris Yates – a photographer and a brilliant writer who might be said to have inherited 'BB's mantle as a chronicler of the poetic, lyrical side of angling, but is also an amazingly accomplished catcher of big fish.

The angling landscape was being reshaped in many directions. Salmon fishing and river fishing for trout and grayling were comparatively untouched and essentially continued much as they had before the war. But the creation of new trout fisheries from reservoirs and gravel pits had stimulated a great and rapid expansion in fly fishing. These waters, stocked mainly with fast-growing, hard-fighting rainbow trout from trout farms, demanded novel techniques, different kinds of rods and lines, new approaches. Once again Richard Walker led the way, and as time went on he concentrated on reservoir trout fishing and wrote much less about coarse fishing.

As his influence in the coarse-fishing arena waned, the orthodoxies he had proclaimed were challenged. Walker had told his followers not to bother with artificially flavoured baits for carp – they just didn't work. A later Redmire regular, Rod Hutchinson, turned this doctrine on its head. He experimented with a range of baits including hemp, tares and compounds made from seeds and bird food and other ingredients flavoured with crab and even rancid butter and found that the carp loved them. Carp fanatics became amateur laboratory scientists. The biggest breakthrough was the development of compounds of products such as powdered baby milk, fish meal, bird food, egg powder, salmon and cod oil and a host of others which were rolled into balls and boiled – hence their generic name, boilies.

Boilies took the carp-fishing world by storm. A key advance was the discovery that if the boilie was worked onto a spur of stiff nylon next to the hook rather than being on the hook itself, carp were much more likely to take it. The hair-rig, as it was termed, and the boilie became the new creed among the new generation of hard-core carp addicts.

The carp world divided into two strands. One could be defined as the traditionalist, and was personified by the bearded, tweedy, vaguely Victorian figure of Chris Yates. The traditionalists resolutely employed old-fashioned tactics and tackle, often preferring retro cane rods and centrepin reels. They fished the kinds of lakes and ponds that 'BB' wrote about – reed and willow fringed, speckled with beds of lilies, hidden in deep countryside, waters with history and carp that had been there since arriving from Donald Leney's Surrey Trout Farm a couple of generations before.

They pursued, and today still pursue, their notion of carp fishing. But in terms of attention, media hype and importance to the tackle industry they have been entirely eclipsed by the modernists. The modern carp man (it remains an overwhelmingly male domain) is defined by his equipment. He fishes with three, sometimes four, identical rods and reels which are lined up like an artillery battery, each fitted with an electric bite alarm to alert the angler if the bait is taken. A giant landing net is propped against the bankside vegetation. Close by is a small tent, muted green in colour, in which the carp man sits or lies when it is raining or when he needs rest. He will often take his nourishment in his bivvy, as the tent is called.

Beside the bivvy or in it are the bucket or buckets of boilies that he will need for the session, which may well last over a weekend or longer. There are boxes containing hooks, weights, spools of spare line, prepared rigs of one kind or another. There may well be a bait boat, which looks rather like the kind of boat a child might use on a pleasure park pool, but is actually designed to carry a payload of boilies out to the target area eighty yards or more away, where a release mechanism controlled by a hand-held transmitter deposits them. An alternative method of delivering bait is known in CarpSpeak as spodding – it involves attaching a bait-packed device resembling a small cluster bomb to the end of the line and hurling it a hundred yards and more out to the desired spot where a quick tug releases the load.

The rapid march of technological innovation took carp fishing far away from its origin as a contest between angler and fish in which the odds were generally stacked in favour of the fish. The angler, armed with irresistible bait and an arsenal of high-tech weaponry, acquired the upper hand. This decisive tilting of the balance inevitably fuelled a revised approach to the provision of the fish themselves. Those generations of Leney carp were dying out, and where they did survive were insufficient in numbers (as well as being very hard to outwit) to satisfy the expanding demand.

Canny fishery owners saw the potential in the extreme and often obsessive dedication of the carp-fishing community. They began buying outsize specimens from specialist fish farms, releasing them into customised waters and advertising their availability to those prepared to pay. Bearing in mind that a twenty-pound carp costs about £1,000, a thirty-pounder £3,000, and a forty-pounder as much as £15,000, this kind of stocking was done on a very limited scale. But once a monster had been caught, and its picture had appeared in the angling press, competition for access could become intense. One angler waited seven years to become a member of the syndicate on a lake west of Reading. Once in, he soon established his reputation as a 'legend' by catching a succession of leviathans culminating in a new British record of sixty-eight pounds one ounce, a mirror carp known as The Parrot on account of its strangely disfigured mouth.

The rise and rise of specialised carp fishing on closely managed and highly artificial fisheries was fuelled by mushrooming media exposure. Magazines for the devotees proliferated – *Maximum Carp*, *Advanced Carp Fishing*, *CarpTalk*, *Total Carp*, *Crafty Carper* and others – as did websites, generating a great swelling tide of chat and comment. The growth of satellite TV produced a new species of presenter, far removed from the avuncular, pipe-smoking Bernard Venables, who fronted the BBC's *Angler's Corner* in ancient days – or, indeed, Chris Yates and Bob James, the faces and voices of Hugh Miles's *Passion for Angling*, a six-part series screened by the BBC in the 1990s whose production values set a standard never approached before or since.

Cheap and cheerful series such as *Carp Wars* and *Monster Carp*, in which assorted 'legends' swapped banter and passed on expertise, fed the carp fever. A fairly recent recruit to the stable has been *Bivvy TV*, an internet station featuring ten professional anglers who make their livings promoting their brand of carping on behalf of sponsoring tackle firms and fishery owners.

The trend towards this kind of manufactured angling did not end with the import and stocking of genetically engineered carp fattened to a size way beyond anything a natural water could sustain. Ingenious fishery owners began to look further afield. Size was everything in this market, and there were two species of European fish that dwarfed even the most monstrous monster carp.

In eastern Europe the catfish, *Silurus glanis*, has been recorded at weights of several hundred pounds. With its broad, flattened head, its hugely wide mouth with flickering barbules at either side, and its smooth, slimy, mottled green body tapering to a long, muscular tail, it is not a creature of beauty. Although some were successfully transported from Germany to the lakes at Woburn by one of the Russell family in the 1880s, in general the catfish was unknown in Britain until a handful of enterprising fishery owners began quietly introducing them twenty or thirty years ago, mainly from fish farms in Croatia.

The story of the sturgeon is very different. There are numerous records of this enormous wandering relic from the primitive order of scaleless ganoid fishers turning up unexpectedly in British waters over the last thousand years. In most cases they were caught in fishermen's nets, but there have been a number of well-documented cases in which a solitary sturgeon – perhaps dimly recalling its spawning responsibilities – has come to a sticky end after making its cumbersome way up one river or another.

The most celebrated of these occurred on the Tywi at Nantgaredig in Carmarthenshire on a stretch rented by Alec Allen, a keen fisherman who worked as a travelling rep for a fishing-tackle firm. One July evening in 1933 Allen hooked what he initially thought was a log, which then began to move slowly upstream. After a time he managed to drag the monster into shallow water where he proceeded to beat it over the head with a rock until it was dead. With considerable difficulty Allen and the local farmer plus other assistants dragged it up the bank. No one knew what it was; then someone suggested it must be a sturgeon, and as such was the property of the reigning monarch. A telegram was sent to Buckingham Palace, but George V was not in residence and was presumed to have no need of it, so it was sold – all 388 pounds and nine foot two inches of it – to a fishmonger in Swansea for £2 10s.* The caviar with which the great fish was laden dripped onto the ground where it was eagerly mopped up by the farmer's pigs.

These unhappy wanderers were specimens of the European sturgeon, *Acipenser sturio*, once widely distributed from Norway down to the Bay of Biscay but now extremely rare. However, smaller sturgeon of other species have long been available from aquariums for keeping in tanks and ornamental ponds, and a shadowy trade in rearing hybrids for stocking fisheries developed. Eventually the import of live sturgeon was banned, and since the successful prosecution by the Environment Agency of the owner of a lake near Thetford in Norfolk for illegally putting in sturgeon and selling tickets to fish for them, the trade has diminished. Even so, there are still fisheries advertising sturgeon to be caught and specimens are reported by Trent anglers every now and then, although no one knows where they come from.

The EA has also tightened controls on the import of catfish, but there are plenty of licensed fisheries which offer the growing number of enthusiasts the chance to catch them. The agency believes there are now breeding populations in the Thames, the Great Ouse and elsewhere, resulting from escapes in less regulated days.

This kind of synthetic angling – particularly for outsize carp – arouses violently conflicting views. It receives a huge amount of hype and media coverage, but it's worth remembering that it represents a minority interest. Many anglers despise it and have nothing to do with it and continue to pursue a version of the sport that would be entirely recognisable to 'BB' and others of the old school. They fish on rivers that run as they always have, on lakes and ponds that have been there for decades and centuries, for native species that wax and wane as they always have.

* * *

* Two pounds ten shillings, £2.50 in decimal currency.

I wanted to see how 'BB's Wood Pool had fared in the sixty-odd years since his 'ding-dong battle of pully-hauly' with his biggest carp. Mark Walsingham – a carp fisherman, fishery manager, consultant and general authority who belongs very firmly in the traditionalist school – kindly gave me the location, but it still took a little finding.

In the final chapter of the book, 'BB' describes a last walk to the pool and a last row on its waters in October 1957. 'Alas! The days of this lovely wilderness are numbered,' he wrote. 'Within a month or two this beautiful paradise, where I have had so many happy times, will be bulldozed flat and all the hawthorns will be uprooted, all will be nice and tidy.'

It's not at all clear what he was referring to. It certainly wasn't housing, because there is none. It may have had something to do with the widening of the A14 trunk road, which now – in dual carriageway form – runs no more than a hundred yards or so north of the pool, and fills what was once the peaceful Northamptonshire air with the ceaseless roar and snarl of traffic. But the approach to the pool is far from neat and tidy, and the hawthorns, willows, alders and the rest are doing fine.

The boathouse, which 'BB' fitted with an oak door from his cellar, is still standing, just. The corrugated roof has mostly collapsed, the beams sag, the walls lean as if about to topple over altogether, and the door through which he passed to get to the boat is an open gap. His Congo Channel snakes between the reed beds towards the island, on which the silver birches he described as swooning towards the water are still swooning. The spring feeding the boathouse pool down a concrete culvert and the spillway at the eastern end are much as he depicted them, as are the big trees around the southern side.

Take away the road, and the setting of Wood Pool struck me as entirely characteristic of the rural Midlands countryside that 'BB' knew all his life. Sheep grazed the rough meadow. Rooks disputed the tree tops. Pigeons whirred over the cut wheat-fields.

What remains of 'BB's boathouse.

But the pool was a pool no longer. The whole of the wider part marked on 'BB's map as Open Water and Deep Water was entirely choked with reeds, rushes and solid beds of water lilies. The small patches of open water were no more than a few inches deep. The island had grown and spread like some insatiable animal, and there was no visible water between it and the margins. I walked around the pool twice with polarised glasses. Where there were patches of open water, it was very clear, just a thin sheet above the mud. A family of swans cruised Congo Channel and I could hear coots in the rushes. If there had been carp I would have seen them, or signs of them, but there were no sizeable fish.

I sat on the shattered trunk of a fallen willow next to the boathouse and made some notes, with my copy of *The Wood Pool* beside me. I wondered how long the carp and tench he put in had lasted. They might well have perished in the tremendous freeze of the winter of 1962–3. One way or another, once he had gone there was no one to clear the weed, maintain the boathouse, check on the fish. The land had begun the slow, inexorable process of claiming the pool – or reclaiming it, since it was only ever a man-made thing.

'BB' prefaced many of his books with these lines, which he said he found inscribed on a gravestone in a churchyard in Cumbria:

> The wonder of the world
> The beauty and the power
> The shape of things
> Their colour, light and shades
> These I saw
> Look ye also while life lasts.

They seemed an appropriate epitaph on what was once his Wood Pool.

CHAPTER TWELVE

Salmon Plunder

There is a path through the trees from the car park of the Berwick
Garden Centre on the western edge of Berwick-upon-Tweed
that leads to the broad expanse of the tidal River Tweed. To the
left is the flat, functional concrete bridge taking the A1 north.
A little way downstream, set back from the water and half-choked
in nettles and brambles, is the shell of a small rectangular stone
building. The roof and upper parts of the side walls are missing.
Inside, fixed into one of the end walls, is a blackened fireplace
and brick chimney.

When it was in use it would have had a central dividing wall,
with bunks for the crew, a separate space for the skipper, and
room for a table and benches or chairs. Outside was a flat platform or stand on which the nets and other gear were heaped.
Along the bank, dug into the earth, was a semi-circular brick
chamber: the ice house, where the fish were stored until the boat

came to take them down to Berwick for sorting and dispatch to Billingsgate in London.

Ice house upstream from Berwick-upon-Tweed.

The shiel – the name given to the stone building – was aligned so that the window gave a view across a great sweep of water to where the river swings east towards Berwick Castle and the town.

In the season, which ran from mid-February to mid-September, the skipper would generally sit at the window scanning the water while his men smoked, played cards, snoozed or swapped stories. He would check the state of the tide and the wind, how the weather was shaping. Long experience would inform him when the fish might be expected. Sometimes he could see them, heads and backs breaking the surface as they forged their way upstream. He would give the order. Within minutes the boat would be out on the stream, the sweep net being paid out from the stern. By the time that pulse of salmon arrived, the net would be ready for them.

Upstream from the A1 road bridge is another ruined shiel. There are two more further up, hidden in the trees. Further downstream are the remains of one of the few twentieth-century shiels, a plain and ugly thing of concrete that replaced a stone one washed away in the epic flood of August 1948, when the Tweed rose seventeen feet above normal and almost filled the arches of Coldstream Bridge. Others are dotted along the banks of the river from Berwick up to Coldstream, fifteen miles away. Some have been erased altogether; one or two have been turned into dinky holiday cottages.

Each of them served one or more of the netting stations which had historic rights to take salmon. The one near the garden centre was Clayhole, the one immediately above the road bridge was Needle's Eye. Below Clayhole on the south bank were Ween, Old Toddles, Toddles, Upper Yarrow and Yarrow, with English New Water and Black Goat on the other side. Upstream from Needle's Eye were Cove Sands, Canny and Heughshield, with Ethermouth and Bow for Nought opposite. The netting stations extended all the way through Berwick to the sea: Gardo, Davie's Batt, Tweedmouthstell and others.

Over time some of the thirty-nine stations between Coldstream and Berwick detailed by W.L. Calderwood in *The Salmon Rivers and Lochs of Scotland* had lapsed or combined with others or been divided, so that names changed. To the uninformed eye it would

Sweep netting on the Tweed at Paxton.

have been impossible to tell where one ended and the next one started. There were no boundaries marked, and the river was just one river.

But to the fishermen each was distinct, with special features demanding specialised knowledge. The crews knew every rock, every channel, every mudbank or sandbank on their stretch. They knew how the state of the tide and the weather and the height of water would affect where the salmon would be, where they would linger, where they would hurry, where and when the net should be swept.

This knowledge had been acquired over centuries, added to, adapted, passed on by word of mouth and example, never written

Retrieving salmon from a stake net near Montrose.

down, but stored in the minds of men born into the way of life. It formed a great and irreplaceable part of the river's history and heritage. When that way of life ended – as it did quite abruptly forty or so years ago – the knowledge was retained for a while. But being of no practical use any more it soon decayed and was lost.

Now the names of the netting stations are recorded, but they are no more than names. The memories of the surviving fishermen have been dutifully deposited on CDs and transcribed, but they are just words. All that remains is the river, and the salmon, although they are sadly reduced.

Most of the fish caught in the Tweed river nets and by the fixed-net stations along the coast north and south of the mouth of the river were sorted and sent on their way by the Berwick Salmon Fisheries Company. They also controlled some of the stations, but by no means all, and faced competition as wholesalers in Berwick from another company, Ralph Holmes and Sons.

Further north, at Montrose, the dominant force in the commercial salmon fishing on two productive rivers, the South Esk and the North Esk, and along eighty miles of coast from near Stonehaven in Aberdeenshire to Kirkcaldy in Fife, were Joseph Johnston and Sons. They had been a major force in the industry since the middle of the nineteenth century and had expanded their operation in Montrose Bay and beyond into the most systematic and productive salmon fishery in Scotland. In 1939 they employed two hundred men during the season – among them a young apprentice, Michael Forsyth-Grant, whose family owned Ecclesgreig Castle, a baronial extravaganza near St Cyrus.

In his memoir, *A Salmon Fisher Remembers* (1995), Forsyth-Grant provided a colourful account of his own varied career and what he referred to as the golden age of salmon netting, which he dated between 1952 and 1977. It was golden principally because of the abundance of fish coming in from the sea, which was generally sufficient to keep Johnston's fishermen busy and the anglers on the two Esks happy. There was no serious competition, so Johnston's were able to control supply to keep prices buoyant. Forsyth-Grant recalled one opening day, 16 February, when the early run of spring salmon had been held up in the pool below Morphie Dyke Dam, a mile or so up the North Esk from the sea. The fishermen reckoned there were two thousand fish confined there, unable to ascend because of the height of the water. They took 150 good salmon between 6am and 7am, leaving the rest for another day and moving up to Kinnaird at Craigo where they had another 150 knocked on the head and boxed by 10am.

In 1960 Forsyth-Grant became Johnston's joint managing director. The salmon fishing, with the associated trades of net-making and boat-building, plus the processing, were integral to the economic health of Montrose, and any threats to it were dealt with in severely practical ways. Seals, for instance, which made a considerable nuisance of themselves by devouring the salmon in the nets, were shot or poisoned with strychnine and no one protested. Business was good and had been good for as long as anyone could remember. Too good to last.

In January of that year, 1960, a handful of boats from the small Northumberland port of Seahouses sailed a short distance north and took up position off the mouth of the Tweed. The Seahouses fishermen were in a bind and were resorting to desperate measures. The virtual collapse of the North Sea herring industry, on which their port and many others had depended for so long, was threatening their livelihoods. They either had to find an alternative catch or go out of business.

They had their boats and they had their nets, drift nets made from hemp that fished the top ten feet or so of water suspended from a cork-floated rope. Each boat worked nets extending a mile or so in length – it was a deadly way of catching herring while there were still herring to catch, and the Seahouses men were set on finding out if it could be equally effective for Atlantic salmon.

The Seahouses vessels – forty to fifty feet long with crews of four to six – began operating just outside the three-mile coastal limit and they immediately hit good catches of salmon. News of their success spread, and they were joined by boats from the Borders ports of Burnmouth and Eyemouth. By the end of May, when the runs tailed off, around nine thousand salmon had been taken. The following year the scale of operations expanded rapidly. The Seahouses men found themselves competing for space with boats from all the Berwickshire ports and beyond. The drift netting spread to Montrose Bay, where the fish came in later, and by July forty boats were at it there. Being outside territorial waters, the drift netters were beyond the reach of bye-laws and regulations and could fish day and night seven days a week. Some boats migrated north to the Findhorn, and even the Helmsdale on the Sutherland coast. More than forty thousand fish were recorded for the 1961 season, and plenty went unrecorded.

Inevitably the bolder skippers began to transgress inside the three-mile limit – aware that the nearer the salmon got to their birth river, the closer they came together and the easier they were to catch. On 15 June 1961 the *Daily Express* reported that one-and-a-quarter tons of salmon had been landed at Arbroath by 6.30am, to be sent to London. Michael Forsyth-Grant wrote that there were yawls from Gourdon and Arbroath everywhere across the Bay of Montrose, with miles of nets at work. Johnston's, alarmed by the inroads into their business, sought and were given authority to deploy a seventy-foot patrol boat against the interlopers. One Gourdon skipper, James Cargill, was caught drift netting within the three-mile limit, had his nets cut, and was escorted into harbour where two hundred of his supporters staged a mini-riot.

The following season the bonanza got out of hand. Around 160 boats were drift netting along and often inside the three-mile limit on the east coast, sixty of them off the Tweed. Altogether 115,000 fish were declared, the equivalent of 30 per cent of the total Scottish commercial catch by other means. In an unusual display of urgency, the government took decisive action in response to the clamour from riparian owners and legitimate netting interests, and the dire warnings about overfishing from scientists. In September an order was made banning drift netting at sea and the landing of any fish caught by such means at any British port.

For a time the golden age remembered by Michael Forsyth-Grant was restored. The salmon runs into Scottish rivers – and English, Welsh and Irish rivers – remained plentiful into the 1970s, filling nets and providing the halcyon angling still remembered with a nostalgic sigh by those fortunate enough to have enjoyed it. But other factors were at work – or soon would be – that would bring that golden age to a sudden end.

* * *

In the late 1950s a discovery was made that would over time imperil the very survival of the Atlantic salmon. It had long been known that they left their native shores as smolts, travelled far away to feed and mature, and then returned – sometimes after one year at sea, sometimes as multi-sea-winter fish – to spawn. But their migratory routes were a matter of guesswork, until boats operating off the south coast of Greenland began catching them in abundance on their summer feeding grounds.

The Greenland drift-net salmon fishery, stoked by investment from Denmark, took off. In 1961 it took 127 tons; ten years later the figure was 2,700, amounting to about three-quarters of a million fish. It was completely unregulated, with no quotas or size limits, and the switch from using hemp to make the nets to monofilament nylon – in effect invisible to salmon – made it even more deadly. The tagging of salmon on their native rivers revealed that it was also undiscriminating: the fish originated from rivers along the east coast of Canada as well as from all over western Europe.

The Norwegians soon opened their own drift-net fishery, and the Faroese developed their own version, using baited long lines. A multi-nation free-for-all developed in the open seas east of Greenland, with an unknown number of boats helping themselves to an unknown but vast volume of adult salmon. Drift netting boomed along the west coast of Ireland, producing a declared catch of up to two thousand tons a year (plus a great deal un-declared). At the same time a smaller but lucrative drift-net fishery developed off the north-east coast of England, taking fifty thousand plus fish a year – most of them heading for the prime Scottish east coast rivers.

No natural resource could sustain such pressure for long. Fishery scientists expressed alarm, and governments – particularly those of countries whose rivers were suffering – took notice. The establishment of the North Atlantic Salmon Conservation Organisation (NASCO) in 1984 was an important step towards restraining the excesses of the salmon boats and led to an internationally agreed ban on netting beyond a twelve-mile coastal limit.

Even more significant was the setting-up in the early 1990s of the North Atlantic Salmon Fund by the Icelandic businessman and salmon angler Orri Vigfússon. His strategy, sustained by amazing energy and driven by an almost messianic zeal, was to raise money from angling and conservation interests and use it to compensate commercial fishermen for giving up or restricting fishing. In 1992 Vigfússon negotiated a moratorium with the Faroese fishermen, and the following year the Greenland fishermen also accepted a deal that drastically limited their catch. Over the succeeding years until his death in 2017, Vigfússon hammered away at the surviving commercial fisheries with varying degrees of success. A significant breakthrough – which he claimed as a victory although it was actually due largely to pressure on the EU authorities – was the closure in 2006 of the Irish drift-net fishery.

The salmon plundered so recklessly from the North Atlantic and along the coasts and up the rivers of Europe was wild, a prime eating fish, a luxury item on the table. Even when supplies were dramatically increased as a result of the vastly expanded commercial fishery, salmon did not lose its status as a prestige food in the markets and restaurants. It was not like herring or cod. However many were harvested by the nets, there were never enough for it to become an everyday staple.

Salmon farming changed all that and delivered the fatal blow to large-scale commercial fishing for wild salmon. In the late 1950s two brothers, Karstein and Olav Vik, built a dam on the River Vikelva which ran by the family farm into Sykkylvsfjord in western Norway. They created three pools of salt, brackish and fresh water, stripped several brood salmon of their eggs, fertilised them in a tiny hatchery, grew them to smolts and then confined them in floating wooden cages and fed them. They established a company to market the salmon and discovered that they sold much better if crushed shrimp was added to the feed to turn the flesh from pallid white to pink.

Word of the Vik brothers' pioneering work spread in the food production world, which was becoming keenly conscious of the commercial potential of aquaculture. Karstein Vik was invited to Britain to speak at a research group meeting in Cambridge, where he was approached by a representative from the Anglo-Dutch corporation Unilever. The brothers were offered £20,000 to develop a research facility to take their experimental work to the next stage. A site was found beside Loch Ailort and close to the River Ailort, west of Fort William in western Scotland. Unilever's biologists took over, in effect sidelining the Vik brothers. In 1965 Unilever set up a company to run the enterprise at Lochailort and called it Marine Harvest.

Lochailort produced its first farmed salmon for sale in 1969. At around the same time production was getting going in Norway, where it grew rapidly. By 1975 Norway was producing a thousand tons of farmed salmon a year; by 1986 it was forty-five thousand tons. Scotland lagged behind because it had fewer suitable sites, but by the late 1980s had 170 farms producing fifteen thousand tons annually.

Salmon farms require protected saltwater sites, ideally with a strong tidal flush to get rid of the waste. Over this period virtually every suitable fjord and sea loch in western Norway and north-west Scotland saw the establishment of at least one farm, and often multiple farms. Salmon aquaculture also took off in British Columbia, around the west coast of Ireland, and – most spectacularly – along the Pacific coast of Chile. Throughout that time Marine Harvest remained the dominant power, although the control of the company was shifted from Unilever to a purely Dutch corporation and then through various pairs of hands until it was secured by the Norwegian shipping magnate, John

Fredriksen, and brought to Norway. Today it still controls almost a third of global production of farmed salmon through operations in Norway, Scotland, Canada, the Faroe Islands, Ireland and Chile.

The dawn of the age of salmon aquaculture was full of promise. Almost at a stroke it did away with the worst excesses of the wild salmon fisheries by offering a consistent and increasingly plentiful supply of fish at a much lower price. As a result it was hailed as a saviour by anglers and the owners of salmon rivers. It created jobs and brought investment in remote places where there had been none in living memory. Long moribund settlements were brought back to life by the coming of the salmon farm and its secure year-round employment.

As far as consumers were concerned, the product looked much the same as its wild cousin. Its flesh was the same colour, albeit as a result of adding dye to its food. It was easy to prepare and cook, tasted distinctly but not excessively fishy – quite like wild salmon, in fact. It was cheap and getting cheaper all the time; in fact it became significantly cheaper than cod and haddock. And it was healthy – the medical experts all said how healthy it was, packed with protein and vitamins and Omega 3 fatty acids.

As with all false dawns, it took time for the glow to start fading. In the late 1980s reports began to filter into the angling press of an unprecedented disaster that was overtaking sea trout in remote parts of north-west Scotland and western Ireland. Sea trout are actually brown trout that have adapted over the ages to feeding along coastal fringes and in sea lochs and loughs before returning to fresh water to breed. The reports were of a crash in numbers, and of surviving fish being infested and ravaged by a parasite, the sea louse. It did not take a great deductive leap to work out that this was happening in areas where salmon farms were located.

Sea lice in small numbers are a common sight on wild salmon

caught on rod and line – indeed were always regarded as a sign that the fish was fresh in from the sea, as they drop off when exposed to fresh water for any length of time. But where artificially reared salmon are densely confined in cages in salt water, infestations of sea lice multiply exponentially. Untreated, the salmon soon become a mass of parasites and are eaten alive. From the start, controlling sea lice in the cages represented a major challenge for the industry, which was met by dosing the cages with pyrethroid chemicals which have the effect of causing the lice to release their hold but do not kill them.

Forced away from the cages, the lice drifted in clouds, searching for new hosts. When they encountered sea trout foraging the margins of the loch – or salmon smolts returning to the sea – they fastened on with catastrophic effects.

The most notorious example of the impact of sea lice was the collapse of the celebrated sea-trout fishery on Loch Maree in Wester Ross, which had drawn generations of anglers to fish and stay in the Loch Maree Hotel. This was a stable population of slow-growing fish, some of considerable size, that was well able to sustain the modest depredations of the anglers. Salmon farming had begun in Loch Ewe – which connects Loch Maree to the sea via the River Ewe – in 1987. In 1985 a thousand takable sea trout were caught on Maree; in 1989 it was fewer than two hundred. The big fish that kept the hotel thronged and boatmen employed through the summer season were wiped out. Stocks never recovered, the anglers ceased to come, the hotel closed.

The fate of Loch Maree was mirrored all around north-west Scotland and western Ireland. In the early 1990s I was commissioned by the *Daily Telegraph* to write an article about the industry hailed as the salvation of the rural economy in Scotland. Among the sea lochs I visited was Loch Sunart, which cuts deep inland between the Ardnamurchan and Morvern peninsulas almost

Fishing boats at the Loch Maree Hotel, before disaster struck.

opposite the Isle of Mull. It was a place of special resonance for me. My father and mother had spent their honeymoon on a small island, Carna, at the seaward end of the loch, and as children we had had wonderful holidays there and had caught surprisingly large sea trout when a spate brought the burns racing down from the hills on the Morvern side.

Coming back, I walked into an ecological horror show. The loch's size and protected location had made it a prime salmon-farming site, and the cages had proliferated in every accessible spot. But overcrowding had also made it a prime breeding ground for disease. Successive outbreaks of infections had killed thousands of salmon, many of which were surreptitiously buried along the shore, allowing the decomposed tissue to leach into the water. The absence of an adequate tidal flush meant that much of the bed of the loch had been turned into a biological dead zone by the soft, grey mantle of deposited salmon faeces and uneaten food. The sea trout that we, as boys, had fished for in the burns had been wiped out by infestations of sea lice expelled from the salmon cages. An insistent whiff of fish food and fish shit hung in the air. I have not willingly eaten farmed salmon since.

Not a lot has changed in the last twenty-five years. Production of Scottish farmed salmon has increased steadily to its current level of more than 180,000 tons a year. Successive Scottish governments have been uncritically supportive of the industry, resolutely ignoring its abysmal environmental record and taking every opportunity to trumpet this 'Scottish success story' and denigrate anyone who dares challenge it.

The industry itself – still largely controlled by Norwegian companies eager to operate away from their own country's more rigorous regulatory system – steadfastly refuses to take responsibility for the damage it has done and is doing. It continues to deny that salmon farming has had a devastating impact on sea trout, despite the steady accumulation of evidence to the contrary. It does everything it can to prevent information about sea-lice infestations and its inability to control them reaching the public domain. It insists that the regular outbreaks of disease – such as ISA (Infectious Salmon Anaemia) and AGD (Amoebic Gill Disease) – are a normal and acceptable aspect of husbandry, even though hundreds of thousands of fish have to be destroyed each year and their bodies disposed of. It offers a similar explanation and defence of the mass escapes from defective cages and dismisses as unfounded or unproven the fears of scientists about the potential weakening of the wild salmon's unique homing instinct from interbreeding with artificially reared escapees.

Locked into a pernicious 'maximum production/low cost' stranglehold, the salmon-farming industry has been permitted by Scotland's politicians to operate welfare standards that in any other branch of livestock farming would have provoked a public outcry and root-and-branch reform. It has been given licence to trash the marine environment along some of the wildest and loveliest coastline in Europe. Recklessly urged to expand at all costs – most notably by the former First Minister, Alex Salmond – it has been left to inflict untold damage on the native sea trout, on wild salmon smolts, and on the genetic integrity of the adult wild salmon.

In recent years cracks in the marriage of convenience between the politicians and the salmon-farming companies have begun to appear. A constant flow of negative publicity in newspapers and magazines and on websites, local radio and TV and, increasingly, the national media, has forced the industry onto the defensive. Local campaign groups have resourcefully and sometimes successfully challenged individual proposals for new farms. The Salmon and Trout Association – now renamed Salmon & Trout Conservation UK – has devoted huge energy and financial resources to a campaign which led, in 2018, to committees of the Scottish Parliament conducting inquiries into salmon farming and producing highly critical reports demanding radical reform.

Salmon & Trout Conservation UK, of which I was a trustee until my term ended in autumn 2018, is not calling for an end to salmon farming. In the short term we, and everyone else who cares about wild fish and their habitats, want to see the conclusions and recommendations from the Environmental, Climate Change and Land Reform Committee accepted by the industry and acted upon. In summary, these were that the industry had shown itself incapable of addressing key issues, particularly sea lice; that further expansion without addressing those issues would be unsustainable and could cause irrecoverable environmental damage; and that the existing regulatory system was inadequate.

The committee also called for a full analysis of the alternative system of rearing salmon – on land, in closed containment units that prevent any contamination of the sea or contact with wild fish. In the longer term this may well represent the way forward.

* * *

'If anyone wanted to make a living out of salmon fishing,' Michael Forsyth-Grant wrote in *A Salmon Fisher Remembers*, 'it would be wiser to do it through angling than netting.' That was his postscript on the decline of commercial netting from 1980 onwards.

By then his company, Joseph Johnston and Sons, had wound down its operations to the extent that it was netting only between Milton Ness, near St Cyrus, and Boddin Point, a few miles south of Montrose. The writing was on the wall for the netsmen all over Scotland. On the Tweed they were being squeezed from all sides. The easy availability of farmed salmon had depressed prices. At the same time, in one of those great and mysterious shifts in the pattern of salmon migration, the majority of the fish were now returning in the autumn, after the end of the netting season. Furthermore, the supply of summer fish had been significantly depleted by the activities of the north-east England drift-net fishery, which was harvesting a declared catch of fifty thousand plus salmon a year (probably half the actual total) – many of which would have been intent on spawning in the Tweed and other east coast Scottish rivers.

Some of the netting stations between Berwick and Coldstream had ceased operations, and others were just going through the motions. In the mid-1980s, armed with a fund of £750,000 donated by the owners of rod-fishing beats, a small delegation from the Tweed Commissioners began to negotiate a buy-out of the netting stations. The process began with those highest up the river and worked down – the negotiators were keenly aware that it must be all or nothing and progressive, because if one station continued fishing when the others had stopped it would have a bonanza.

The approaches were made very quietly and discreetly and encountered very little resistance. The owners of the netting rights and the fishermen who exercised them knew well enough that their days were numbered, and they were quite prepared to take the substantial sums on offer. In 1987 netting upstream from Berwick ceased; netting stations in the town continued to operate until the early 2000s, when they were bought out, as were the surviving coastal rights north and south of Berwick.

Leftish-leaning academics and social historians are inclined to portray the closing of chapters such as the commercial netting of wild salmon as yet more examples of the privileged, moneyed elite trampling on the already downtrodden working-class; a political process in which, through economic power, one interest secures the upper hand over another, leading to the extinction of a way of life and its associated cultural heritage, body of experience and wisdom.

It is certainly the case that the 1987 buy-out of nets on the Tweed stimulated a spike in the salmon runs that the owners exploited to their advantage through substantially increased rents for their fishing. It also eliminated a river-working life that had lasted for centuries and was culturally rich as well as being steeped in history. But the buy-out did not cause the end of netting, which was dying anyway. It provided a clean end, from which the netsmen walked away with payments that would have taken years of hard graft to earn. That is what they call a harsh economic reality.

My guide to the shiel near the Berwick Garden Centre was Ralph Holmes, whose family were involved in the Tweed netting business until the very end, and who has since made himself an unrivalled source of information about that strand of the river's history. I followed him down to the car park at Spittal Point, on the south side where the Tweed, having executed a reverse S through the town, meets the sea. He had other business to attend to, so I walked on my own across the gritty sand in the direction of the lighthouse.

I had a map Ralph had given me marking the names of the netting stations on either side: Tweedmouthstell, Carr Rock,

Ellstell, Hallowstell along my side; Outwaterstell, Crabwater, Dun Cow and others across the water where the breakwater stretches a thin finger seawards. To the south the coast stretched away towards Holy Island. More netting stations – Far Seas, Middle Seas, Huds Head, in the far distance Cheswick and Goswick. They are all just names now, with the occasional ruined shiel to show where a crew once gathered to get the nets ready, to wait for the tide to be right and for the fish to come.

The tide turned. I watched a cargo vessel come in and make for the harbour. It was followed by an Environment Agency boat engaged on sampling work. Her crew put to shore in an inflatable and hauled in a set of fyke nets and a sweep net. I went over to ask what they had got. The answer was some small cod and plaice, sticklebacks, one freshwater eel. No salmon.

It was 20 September, and if the pattern of recent years had been followed, the salmon should have been streaming in from the sea. It wasn't and they weren't. This was the second year that the autumn run had failed, and it has got worse since then.

From Spittal I drove south to Seahouses, where the short-lived drift-netting frenzy had originated. I was expecting to find a ghost port living off the past and tourist trips to Holy Island and the Farne Islands, but my expectations were confounded. It is a holiday resort of the cheap and cheerful, bright and breezy variety, with caravan parks north and south and suburban creep inland. But the little harbour was hard at work. There were boats plying the excursion trade, but there were half a dozen others that were unmistakably fishing vessels: crammed with pots and blue and white plastic boxes, heaps of rope, a winch at the back, orange buoys bouncing at the sides, all overseen by tough-looking blokes in tee-shirts and yellow chest waders.

And the boxes were full, of dark blue, yellow-speckled lobsters and pale terracotta crabs. The vans were lined up along the quayside being loaded. Most of the catch would soon be on its way north to the processing centre at Eyemouth to be sorted and dispatched – 80 per cent to continental Europe. I asked one of the tough-looking blokes how business was. Good, he said: plenty of lobster and crab about and no quotas to worry about. He remembered the end of the whitefish in the 1990s, strangled by quotas and declining stocks.

But no one remembered the days when Seahouses men left port to help themselves to the silver harvest in the seas off Berwick.

CHAPTER THIRTEEN

Vanishing Act

We gathered in an old-fashioned boozer in Brentford, west London, to celebrate our most secretive and tantalising freshwater fish in song and poetry, and to lament its current condition. The event, entitled The Eels Have Eyes, was organised and compered by a man in a pale lilac suit and a beard that looked as if it had been borrowed from a 1920s Bloomsbury Set tea party. There was a band of seasoned musicians in the corner ready to improvise accompaniments in whatever style was asked.

Some of the compositions were a touch cheesy – a song from ELVERS Presley, a chorus of All-EEL-uia. Others were heartfelt and lyrical – '*Leptocephali*, away from the Sargasso Sea / *Leptocephali*, you look pretty good to me.' The theme of others was elegiac and slightly mournful, all about the many threats and dangers and pressures.

The invitees included me – because of my *Book of Eels*, written many years before – and volunteers recruited by the Zoological

Society of London for a project to monitor eel abundance at eleven sites on London's rivers and streams. Brentford's river is the Brent, which meets the Thames opposite Kew Gardens. The eel trap is at Stoney Sluice, off Tallow Road a little way upstream, and those who check the numbers were out in force, clearly moved by a strong impulse to praise the object of their attentions.

Knowing nothing at all about the monitoring programme, and never having even heard of the River Brent, I was expecting to hear a familiar dirge about the decline and fall of the eel, in line with the picture presented by the scientists of a species sliding towards and possibly on the edge of extinction. I was surprised and heartened to hear that the monitors on the Brent had recorded a total of more than 63,000 juveniles in their trap over the summer of 2018. This was twice as many as the previous year, the figure for which was more than twice that for 2016.

So why the gloom? It was pointed out to me that the Brentford haul represented three-quarters of the total for all eleven monitoring sites, on the Medway, Mole, Lea, Wandle, the Thames itself, and some others – several of which had reported hardly any eels at all. It struck me as strange that the Brent should be such a draw. But then again, almost everything that is known about the eel is strange, and the plenty that is unknown must be stranger still.

This is a fish that is classified as a freshwater species but is just as able to function in salt or brackish water. Its birth is presumed to take place in the deep, still, salty waters of the Sargasso Sea but no one has ever witnessed it or the act of procreation leading to it. As a fragmentary, leaf-like larva it drifts three thousand miles across the Atlantic, an involuntary migration that can last three years. The *leptocephali* – thin-heads – cannot swim and have no homing instinct, so they are at the mercy of the currents. Some will be pushed north towards Finland, Iceland and

Scandinavia, some south into the Mediterranean, reaching Turkey and the North African coastline, a few penetrating the Black Sea.

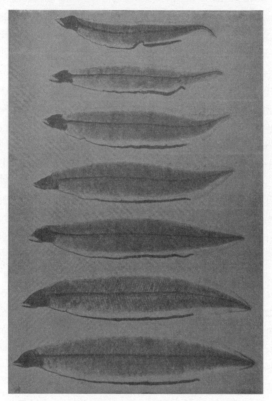

Eel larvae at advancing stages of development, photographs by the Danish marine biologist Johannes Schmidt.

This process of distribution is not so much poorly understood as not understood at all. But we know that it takes many months. The first *leptocephali* arrive off Portugal in the early autumn; they reach the Bristol Channel in early spring. As they near land their shape becomes more eelish and they enter a phase in which they become what we call elvers but are known generally as glass eels because they are still translucent. Pigmentation follows, and as they reach their place of residence they grow and become yellow eels.

Their assumption of gender is most peculiar, and biologists are still arguing about it. They progress from being gender neutral through a period of femininity and one of hermaphroditism before going one way or the other with maturity (although there is evidence that they retain the ability to switch the other way should circumstances make that desirable). The males, which are smaller, tend to remain in estuaries, lagoons and brackish water while the more enterprising females push inland.

They settle down. They feed. They grow, slowly. Their lives are almost entirely hidden, but you may happen on one or more in clear water – they used to be common in the chalkstreams, but no more – hugging the bottom, a dark, slender shape pulsing ever so slightly, occasionally drifting sideways or creeping upstream, mouth down, seeking morsels of food. After years of the quiet life a proportion of the adult eels are roused by some instinctual stirring. Their eyes expand, their skins silver, they deposit layers of fat. One autumn night, generally dark and stormy, when the atmospheric pressure is low and the water level high, they slip downstream – to the sea, out to the ocean, back to the Sargasso where they mate and die and their bodies sink slowly down to the layer of ooze fifteen thousand feet below, to be consumed by eyeless, jawless fish and scavenging crustacea.

That is a condensed version of the accepted account of the life cycle of the European freshwater eel – a mixture of tested knowledge and informed assumption. It has not changed significantly since I wrote *The Book of Eels* in 2002. I was struck then – as I ploughed through literally dozens of learned scientific papers from all over the eel world – how meagre were the returns in terms of proven data in proportion to the expenditure of time and effort. That has not changed either. The volume of academic literature on every aspect of the eel's birth, life, death and everything in between has gone on growing steadily, with remarkably little to show for it.

A comparatively recent review of the orthodox scientific assessment was compiled and presented with exemplary clarity by Doctors Matt Gollock and David Jacoby of the Zoological Society of London. Their paper strives to strike and sustain a tone of authority, but this is somewhat undermined by the heavy sprinkling of caveats and qualifications demonstrating how incomplete the state of knowledge actually is. The element of the overall population resident in estuarial, lagoon and coastal waters is 'particularly poorly understood'. With reference to the spawning stock, 'data sets are very rare . . . the relationships are poorly understood'. 'Data are particularly sparse for Mediterranean and North African populations.' 'Only a very small amount of data are available for silver eels.' 'There is still practically nothing known about the dynamics of the oceanic phase of the eel's life history.' And so on.

Such admissions of the limitations of knowledge are admirable – there is nothing shameful about not knowing the unknowable. The problem with the work is that it was carried out to justify and support the listing by the Convention on International Trade in Endangered Species (CITES) of the European freshwater eel as 'critically endangered'. This classification on the CITES Red List puts the fish one stage beyond endangered, and just one short of 'extinct in the wild'. It states that there has been a decline of 90 per cent in recruitment of glass eels since 1990, and a decline of 50 per cent in the adult population. The authors admit that the listing – first made ten years ago – is 'borderline' and that the data is patchy. For instance, several of the countries with marginal eel fisheries, including Morocco, Tunisia, Egypt and Algeria, do not report at all.

On the basis of the estimates of population decline and the CITES listing, EU member states were instructed to draw up management plans whose guiding principle has been to mitigate, restrain or, if possible, get rid of altogether, human impacts on the eel. Recommended measures include improving habitats, adapting weirs, dams and other obstacles to migration, and installing passes around hydro-electric plants so that the fish do not get chewed up in the turbines. All these steps require considerable spending and therefore tend to remain theoretical rather than being put into practice, and their effectiveness is very hard to measure.

The one 'quick win' that the scientists can agree on and the officials can implement is to clamp down on fishing. There are many eel conservationists who believe that all commercial fishing at all life stages should have been stopped. That would at least have had a brutal logic to it, but political considerations intruded. The glass-eel fisheries in Spain, France and Britain, and the surviving wild-eel fisheries, are economically insignificant except to those involved in them, but no politician wants to be seen stamping on fishermen of any kind.

The situation is further complicated by eel aquaculture. Fish farming is supposedly a benign form of husbandry that takes the pressure off the wild species, and there are eel farms in Holland, Denmark, Germany, Italy, Greece and a handful of other countries which continue to satisfy a steady market for smoked and fresh eel. The problem is that no one has yet devised a way of persuading the eel to breed viably in captivity, so these farms are entirely dependent on obtaining glass eels from the wild to stay in business. The same is necessarily true of the EU's obligatory stocking programmes – the infant eels have to be supplied by hard-nosed, profit-incentivised professional fishermen.

When I was writing *The Book of Eels* the trade in glass eels had been energised to an amazing degree by demand from China. Chinese fish farms had developed a lucrative business supplying the insatiable Japanese longing for *kabayaki*, eel fillets steamed, grilled and dipped in soy sauce. Chinese buyers were not fussy about where the glass eels came from or how they were caught, and were prepared to pay what seemed like stratospheric sums for air-freighted shipments of the little slivers of eel life. The trade was secretive and wholly unregulated, and no one had a clue what proportion of Europe's diminishing influx was being spirited away to the Far East.

In 2010 the EU banned it, with the predictable outcome that it went entirely underground. Each country with an established glass-eel fishery was allotted a quota to meet demand from within Europe; when that quota was caught, the fishermen were supposed to stop. Alas for dreams! In the absence of any meaningful policing of the ban, the fishermen did nothing of the kind.* In France, which had the biggest quota, around sixty tons a year, control of the black market was seized by criminal enterprises which saw the potential of a product more valuable, judged by weight, than cocaine.

Instead of organising a regulated and properly monitored export trade in glass eels, EU officialdom preferred to take refuge behind the fig leaf of its ban. One of the consequences is that the official data on catches is useless. The Sustainable Eel Group, which campaigns on the eel's behalf across Europe, estimates that well over half the total catch is being illegally exported. It's worth pointing out that the English fishery, based in the Bristol Channel, is largely exempt from the strictures – it is closely regulated, and the licensed fishermen have to use traditional hand nets, a far cry from the French and Spanish industrial methods.

In these circumstances, it is clear that the 90 per cent fall in glass-eel recruitment used to justify the management policies is nothing more than a guess. The scientists and officials have very little idea how many glass eels are arriving in Europe, what

---

* That has now changed. Arrests and seizures by the EU's enforcement agency Europol has had a significant impact on the illegal export trade with China. At the same time the decline in the numbers of glass eels reaching European waters has been reversed, with a steady increase over the past few years.

Traditional eel fishing was still booming in the 1940s.

proportion fall victim to the host of predators waiting for them, what proportion are taken by the fishermen, what proportion survives to maturity. The figure takes no account of the startling fluctuations in the size of the influx. Over the past fifteen years the English fishery has recorded seasons when no more than two hundred kilos were caught, and others when the quota was easily achieved. The autumn of 2018 saw a bumper harvest, as a result of which the French boats caught their quota in record time – what happened thereafter is anyone's guess.

At the same time, no one involved in the science, in angling, in volunteer monitoring, in commercial fishing or any other matter affecting eels denies that there has been a drastic reduction in eel stocks over the past half century. All over Europe they have disappeared from rivers, lakes, canals and other waterways where they were once common. No one disputes that the eel needs all the help it can get and that measures to protect it and to enhance its habitat and thereby improve its overall chances of surviving long enough to reproduce successfully are urgently needed.

The flaw in the current conservation approach is that it is focused on the easiest target: those who fish for infant and adult eels. For example, no country in Europe apart from Germany is close to achieving its stocking target. The authorities say the problem is obtaining sufficient supplies of glass eels – yet tens of millions of the little creatures are being spirited out of Europe by organised crime. In England the Environment Agency has, in effect, declined to involve itself at all in stocking, apparently because of fears that it could spread *Dikerogammarus villosus*, the dreaded killer shrimp.

Enough of depressing statistics, trends, assessments, predictions. Sixty thousand juvenile eels were counted going up the River Brent over one summer, and there are other places where the fish is doing fine – even if no one can work out why. One of them is our largest tidal lagoon, the Fleet, on the Dorset coast.

It is a strange and fascinating sheet of water which becomes more fascinating the more you learn about it. Trapped between gently sloping Dorset farmland and the pale, shingly rampart that is Chesil Beach, the Fleet is eight miles long and between a hundred and nine hundred yards wide. It is fed by a channel to the sea at the Portland end, so that the water is brackish and subject to tides that diminish in strength the further west you are. It is shallow and rich in aquatic flora, notably the eel grass that used to feed the famous colony of swans at nearby Abbotsbury (they depend on artificial feed these days). It is also rich in the shrimps and little prawns and crabs that eels near the sea like to forage. Eel fishing has been part of the life of the Fleet throughout the ages.

I found my eel man, Alan – one of a pair of eel-fishing brothers – at the back of Abbotsbury, the picturesque old stone village that straggles along the road behind the western end of the Fleet. His semi stands well back from the lane. In the front garden is a boat and a miscellany of pots, nets, buoys, coils of rope and the other gear that a fisherman accumulates over a lifetime and retains, always half-thinking that whatever item it is will come in handy again one day. Abbotsbury born and bred and permanently resident, Alan talks readily about a life in which fishing – from the sea, from the Fleet, from rivers, from anywhere with fish – has been the constant theme.

He left school at fifteen to fish with his uncle, chiefly for the mackerel off the Chesil. The boats were kept on the shingle and had to be dragged down to the water, and it became Alan's job to study the crash of the waves and work out when a momentary calm would allow the boat to be launched and pulled out on the oars. Seine netting for mackerel was the staple business, but he fished eels when the time was right. In the early days they used baited traps, but the appearance in the 1970s of the new-fangled fyke nets – used to catch eels on the Continent for at least a hundred years – made the job a whole lot easier. The fyke net consists of a wall of netting known as the leader, which guides the eels towards a hooped trap with internal funnels to stop them swimming out again, and an enclosed chamber, the cod end. Several of these are strung together to make a barrier that is placed across the eel's feeding routes; the fish work their way along it and into the trap where they are happy to sit quiet until disturbed.

They had some great days on the Fleet in them days, Alan said in that tone of voice fishermen always use when looking back to a distant past. The best was one summer when they averaged three-quarters of a ton a week for ten weeks, and the nets were jammed every time they lifted them. He did elver fishing as well back then, journeying over to the Parrett or the Brue in north Somerset to compete with some hardened Somerset elver men for room to dip the big net. He used to rayball for eels on the Frome, weaving worms into balls of wool so that their teeth got snagged and you could lift them out and drop them in a sack. You could get thirty or forty pounds in a night, good fat eels, Alan said, still in that tone.

It was a roasting day in that roasting August of 2018 and the Fleet was shimmering in the heat by the time we got down there to check the nets. We bumped along the track from Langton Herring past a row of what had been built as coastguard cottages, now tarted-up holiday homes, down to the water's edge. Boats of many colours, shapes and uses formed a wavering line where they had pulled up on the rough grass. Alan's, a slender, flat-bottomed sixteen-footer in blue fibreglass, was tethered in the water ready for action. The man himself, in matching blue tee-shirt, battered sunhat and much-patched yellow chest waders, dumped a large plastic bucket – also in royal blue – in the boat, ushered me in and took the oars.

The water was as flat and smooth as glass. Behind the shore extended pale, parched low hills, almost white where the wheat had been cut. The water was no more than three feet deep and clear, the bed cloaked in dark green eel grass. To the west the swans of Abbotsbury, white flecks on blue, were cruising the shallows near the swannery for the benefit of the visitors and their cameras. Closer at hand, lines of misshapen poles like bones or toothpicks protruded a foot or two above the surface to show where the other fishermen's nets had been laid.

Puffing somewhat and sweating considerably, Alan rested the oars and leaned over the side to retrieve the first line of nets. They were stretched between poles, the hooped traps resting on the eel grass. He pulled them in, plucking off the clumps of weed, examining each one. 'Rubbish,' he said impatiently, 'not worth the trouble.' I felt bad, as I had been on at him for weeks to take me out and now here we were and it was hellishly hot and the fishing was rubbish.

But there were eels, nothing bigger than three-quarters of a pound, but some above the size limit and worth dropping in the bucket. The rest went back along with the crabs and the handfuls of weed. He got to the last trap, by which time the others were neatly stacked on the stern. He extracted what it had to offer before pegging it back in position and taking the oars again. As he rowed back towards the shore the whole string was flipped off the stern in sequence, an impressively efficient operation. Alan stopped every now and then to fix and tighten the string until we, and his nets, were back where we started.

We rowed over to another string and repeated the process. The catches were better and Alan grunted with satisfaction as he dropped them into the bucket where they slithered and writhed exactly as eels should, whipping up a white froth of slime. Attached to the end were two string sacks in which the accumulated haul of the past few days was stored. Alan lifted one out and opened it so he could add that morning's tally. He reckoned there were about thirty kilos in each sack. Several of them were silvering in preparation for the sea migration they would now never make, which seemed a bit sad. The eels would keep quite happily there for a week or more, until the Dutchman came with his truck and aerated water tanks to pick them up, pay for them and take them off to Holland where they still appreciate such delicacies.

The size of the Fleet eels suggests that most were males, which would fit the theory that they prefer a saline habitat while the females tend to seek fresh water. Since a fertile migrating female can carry anything from two million to twenty million eggs, a distinct gender imbalance is clearly allowed for in the breeding equation. On the Fleet, as elsewhere, the population dynamics are a mystery. A few years back, Alan and his regular partner started and continued catching what he termed 'a lovely lot of fat silvers'. Were they females (establishing gender in an eel requires careful and expert autopsy)? If so, where had they come from? And if they were males, why were they so much above the average weight?

This profound and chronic unpredictability breeds a corresponding tolerance in the fishermen reminiscent of the Buddhist *samatha*, a calm abiding. That which cannot be understood cannot be changed, only accepted. But it would be untrue to say that this placid indulgence towards the fish extends to embrace those who control the fishing – Ilchester Estates, which charges Alan for access to the Fleet and for keeping his boat there, and the Environment Agency, which licenses his nets. Resentment against the EA on account of their rules, their ignorance, their lack of interest and sympathy bubbled through Alan's conversation like a stockpot. 'Know nothing, they don't,' he grumbled. 'And they don't care. They'd like to get rid of us, they would. We're just an administrative burden to them.'

All very unfair, of course. But it would be difficult to characterise the EA's attitude to eel fishing as positive and encouraging. Its unspoken operating principle seems to be that catching eels in the wild is a bad thing and should be phased out by the simple tactic of restricting licences to those who already have them – around nine hundred across the whole country – and not issuing any new ones. The EA refers to a 'presumption to prevent the fishery expanding', i.e. to allow the fishery to die. In fact it is already tiny – twenty-five tons or so a year, one per cent of the European total – and is shrinking steadily as age and infirmity take their toll of those fishermen that remain.

Interestingly, if you add the eel catch of Northern Ireland to that of mainland Britain, the UK total rises from near the bottom of the European table to fourth behind France, Sweden and Denmark. This is entirely due to the survival on the country's biggest freshwater lake, Lough Neagh, of by far Europe's biggest wild-eel fishery. They harvest around three hundred tons a year – which is more than the eel farms of Germany and twice as much as those in Holland.

Lough Neagh might have been designed for the comfort and

convenience of eels. It is mostly fairly shallow, which helps the
water to warm in summer. It is nutrient-rich, its sandy or muddy
bottom seething with a limitless abundance of tiny larvae and
invertebrates for the eels to graze on to their stomachs' desire.
It has its vital artery to the sea, the River Bann, which historically
allowed in the elvers to replenish the lake's stock and the fat
silvers to embark on their final voyage. An Irish naturalist,
William Thompson – writing in the 1830s – described the weir
known as The Cutts as being 'black with the multitudes of young
eels . . . hay ropes are suspended over the rocky parts to help
them'. Thompson was told of a catch of seventy thousand
migrating silver eels in one night at the trap below Toome, the
village near where the Bann leaves the lough.

Lough Neagh was fished for its eels from the time of the first
human occupation several thousand years ago. But until the
middle of the nineteenth century consumption was local and
trade minimal. The growth of the rail network changed all that,

Lough Neagh eel fishermen returning to base.

as so much else. The fish merchants at Billingsgate in London began shipping live eels over to Liverpool from Coleraine, the port near the mouth of the Bann, and then by train to London. The trade was much helped by the eel's remarkable tenacity in clinging to life – kept cool and damp, they comfortably survived transportation, and on arrival could be kept in good condition in tanks for weeks.

Quite suddenly Lough Neagh's eels became a valuable commodity. I told the long and complicated story of the struggle between the fishermen and the landowners over who had the rights to take them in *The Book of Eels*, and I do not propose to retell it here. Suffice to say that – as any student of history would expect – the courts and the judges consistently favoured the landowning and capitalist class over the working class. The upshot in modern times was the acquisition in 1959 of the company that controlled the fishing by a consortium of Billingsgate merchants. It was headed by a Dutchman, Hans Kuijten, whose company, based at Maldon on the Essex coast, had been a major customer for Lough Neagh eels for many years.

Kuijten and his partners had a clear business strategy. They wanted more of the silver eels, which were best for smoking and eating, could be kept alive for weeks in his storage barges on the Blackwater estuary, and could be caught with comparatively little effort in the traps on the Bann. They were much less keen on the yellow eels from the lough itself because they were generally smaller, not so firm and tasty, and came with the hooks on which they had been caught still rusting in their mouths. But for the several hundred fishermen, the yellow eels were the staple; not being able to sell them would be tantamount to losing their livelihoods.

The consortium attempted to enforce its preference. The fishermen resisted. Smuggling across the Irish border became rampant, as did poaching. The merchants went to court to stop the anarchy; they won their case, but in time lost the war. This was as a result of the formation of the Lough Neagh Fishermen's Association under the direction of the priest of Toome, Father Oliver Kennedy. The Billingsgate consortium wearied of the struggle and in 1971 the association – now transformed from a trade union into a members' co-operative – raised the money to buy the company.

When I first visited Toome in 2000 to research my book, Father Kennedy was still very much running the show. I described him as looking remarkably like a rounder, more substantial version of Alec Guinness, but he was a formidable operator and exercised dictatorial power over the co-operative. At that time the annual eel catch still averaged 750 tons – two-thirds of them netted or caught on long lines on the lough, the rest migrating silvers caught in the traps in the autumn. The business turned over £6 million a year and provided part-time livelihoods for three hundred or so fishermen. In return, they were generally content to tolerate their priest's habit of treating them like children who, left to their own devices, would poach and overfish the eel to extinction.

Even then clouds were gathering over the heads of Father Kennedy and his flock. The run of elvers – which historically were collected at Coleraine and brought to the lough overland because of the many obstacles on the river – had pretty much collapsed. The co-operative thus became dependent on stocking elvers from elsewhere – chiefly the Severn – but the pressure of competition for them had forced the price steeply upwards. Furthermore the biologists were agitating about the crash in wild-eel stocks across Europe, and some were arguing that a ban on fishing wild eel was the only appropriate response.

Father Kennedy died in 2013, and until late in life maintained his pugnacious defence of the fishermen and the fishery's unique status. He fought successfully for it to be recognised as a 'protected geographical identity' and kept it alive and kicking while elsewhere – in the Irish Republic for instance – wild-eel fisheries were shut down. Today Brexit again threatens the export trade on which the Lough Neagh fishery depends. The annual catch is down to around three hundred tons, and the number of fishermen to below two hundred.

The lough is also in the throes of a wider environmental crisis. Its natural resources are being plundered on all sides – most notoriously by the dredging from the bed of the lake of more than a million-and-a-half tons of sand each year for use in the construction business. This extraction, not far from Toome, proceeds without benefit of planning permission, with officials from the Department of Infrastructure seemingly content for it to do so indefinitely. Nitrate and phosphate pollution from intensive farming, and sewage from defective septic tanks have enriched the water's nutrient content well beyond historic levels, setting off damaging algal blooms. Illegal netting for the lough's pollan (a whitefish which looks like a freshwater herring) and its unique strain of Dollaghan brown trout is persistent, and the policing of it clearly inadequate. In January 2018 a new patrol boat bought by the Fishermen's Co-operative for £60,000 was set on fire and destroyed.

Northern Ireland suffers from the lack of independent monitoring of environmental standards. Its own toothless environment agency is merely part of the Department of Agriculture, which itself is committed to promoting an all-out expansion of industrial farming without any evident regard for the environmental consequences. The collapse and subsequent suspension of devolved government and the inability of the politicians to agree on anything has made a bad situation worse.

In my eel book I noted that the fishing community of Lough Neagh was something of an anachronism in our world, surviving by exploiting a natural – or semi-natural – resource in ways that had not materially changed in two thousand years. The lives of the fishermen I met were a lot easier than those of their forebears, but a lot harder than is commonly the case these days. Try this for a working schedule: going out in the afternoon to bait two thousand hooks with worms and set a line the best part of a mile long; back out that night to cast and retrieve a draft net for six hours until dawn breaks; back out again in the day to retrieve the long line, cutting off the sizeable eels with a knife to drop in the bucket; and all of it on a lake that can turn thoroughly nasty in the wrong kind of wind. I did that once, in an observer status, and it nearly did for me.

I wondered then how long it could last. Last it did, but again I am wondering.

It seems highly likely to me that, within a generation, eel fishing in this country will have joined commercial salmon fishing as a historical curiosity, something to be recalled in museums where visitors will pause in front of displays of eel grigs and spears and fyke nets and elver nets and black-and-white photographs of the eel men of old posing with a seething confusion of eels and wonder what that was all about. Eel fishing never approached salmon fishing in economic importance, and salmon fishing was never of more than local significance. But the eel was, in Walton's words, 'a dainty dish' and one for which, until fairly recently, the English retained a considerable fondness.

Across the Fens and the Somerset Levels, along the Thames and the Trent and the Humber, on the chalkstreams and the slow streams, on lakes and meres and canals, fishermen netted, speared, trapped and put out baits for eels, and ate them and traded them. The Dutch came and took over the London eel business and floated their eels across the North Sea in strange semi-submerged barges known as *schuyts*, and took ours home in return. The Irish and the Ulstermen shipped them to Liverpool. Londoners ate them in eel pie and jellied them and stewed them to be served with 'liquor' (green parsley sauce). But now only vestigial markets remain, and a niche market for smoked eel. We have largely lost our taste for this delicious fish, and soon we will lose our eel fishermen.

I phoned Alan on the Fleet to find out how the season had been. Not bad, not bad, he said – he reckoned that between the four of them still doing it properly, they'd had about six tons all in. The biggest share had been caught by his brother, which was a bit annoying like. But that's eel fishing for you, Alan said, philosophical as ever. I asked if he'd be out for the next season. He reckoned so, as long as there was someone to buy them. He'd heard that the Dutchman had sold out to two lads from Honiton, so maybe they'd take them.*

But after we've gone there won't be any, Alan told me. I asked if his son was interested. My son, he said – articulating the words carefully – is a patent lawyer. Doesn't really go with eel fishing, does it?

* They did and Alan fished through the 2020 season and did pretty well, thank you.

CHAPTER FOURTEEN

Death and Transfiguration

I could have imagined myself on a Slovenian mountain stream, almost. The sides were steep and rocky, densely wooded with alder, willow, sycamore and ash, in full summer leaf. The branches hung low over the water, meeting to shade it from the sun blazing in a pretty much cloudless sky. There were dippers and wagtails looping and skipping from rock to rock.

The water tumbled down chutes between the sandstone blocks and crashed over miniature falls, spread past gravel banks to lose itself in slow, reflective pools, then gathered its strength to surge past gnarled tree roots towards the next riffle. It was cool in the shade. The air was fresh and filled with cadences of moving water mixing with birdsong.

But I was not afoot in the Julian Alps, wading the upper Baca or the Trebuscica beneath karst crags and alpine meadows, far from any human habitation. I was actually half a mile or so from the centre of a town densely packed with terraces and little streets

of cottages. I was breathing sweet summer air, but a century ago
– even half a century ago – it would have been heavy and acrid
with the smoke from a forest of factory chimneys. A century ago
– even half a century ago – this stream was no more than a
stinking sewer, a byword for filth, running orange in the morning
and black in the afternoon, dead and toxic.

And I was wading it, rod in hand, with wild brown trout on
my mind.

In Manchester's imposing art gallery there is an extensive
collection of paintings by a remarkable artist, Pierre Adolphe
Valette, a French Impressionist who deserves to be much better
known than he is. As a young man he came to London after
studying in Bordeaux, subsequently moving to Manchester where
he supported himself with commercial artwork while attending
evening classes at the city's School of Art. He impressed his
teachers enough to be offered a post there himself and remained
on the staff until 1920 – among his pupils was L.S. Lowry, who
counted Valette as a great influence even though their styles
differed radically.

Eventually he returned to France, moving to the Beaujolais
region where he died in 1942. He continued to paint but received
little attention and no acclaim until long after his death, when
Manchester discovered that this obscure foreigner had captured
something about its past that no one else had and set about
buying everything of his that it could lay hands on.

Valette's particular genius was to find beauty where everyone
else – writers, journalists, social observers and the rest – found
only the ugliness and din and dirt of a great industrial city. He
found it in the greasy cobbled streets, the cabs and horses that
clattered along them, the dark smudged figures walking the
pavements, the shapes of iron railings and lamp-stands, the smoke
rising from the little domestic chimneys and the great factory
chimneys, in the light blazing into the gloom from the windows
of the new office blocks. He found it in the thick, smoky, smoggy,

fume-heavy air, and in the way the impression of objects, buildings, people and animals was diffused in that air. He found it, most surprisingly, in the Irwell, the black channel of effluent that crept through the western edge of the city.

His 1912 painting *Under Windsor Bridge on the Irwell* shows a smoke-belching barge approaching the space between bridge and water, slowly and implacably. In the foreground a dark figure in rounded hat and short coat, hands in pockets, watches from the quayside, shoulders hunched. On the far side, beyond the bridge, is the outline of another barge reflected on the pale surface of the river like a ghost ship. An earlier work depicts the same bridge from downstream, the lattice ironwork silhouetted against a thick, heavy grey sky hanging below an unseen sun which throws its light over the dark mass of the warehouses onto the river's surface, where it meets the reflection of the bridge.

In *Bailey Bridge, Manchester 1912* (actually the Albert Bridge connecting Salford with Manchester) the sky is recognisably blue, the light from it pearly as it reaches the smoke over the city. Again, the bridge is framed between the brooding bulk of factories and warehouses. Windows are lit in defiance of the smoke, the two brightest sending shafts of light along the water in silver lines. Through the arch distant barges are pouring forth smoke from their funnels. Another barge is tied up at the quayside in the foreground, a smudge of a figure beside it.

Valette discovered this silent beauty in Manchester's river and the way it spoke for his adopted city. But he would have been ill-advised to fall into it or have any direct contact with it, and like everyone else he must have found its stench overpowering. By the time it had reached the heart of the city – twenty-five miles or so from its source beyond Bacup – the Irwell had been systematically abused and poisoned by one of the most intensively industrialised areas of Europe.

This was it in 1862 – 'a flood of liquid manure in which all life dies whether animal or vegetable, and which resembles

Pierre Adolphe Valette's *Bailey Bridge, Manchester 1912*, an Impressionistic, smog-ridden view of the River Irwell.

nothing in nature except perhaps the stream thrown out in eruption by some volcano'. And in 1867 – 'a poor, blackened, suffocated, poisoned, demoralised monstrous piece of river misery . . . day and night pipes spitting fitful white rods of steam, from others all the waste filths of industry, bilges and rinsings and disgorged greases suppurate slowly and cake the walls coat by coat'.

This was, of course, the common fate of rivers and streams in our great industrial age: to be used for transport when suitable, to provide water to power millwheels and for treating textiles and other processes, and as channels in which to deposit the industrial wastes and to receive the human waste of the multitudes required to run the machines. What was unusual about the Irwell was the extent and thoroughness of its abuse. Other intensely polluted rivers – the Trent, the Tyne, the Thames for instance – had upper reaches beyond the smoking towns and cities where the water ran through moorland or open countryside and was pure enough for fish and other creatures to live.

But the Irwell was put to work as soon as it became a viable flow, with cotton mills and coal workings close to its source in the parish of Cliviger. Bacup, a couple of miles downstream, spun cotton, dug coal, quarried stone, made shoes, and took the Irwell's water and returned it a different colour. At Rawtenstall – itself a thriving cotton town – the river received the Limy Water, thick with effluent from textile-printing works. Each working town – Ramsbottom, Bury, Radcliffe, Farnworth – poured its filth into the river. Each tributary – the Ogden, the Croal, the Roch, the Irk – added its load. Every industry – coal mines, spinning mills, bleachworks, dyeworks, textile printers, tanners, paperworks, soap and candle makers and the rest – depended on the river in one way or another. Soda ash, bleaching powder, grease, mordants, potash salts were just a few of the ingredients released indiscriminately into the nearest watercourse. Add to that the millions of gallons of untreated sewage pouring from where the tenements and terraces were crammed together, and it is hardly surprising that nothing could live in the Irwell, unless you counted sewage fungus and other rank algae.

This ruin was accomplished so quickly. In 1879 Edward Corbett, the father of Salford's borough engineer at the turn of the nineteenth century, contributed a paper to the Manchester Anglers' Association entitled 'Angling on the Irwell'. He recalled being told by the old-timers of the salmon and trout that they used to catch back when George III was on the throne. He wrote of watching innumerable fish – mainly gudgeon – around the piers near the New Bailey bridge; the year was 1819. The insect life brought out so many swallows and martens to feed that the boys used to whip the birds out of the air from the bridge. A few years later Corbett and his friends would spend the day fishing up from Pendleton; their favourite spot for dace and chub was between Douglas Mill and Agecroft Bridge.

'About 1825', Corbett wrote, 'I became acquainted with practical fly fishing and made flies that caught fish.' He had studied an angler below Agecroft Bridge catching a hundred or so dace, roach and chub, using two flies and often getting two fish at a time. But by 1850 the fishing was finished – 'there was scarcely a blade of grass or a bunch of rushes near the river itself . . . and only such trees as were high enough to keep their roots out of its reach'. Apart from bargees and lock-keepers, rats and 'now and then a melancholy-looking sandpiper . . . there was not a thing with life to be seen'.

And, despite the regular cries of protest from public health officials, that is how it remained. No one in authority seriously questioned the assumption that a dead, toxic river was a price worth paying for Manchester's wealth and standing. In 1950 the Labour MP for Roxendale, Anthony Greenwood – later a cabinet minister in successive governments – alerted a wider audience to the state of the Irwell in a speech in the House of Commons. He referred to it as 'the hardest working river in the country', with more than one hundred cotton mills beside it and its tributary, the Roch, as well as a host of other industries.

But Greenwood was appalled that it should contain no fish, no insects, no life – 'that the purest water to be found should be sewage effluent'. He instanced the dumping of caustic soda by the papermills and the spent dye from the dyeworks, turning it 'all the colours of the rainbow'. Greenwood quoted a report from the chairman of Bacup Council's general purposes committee describing how at 8am the water was a vivid orange colour with suds rising eighteen inches high, and by noon it had changed to an intense black.

*   *   *

The fortunes of Ramsbottom followed a familiar trajectory for a Lancashire mill town. In 1783 the textiles firm of Peel and Yates – the Peel was the father of the future Prime Minister, Sir Robert – expanded their existing business in Bury to Ramsbottom by building a calico-printing and bleaching factory in what is now the centre of town, using water pumped from the springs that fed the Irwell. Subsequently they added another bleaching works near what would later become Ramsbottom's famously characterful cricket ground. In 1802 two brothers, Samuel and Thomas Ashton, established a substantial spinning mill on the river.

But it was the arrival a few years after that of another pair of brothers, William and Daniel Grant, that led to the transformation of the town. They had migrated south from Strathspey in Scotland, where the family farm had fallen on hard times; when they first looked down on the Irwell it reminded them of the famous salmon river of their home valley. They began as small-scale calico printers in Bury and then Manchester. In 1806, having been joined by two other brothers, and then by their parents, they acquired Sir Robert Peel's factory in the centre of Ramsbottom, set up home in what is now the Grant Arms Hotel, and began developing more mills along the river.

As well as their enterprise and dedication to hard work, the Grants brought with them from Scotland their religion and sense of civic duty. They built a Presbyterian church and Sunday school, gave lavishly to local good causes, and immersed themselves in the life of the town. The example they set reached far beyond Ramsbottom. In the 1820s Charles Dickens, on one of his many visits to Manchester, heard of them and became curious about them, and eventually – despite never actually meeting them – fashioned them into the characters of the Cheeryble brothers in *Nicholas Nickleby*.

William Grant died in 1842, Daniel thirteen years later. By then the railway had reached Ramsbottom, sealing its position as a medium-sized industrial powerhouse. Squeezed into a cleft in the Pennines, its mills and factories and workers' cottages were all crammed together in one noisy, smoky and unhealthy whole, united in the common enterprise. The 1893 Ordnance Survey map shows industrial sites lining the river, with numerous artificial channels, leats, holding pools and other engineered alterations attached, and the rows of new housing up the slope to the west.

The Lancashire cotton mills hit peak production just before the outbreak of the First World War, but the slump set in afterwards as what had been customer nations set up their own textiles industries which, in time, came to compete with and then eclipse the British industry. Hundreds of mills closed between the wars, and although there was a resurgence during the Second World War and immediately afterwards, the pattern of decline then reasserted itself. This time there would be no recovery. By the 1980s the textiles industry that had made the north-west rich and given it pride had been virtually wiped out.

In Ramsbottom as elsewhere, the mills and factories that had risen were abandoned and left to rot or were demolished. Meanwhile the Irwell, which had brought them into being, began to show signs that it had not been killed off altogether. An article in the *Manchester Evening News* in 1969 had described it as a 'nauseous grey gravy distilled from the toxic effluent of chemical plants, dyeworks, papermills, detergent scum and other less mentionable evacuations'. The only improvement, according to the journalist, was that the rats that had once been able to walk across 'the filth-encrusted surface' had had to learn to swim. But even then there were rumours of roach having been seen near Bury, and in 1971 the Bury Angling Society secured fishing rights along four miles of the river between Summerseat and Radcliffe from Bury Council. The club secretary said that perch and roach had been caught, and 'we are satisfied that the water will support fish life'.

By 1974 the *Manchester Evening News* was able to carry the headline 'New Life for Infamous Irwell'. The main factors in coaxing the river back to something approaching health were the installation of new water-treatment and sewage works and the collapse and disappearance of the main polluting industries. There were many setbacks – accidental and deliberate dumping of chemicals, leaching of toxic waste from old mine workings, break-downs at sewage plants, discharges of fuel and so forth – but by the early 2000s several stretches of the Irwell right into the heart of Manchester had populations of wild brown trout as well as healthy stocks of most coarse fish species.

The story of the Irwell's rebirth was mirrored in many other parts of the country long blighted by heavy industry and inten-sive manufacturing. The Tyne – biologically defunct along its lower reaches for decades – re-established itself as England's premier salmon river. The Thames, devoid of life in its estuary and through London, was restored. Salmon ascended the Don through Sheffield for the first time in a century. The rivers reaching the sea from the South Wales coalfield, stinking chan-nels of muck for as long as anyone could remember, had pike and chub in them, even salmon and grayling. The Trent, which received all the waste from the Potteries and the Nottinghamshire coalfield, became a river of pilgrimage for barbel hunters.

In 2012 a young writer, Theo Pike, who had made a speciality of fly fishing in improbable urban locations, produced a book called *Trout in Dirty Places*. The title was both an acknowledge-ment of the startling, unsung transformation of urban rivers and streams, and an affirmation of their capacity to heal themselves, if we would give them a chance.

Over my angling lifetime many miles of river and canal previously degraded beyond the point of sustaining life have been resur-rected, and you may now cast a fly with a decent chance of catching a wild brown trout in places where, if you'd fallen in half a century ago, you would have been advised to have a health check.

The same period has also seen the birth and maturing of a genuine conservation movement, the recruitment of a small army of volunteers prepared to devote time, money and effort to the struggle on behalf of our waters and the life they sustain. It began in my youth with the Anglers' Co-operative Association, which challenged and often brought to book the polluters who had previously acted with something like impunity, and eventually metamorphosed into the Angling Trust. The Salmon and Trout Association (now Salmon & Trout Conservation UK) grew from an ineffectual talking shop into a potent lobby group. The Wild Trout Trust banged the drum and began to work effectively to repair abused streams and enable them to function again. Rivers trusts were founded in various parts of the country to fight for cleaner waters and to support their fish. The Tweed Foundation (formerly Commission) and the Wye and Usk Foundation have done tremendous work on habitat improvement, to give their game fish the best chance of surviving and thriving.

At a lower level, angling clubs and societies have upped their game. Their primary role used to be securing and running fishing, collecting subscriptions, arranging stocking and matches where appropriate. They have become the police officers of our waters, guarding them jealously and going after those who do them harm, as well as becoming increasingly involved in the citizen science and research side.

More and more, anglers have come to realise that there is more to it than just going fishing: that their pleasure is dependent on a natural resource that requires constant attention and protection; and that it is made possible within the wider context of the whole landscape, which itself is vulnerable, under constant attack, and in need of all the help it can get. The volunteer army – and the professionals who work with them – have achieved some notable victories. At every level, campaign groups have doubled and redoubled efforts to monitor the health of our waters, to identify what is wrong, to promote remedial action, and to hold those responsible to account.

These are all heartening developments. But is the struggle being won? It is not, and never will be. Is it lost? Not yet, but it could be.

The environmental writer Mark Cocker, in a powerful book called *Our Place*, narrated the history of farming and food production and their impact on the countryside in modern times, in step with the emergence and development of the conservation movement. His conclusion was that the conservation campaign groups – RSPB, the National Trust, the various wildlife trusts and the rest – had, despite individual success stories, failed overall to prevent the wholesale degradation of the countryside and the destruction of its flora and fauna.

Cocker pointed out that we were all complicit in what had happened. Fragmentation and rivalry between the various factions within the conservation lobby, and its inability to present a common front and speak with one voice, had been a factor. But the much bigger one was the acquiescence of our wider society in what was happening, our unwillingness to change the way we live and to reject the dual doctrine of maximum production/ cheap food that has engineered and legitimised the laying waste of our land.

Mark Cocker did not deal with our aquatic environment, but the same lessons apply. I have already had my say on the subject of salmon farming: how, as a society, we have been able to turn our faces away from the consequences of our choices because of the way a particular consumer habit – in this case buying cheap, convenient salmon – has worked its way into the fabric of our lives.

Take another staple of the middle-class shopping basket: watercress. This was grown benignly on the chalkstreams from the beginning of the nineteenth century, until the commercial potential of the expanding salad market was recognised.

Exploitation followed the usual pattern: ever-increasing appli-
cations of chemicals to promote faster growth and to keep
disease at bay. On the headwaters of the Itchen in Hampshire
– designated a Special Area of Conservation and as such supposedly under maximum statutory protection – watercress farming
and the associated business of washing salads from elsewhere
have resulted in a steady discharge of chloride-based chemicals,
killing off invertebrates vital to the aquatic food chain and
degrading water quality.

Lorryloads of bags of cress and salad leaves are transported each
week from the industrial washers at the top of the Itchen and are
sold as an essential component of the latest health/low-calorie diet.
The Environment Agency is well aware of how the standards of
chalkstream water quality are being breached, because local campaigners backed by research from Salmon & Trout Conservation
UK have demonstrated it. But to enforce those standards would
mean a fight with powerful interests, using up scarce financial
resources. And no one is actually dying, are they?

This is one more illustration of our society's collective
reluctance to recognise the consequences of our addiction to
convenience food. All over the British Isles and the island of
Ireland, intensive dairy farming has been allowed to inflict
untold damage on the land and watercourses, so that we can
buy milk at fifty pence a litre in the supermarket. Intensive
arable farming has wiped out bird and insect life across great
swathes of our countryside. When I began serious fly fishing
half a century ago, a drive across the chalk downs of southern
England would leave the car windscreen thick with the bodies
of dead insects. That no longer happens. We no longer witness
hatches of fly beginning in the late morning, petering out in
the afternoon, resuming in the evening and lasting into darkness.
The insects are simply not there.

It is true that the ideology that has shaped British agriculture since 1945 – of maximising production to secure supply and keep prices down – is at last being challenged. But it is a very long way from being dislodged.

The campaign groups keep campaigning, and we may hope that, bit by bit, ignorance is chipped away and awareness added to. The outright victories are few and hard won – but when we are dispirited and inclined to question whether the struggle is really worth it, we also need to ask ourselves how much worse the situation would be without us. We have not got rid of the salmon cages, but the excesses of the aquaculture industry have been restrained. The same applies to other sectors of farming, to industry, to the abstraction of water by the water companies. They all attack our waters, but their awareness that we will defend them undoubtedly restrains their worst excesses.

But with some issues we seem genuinely powerless. The crisis that has overtaken the Atlantic salmon is a striking example. Most of what could be done to protect and enhance salmon stocks – from getting rid of commercial netting to maximising the production of fry and smolts on spawning streams – has been done. But the line on the graph measuring the numbers of salmon returning from the feeding grounds to spawn in British rivers continues to slope steadily down.

Inevitably those in charge of our salmon rivers find themselves accused of not doing enough. Much outrage is focused on the hot issue of predation. Put crudely, there are those – generally with the loudest voices – who assert that if enough seals, cormorants, goosanders, mergansers and otters were erased, all would be well. Leaving aside the political absurdity of advocating the mass slaughter that would be needed, the fact remains that predation at all levels – from salmon eating blue whiting in the North Atlantic to those salmon being devoured by seals to mergansers scooping up the smolts – has always been factored into the equation of natural balance.

Cormorant doing what cormorants do.

In the case of wild salmon and – almost certainly – the European eel, something has happened and is happening at sea that is having a profound transformative effect on historic patterns of migration. We can guess what it might be: a gradual weakening in the vast Atlantic circulation system that moves and mixes layers of colder and warmer water of differing salinity – the engine that powers the currents, controls the water temperatures and stokes the weather systems. It may be that the salmon's main food sources have moved further north in response to temperature changes, making the southern part of its migration range – including British shores – less viable because the fish are more exposed to risk and predation to get there. It may be that the production of eel larvae in the Sargasso Sea has been diminished by temperature change, or that the currents that deliver them to

Europe and distribute them north and south have slackened. And it is highly likely that if these factors are at work, they have been generated by climate change.

These are immense imponderables, still well beyond the capacity of science to understand, let alone for humankind to correct in the short term. There is a grim comfort in that: there is little or nothing that we can do except wait and see what happens. All we, as defenders of our waters, can do is our best to keep our own house in order. For what it's worth, my assessment is that – broadly speaking – we are doing that. The results are never everything we would want, but we go on.

The Irwell runs through and over millstone grits, shales and red sandstone, which makes the water look dark even though it is clear enough. I made my way downstream slowly and with care, having reached an age when scrambling and sliding over rocks and up and down steep banks presents a distinct mobility challenge.

The river revealed vestiges of its engineered past: walls of sandstone blocks, a concrete pier, the decayed outlines of impoundments of one kind or another. The black mouths of disused waste pipes showed toothlessly in the stonework. Once they would have steamed and spewed torrents of liquids of many colours to splash on the rocks below. Now they were the haunts of rats and produced nothing more than thin trickles of water.

I saw a few dog walkers on the paths through the woodland, but no one on the water apart from one bloke stretched out on a rock, smoking contentedly, who told me he was taking it easy after his weekend's work. A little way further down was a footbridge, and a little way below that a fat metal pipe spanned the stream. I stopped and rested on a fallen tree and studied the water. There was a shingly beach on my side and a vertical bank on the other, thickly overgrown, along which the current worked purposefully, curling around the roots of the trees. There was no sign of fish feeding, but it looked highly fishy. I tied on a small weighted nymph, with a buoyant dry fly a couple of feet up the cast to act both as an attractor and as an indicator should something take the nymph.

Keeping low at the water's edge and casting low to avoid the overhanging branches, I worked my flies down the pool, moving upstream a couple of yards after every few casts. Towards the top, where the chute of water from the rocks spread and deepened, the floating fly suddenly floated no more. I struck and felt a heavy fish that had taken the sunken nymph. But I was a little slow and after one fierce lunge that put an impressive curve in my rod, the hook came free. I swore but not too violently. I had only just started and there would surely be more action. But there wasn't, not for some time. There were plenty of promising pools and deepish runs which I covered carefully, without another take.

I passed the rock where the bloke had been smoking but he had gone. When I moved from shade to sunlight it was hot, but mostly it was shaded, deliciously so, and still. I could hear the steady buzz of traffic from the M66 which runs along the crest of the valley to the east, but it was counterpointed by the songs of the birds. I reached the footbridge that takes the cycle path over the Irwell just south of Nuttall Park, which used to be the grounds of Nuttall Hall, the grand residence of one of the Grant brothers, demolished in 1945.

Below the bridge the water spilled over rocks and slowed in a wide pool, steep and wooded on the far side, with another pebbly beach on the right bank. It was evidently a favoured place for dogs to swim and frolic, but it was quiet at that time. Near the top of the pool I had a trout as long as my hand, and another a few yards further down, a bit bigger, which regurgitated a fat minnow as I tweaked out the nymph from the corner of its mouth.

I was content. The Irwell had shown that it had wild trout in it, which was what I wanted to know. After I got home I phoned

Mike Duddy to tell him how I had got on. Duddy is the driving force behind the Salford Friendly Anglers' Society, a club formed two hundred years ago when salmon still spawned in the Irwell, which has experienced a marvellous renaissance in recent years as a result of the cleaner river and heroic restoration work. The simple expedient of offering free membership saw numbers leap from a handful to three thousand, which has enabled the club to take a lead role in projects to clean up and restock the Irwell and its tributaries, and to confront the wider pollution issues that persist.

It was Duddy who had suggested that I try the stretch below Ramsbottom. He was pleased that I was pleased with the admittedly modest results. I told him I had been slightly surprised, given the conditions and the nature of the water, not to have done better, and that I had the impression there was not an abundant stock of trout. He told me that just over a year before, the illegal dumping of pesticides in a land drain near Rawtenstall – upstream of Ramsbottom – had destroyed most if not all invertebrate and crustacean life along a fifteen-mile stretch down to the confluence with the Roch at Radcliffe. Two months after that, Tesco had been fined £8 million after admitting responsibility for the leak of nearly 20,000 litres of fuel from its petrol station at Rossendale, killing fish for miles downstream.

Rivers have an amazing capacity to heal themselves from the injuries we inflict on them. But incidents such as these are reminders that the Irwell, and all the other streams in recovery, remain fragile and vulnerable. The struggle for a cleaner natural world will never be won.

CHAPTER FIFTEEN

Growing Up

I suppose it began at the boathouse.

It was on the right bank, below the footbridge. A path led to it past the clipped hedges at the bottom of the formal gardens in which the big white house stood, separated from the river by a smooth slope of lawn. It was tucked in against the bank where the current slackened and was shaded by big trees. It had a corrugated-iron roof whose utilitarian look was softened by an unruly blanket of ivy that had spread across the back half of it and spilled down the sides. The roof was supported on the river side by sturdy posts strengthened by piles driven into the gravel bed. That side was open between the posts but it was planked in on the landward side.

In front of the boathouse was a small landing-stage accessed by a flight of wooden steps that had presumably been installed at the same time as the boathouse. They both looked solid and seasoned, as if they had been there for ages. The path continued along a high bank kept in place by wooden revetments, originally vertical but now sagging outwards. It ended at a gate into a field, beyond which the river had been engineered into a pool which had a wooden shelter on the bank above it. This was known as the Bathing Place; the hut was for changing, and there was a metal ladder to lower yourself slowly into the cool water.

The boathouse

Beyond the Bathing Place the river ran between meadows for a mile or so until it reached the A4 Bath Road, where the land to which we had access ended. There was more grazing between the river and a sister flow a little to the west which is shown on the maps as the Old River but which we called the Second Stream. This had been a lovely wild, overgrown flow until complaints about flooding prompted a brutal exercise in dredging carried out by the old Thames Conservancy which stripped away its charm and left it treeless and featureless.

The big white house was called Bridge House. It and the land and the river and fishing rights were owned by family friends of ours who were happy to give my two angling brothers the run of it – and me, when I was considered old enough. At that time the old colonel and his wife still lived there; they had grandchildren of our age who were not really interested in the wonderful opportunities offered by the river, beyond a little leisurely punting now and then. All the better for us.

The colonel kept his punt and a Thames skiff in the boathouse. Between them and the back of the boathouse was a patch of open water about three feet deep at normal summer flow, and that is where I began. There was a window-sized opening in the side through which a fishing rod could be manoeuvred between the tendrils of ivy. There was just enough room for me to get my head, shoulders and upper body through from a kneeling position. It was not at all comfortable, but when you are eight or nine and you have been given your first fishing rod and reel and allowed to do your worst, who cares about comfort?

The air inside the boathouse was still, dark and cool, and smelled of mud and weed. I used a small, round cork float with an orange tip, kept upright by a couple of lead shot pinched onto the line below, a small worm for bait. As my eyes adjusted to the gloom, their gaze and all my desire was concentrated on my float as I willed it to bob and go under. Sometimes it did, and I would lift out a frantically wriggling fish and swing it back and through the aperture into the daylight.

Once in a while it was a perch, its rough-scaled olive flanks barred with black vertical stripes, its dorsal fin bristling. Perch were the first species of freshwater fish I truly admired and desired. I was by no means unusual in this. My brothers had done their first fishing with our grandmother (when I was considered too young), catching the bold and obliging perch of Windermere and Coniston Water on family holidays in the Lake District. In his book, *The Hampshire Avon*, the nature writer and

The perch, from Herbert Maxwell's *British Freshwater Fish*, 1904.

broadcaster Brian Vesey-Fitzgerald captured the appeal of the perch perfectly: 'This was the fish of my childhood . . . perhaps all men get the same thrill as I do whenever I see a perch, perhaps their minds go back as mine does to that first day, that first tremendous thrill as the float bobbed and I pulled hard and there on the hook kicked a striped green fish with a silver tummy and red fins.'

A perch was a notable capture at the back of the boathouse, but more often it was a gudgeon, which looks like a midget barbel and is rather pretty with its gold and silver tints and tiny black spots. Most often it was a spiny ruffe, which is equally small but nothing like as pretty and arouses little interest among mature anglers. I liked them well enough because they took the worm so obligingly, although they often swallowed it and the hook, necessitating a messy evisceration and, regrettably often, premature death.

That must have been 1960 or 1961. At that time my angling brothers James and Matt, and our nanny's younger brother Ralph, who lived with us, began to keep a fishing record which I still have. In the first flush of record-keeping enthusiasm, every fish

was logged, however small. There are columns detailing innumerable undersized perch, gudgeon, roach, dace, ruffe and bleak.
I do not figure at all in the lists – perhaps because I actually
made my debut later than I thought, or because my tally was
ignored, as was much else about my insignificant existence.

A page from the Fort brothers' fishing diary, 1963.

My first appearance in the record is dated 7 September 1962.
The location was Sonning, a village on the Thames about three
miles from our home in Twyford, where there was a working
mill (later converted into a theatre which is still going). We would
cycle there at dawn in summer carrying rods and boxes of tackle
and a net, the aluminium bucket containing our supply of
lobworms clanging against my eldest brother's crossbar. The
milling waste discharged into the foaming stream below the
wheels attracted an exciting concentration of fish – chub and
barbel, and, lurking with menace on the fringes, pike. The millstream was fierce water, liberally strewn with slabs of masonry
and other snags, and we lost innumerable hooks and lead weights
by getting hooked up. But every now and then the pull was from

a fish. I remember that first capture as being a chub of a respectable pound-and-a-quarter. But my eleven-year-old writing
records it as two ounces. Can it have been so small? Alas for
memory.

Although our little group did have other venues – Sonning,
one or two waters controlled by our local club, the odd Thames
weirpool, a couple of ponds containing smallish carp and stunted
tench – the great majority of our time and effort was expended
on the River Loddon, where the boathouse was, for the simple
reason that we could walk or cycle there easily. In that year, 1962,
there must have been an article in *Angling Times* about the willingness of chub to take chunks of floating bread crust, because
suddenly our book is full of records of chub so caught.

And here am I: 'Loddon, Sept 9 1963, TF, chub, 2 pounds,
floated crust.' Do I remember that fish? I can certainly recall
with ease the powerful emotion that the thought of chub in
general stirred in me. I can see the rough crust torn from a fresh
loaf – dipped for a moment in water to give it weight and lobbed
out into the streamy water below the boathouse – bobbing in
the channel between two beds of the emerald ranunculus that
grew in thick tresses from the gravel, then disappearing in a gulp.
The rest I have to imagine: the lifting of the rod tip, the hook
set, a gallop down the path with bent rod in one hand and net
in the other, a scoop bringing up weed and fish, the hook twisted
from the white rubbery lip, a desperate, disappointed look around
to see if anyone had witnessed this breakthrough event, the chub
slipped back, TF panting and frantic with joy.

Non-anglers will never understand this, but there is no thrill
to match that of lifting the net and feeling the weight of the
fish that you have so intensely longed to land since the second
you hooked it (and no sadness to match that of losing it). From
the age of twelve I was gripped by a passion that was even
more consuming than my other fierce enthusiasms for cricket,
football, later music, books, rugby. I fished, thought about

fishing, read about fishing, daydreamed about fishing, almost certainly dreamed about fishing.

There was a particular favourite daydream, which I conjured and luxuriated in during lessons at school. I was in the punt but downriver, beyond the boundary of our fishing, where the water was bigger, slower and deeper, where the pike were. I was using a live bait, a gudgeon impaled on a treble hook and suspended beneath a fat, brightly painted cork bung known as the *Fishing Gazette* pike float. I watched it intently as it circled a promising eddy, then bobbed violently as if jolted by an electric current, then vanished. I struck, the rod curved. There was a brief, strenuous struggle before the great head broke the surface, the poor gudgeon clamped between the rows of needle teeth, the wide tail thrashing. The net was slipped under it, lifting it to show the olive green flanks dabbed with yellow, its killer's mouth.

This never actually happened because we were almost never permitted – or dared ask for – the use of the punt. But we did a considerable amount of piking at Sonning and on various gravel pits and lakes. My favourite spot was immediately above the lovely, hump-backed redbrick bridge at Sonning, where there was a great submerged patch of what we called cabbages extending up to an overhanging horse chestnut tree. If you swung a live gudgeon or dace up to the top of the cabbage patch and let it drift down, pike would zoom out of the vegetation and seize the bait in the most thrilling way.

Pike went some way – never far enough – to satisfy my longing for bigger fish. At that time I was focused on the desire to be a better fisherman, which would be demonstrated by catching big fish. As this was not something I was particularly good at, the passion was never assuaged. It could have died away – my eldest brother, who had been the keenest of us all, gave it up in his twenties and never came back to it. But it didn't. It continued to burn and still burns, though these days more as a steady glow than leaping flames.

Gradually, almost in spite of myself, my perspective widened. I continued to go fishing to catch fish. That was, and still is, the point. The being outside, the birds and insects, the flowers and trees, the voles plopping into the water and the sheep grazing distant meadows – these are all very well and enhance the angling experience. But those who maintain that that is the point – generally fishing writers of a purple-prose inclination and salmon anglers on rivers where there is no hope whatever of catching a salmon – are, in my view, missing the point.

But as I grew older I was unconsciously educated by the time I spent at the waterside. I fished plenty on ponds and lakes and gravel pits, but was and am happiest beside or in moving water. In the same way you learn a language by studying the grammar – the technique, if you like – and hearing it and speaking it and feeling your way into a state of familiarity, so it was with me and rivers. I came to understand the way they worked. I became aware of the concealed dimension: the beds of weed swinging in the current over the gravel, the silt where the nymphs of damsel-flies and mayflies burrowed until the call came to ascend and hatch, the caddis cases stuck to the undersides of the stones, the darting stoneflies, the freshwater shrimp and snails clinging to the weed, the space behind the boulders, the undercut bank, the whole multi-layered, interlocked, interdependent sub-surface world. And the fish, always the fish.

I learned to interpret the river as a restless, inconstant product of forces that have worked over countless ages, sculpting the stream bed, shaping the banks, engineering the twists and turns through the landscape. The work never ends: like the dunes of the desert shifting before the wind, the slopes of the river bottom migrate downstream in obedience to the water's force. Floods can achieve extraordinary transformations, moving whole banks of gravel, rolling big boulders to new positions, washing banks away, reconfiguring whole pools, stripping silt away to expose hard gravel. The water itself is composed of multiple strands, each following its own path, tangling with and rolling over each other, changing direction, accelerating and decelerating, a dynamic composite held in place by the confines of the banks, a drama with no end. The river lover is a witness to that drama, is drawn into it, becomes a participant.

That process began for me on the river of my boyhood, the Loddon. Our record book was kept going until 1972, by which time our friend Ralph had moved away, my brothers had moved on, and most of the fishing was done by me. Over that summer I caught quite a number of decent chub on the Loddon, up to two pounds ten ounces, on the floating crust, and on lumps of paste made from grated cheese and stale breadcrumb. The last was on 14 August, one-and-a-quarter pounds. I did not catch a significant fish there again.

The Loddon and its sister, our Second Stream, provided the first stage of my angling education. The second – my secondary school, if you like – was on another intimate pairing: the Eden, in what used to be Cumberland, and its sister, the Eamont.

The Eden is a major English river, rising in the north Pennines and flowing seventy miles north-west to the Solway Firth. The Eamont is sent on its way from the northern end of Ullswater and flows nine or ten miles until it meets the Eden upstream from the village of Langwathby. These are the names: lovely names for lovely streams. But only a comparatively short stretch of each – from Langwathby up the Eden to the confluence and then up the Eamont past Udford to the boundary of the Edenhall estate – has concerned me. I have fished that four miles or so of water all my fishing life and have never wet a line anywhere else on either river, which is more a reflection of lack of enterprise on my part than of the exceptional quality of the fishing.

My defence is that I live a long way away and can get there for no more than a few days in the season, and that I could never

The Eden above Langwathby bridge.

tire of it anyway. The Eden valley is a marvellous part of the world, and that is part of the draw, but it has more to do with the infinite, beguiling variety of the water itself. I love the Thames and always will, but its character does not change a lot. I love the chalkstreams, but there is a certain monotony to the even flow and temper of them. The Eden and Eamont remind me – forgive the pretentiousness – of the late piano music of Schubert in the shifts of tempo, key and mood.

But they are very different sonatas. The Eden, as befits the senior partner, is more imposing, more stately. It rolls down wide, deep pools, rushes violently forward where it is constricted, spreads itself to push urgently along rock-strewn streams and over gravel banks, thrusts itself impatiently against whichever high bank seeks to redirect it. The Eamont is lighter-hearted, more carefree, like a younger sister, swinging this way and that over angled shingle banks, turning away to form an eddy under trailing willow branches, slowing into wide, smooth flats then gathering its skirts to dash down the sides of a stony island. Many times, when I was younger and stronger, I spent a whole day walking and fishing up from Langwathby bridge to above

Udford, marvelling at how these partners could speak and sing in so many voices.

As with the Loddon, my brothers and I were lucky in our parents' friendships. Another set of family friends owned the Edenhall estate and the fishing on the two rivers and let us come and go pretty much as we wanted. But for me this demanded a complete and radical change of approach. This was fly fishing for trout, and I knew nothing about it except that I had to put aside my coarse-fishing ways, my ten-foot rod, fixed-spool reel, floats, weights, worms, maggots. I had somehow to persuade eight feet of split cane – hollow bamboo split lengthways and glued into a tapered hexagonal whole – to deliver whisps of fur and feather like thistledown far enough out onto the water to reach the trout. I found it extremely hard – so hard that sometimes I wanted to cry.

It did not help that I had no instructor other than my brothers, who were not that much more accomplished than me. Fortunately the Eden had a large population of mostly smallish trout which were eager for food, or something that looked like food, and not too particular about how it was presented. If you could get your flies out at all, sooner or later there would be a yank at one. Often that's all there was, but sometimes the fish stayed on.

We used ready-made casts of three flies which we bought from a softly spoken, intensely pessimistic tackle dealer in Penrith. We knew the names of the flies and liked saying them – Brown Owl, Snipe and Purple, Partridge and Orange, Greenwell's Glory, Waterhen Bloa. But we had no idea what insects they imitated or when those insects might be expected to hatch. We only changed one if it got snapped off, and we only changed our casts when they worked themselves into an inextricable tangle, which happened distressingly often, sometimes with the first gust of an awkward wind. As an inept caster equipped with an inadequate rod, I suffered badly from tangles and would yell in a torment of frustration as yet again I was reduced to picking away at the confusion of knots into which my nylon and flies had resolved themselves.

In those days the Eden was a notable salmon river, and sometimes we fished for them – not with the fly, because that technique was way beyond our competence, but spinning. This enabled us to use our coarse-fishing gear, and involved flinging an artificial bait – usually a blue-and-silver or oxblood Devon minnow, or a flashing Toby – across the river and retrieving it through holding water. We lost plenty of baits on trees and rocks, but occasionally we got a salmon – on one amazing occasion two fresh-run fifteen-pounders in a morning. But of itself spinning was boring, or so we considered it, and fly fishing – though often very trying to the temper and sometimes wholly crushing of the spirits – was never boring.

Normally we went in April or May, good months for wet-fly fishing on northern streams. One year in the mid-1970s Matt and I were there in June. It was proper summer weather and the trout were reluctant to take flies cast across the current and swung downstream – which was the only method we knew. Trudging back to the fishing hut for lunch I encountered another fisherman who showed me a brace of trout of well over a pound each, bigger than anything I had ever caught. He had taken them on a fly I had never heard of, a Black Gnat, fished dry – that is, cast upstream so that the fly floated. This was dry-fly fishing, which I knew from reading about it was de rigueur on the chalkstreams but had never thought of as applicable in Cumberland.

It was an epiphany, and it nudged me decisively towards learning the technique, which took me in time to the chalkstreams – first the Kennet, later the Avon, the Test and the Itchen – and opened a new field of vision. That switch of focus, away from the coarse fish to the wild brown trout, happened slowly, but it was conclusive and irreversible. I never lost my fondness for the perch and chub and pike that obsessed me in my youth, and I have it still. But the trout, and the challenge of persuading it to take a floating fly, occupied me more and more.

Partly it was the fish itself – the varied beauty of its markings and tints, its spirit and gallantry. Partly it was the places that it drew me to – the Eden and Eamont, the little Barle on Exmoor, smooth English chalkstreams and Irish limestone rivers, Scottish lochs and Irish loughs, crystal-clear mountain streams of the French Pyrenees and the Julian Alps in Slovenia; waters in a dozen countries, all different, all united in giving a home to this fish. Partly it was their feeding habits, their way of taking an insect off the surface which made this deeply wonderful method of fly fishing possible.

There was nothing doctrinal in any of this. I graduated to dry-fly fishing, I was not converted, and I despise the self-regarding notion that it is somehow a higher form of the sport than float-fishing for roach or perch. On the chalkstreams dry fly was the rule. On the Eden and Eamont it was not the rule, but it was much more productive of decent-sized trout than covering the stream with wet flies, as well as being more fun.

There was a day in June 1991. The previous year I had spent several months fishing my way around eastern Europe, in the course of which I had bought a stock of lightly dressed dry flies from an expert tyer in Krakow. I had them with me when I went to the Eden the following season and they looked strikingly suggestive of the medium olives that started hatching in the late morning.

The Eden flows placidly down from where it meets the Eamont. On the far side is a steep, high bank slashed at intervals by slippages to reveal the dark red Penrith sandstone. Along the nearside there is a deepish bit of wading, but the current at summer level is comfortable and once across to the middle you encounter a ridge of boulders extending a way downstream over which the water quickens to create dimples and whorls where insects are trapped in patches of foam. That day there was a steady trickle of olives down this feeding lane and the trout were lined up to help themselves.

The air was warm and slightly soft with retained moisture, which extends the time it takes the hatched flies to free and dry their wings enough to take off, making them easy prey. The fish took those Polish patterns readily, although a number escaped by breaking what were obviously inferior hooks. Even so I netted one after another, almost all of them of a decent size and several of them over a pound. I do not know how long I fished for or how many I caught (I was not bothering with my fishing diary in that period). But I know that I was held in a state of intense concentration and delight, aware of my surroundings and noises and movements but detached from them. All that mattered was the band of water within my casting range, the widening rings on the surface where a fish had snaffled an insect, the swish of rod and click of reel, the press of the river's life force against my legs.

I do not remember ever having another day like that, when the hatch lasted so long. Increasingly we noticed that the daytime hatches were less frequent and more patchy and short-lived; and then rare enough to be remarked upon as an unusual event. More and more we concentrated on the late evening fishing, the magical time when the wind drops and the light fades as the sun sinks towards and then below the tree line. We would have an early supper and be back on the water by nine, watching for the rings on the surface as the trout took the first blue-winged olives. We had some terrific sessions, and I had some big fish — bigger by far than anything I had ever dreamed of in those distant days when all I knew was the wet fly and a half-pounder was a cause to give thanks.

But over time the evening fishing faltered as well. We still came, Matt and I, and fished pretty persistently and went down to favourite places after dinner, drank in the familiar beauty of our river as we always had, and waited for the hatch. If it came it was brief and required a high level of efficiency to produce good results. Often it did not happen at all. I guess we will go on doing it as long as we are able to, because of the memories and, yes, the love. But not so much for the fishing any more.

What happened? The populations of invertebrates on which that kind of dry-fly fishing depends – members of the individual families of the great dynasty of Ephemeroptera to which anglers have given names like Iron Blue, Medium Olive, March Brown, Blue-winged Olive and so on – have declined drastically and in some cases disappeared altogether. This has happened across the country, on all kinds of rivers, anywhere under pressure from intensive agriculture or the expansion of population and housing. Establishing the chain of cause and effect with any exactitude is immensely difficult; addressing the cause – even if established – more difficult still.

The trout haven't disappeared. They have done what species in the wild do to survive and have adapted their feeding habits to changed circumstances. There is food down there – larvae and molluscs and worms of multiple kinds – to be foraged from the streambed or the aquatic plants. They only ever fed on the hatching and hatched insects beloved by anglers because it was worth their while. There is one species, *Ephemera danica*, the mayfly, that is sufficiently big and tolerant of degraded habitat to thrive and hatch in sufficient abundance to bring them to the surface to feast. Otherwise, more and more, they have their noses and eyes down, seeking food that a run-of-the-mill fisherman such as myself (who does not tie his own flies) finds near impossible to imitate.

The trout are not sad about it. But we are. I am.

CHAPTER SIXTEEN

The Spring

I began writing this book towards the end of 2018, coincidentally
the worst fishing season that I had experienced for many years.
My diary entries are liberally sprinkled with depressing adjectives
and nouns – 'poor', 'very poor', 'blank', 'another blank'. It was
bad on the Usk where I went several times in a vain mission to
get a salmon; bad on the Eden; bad on the Naver in northern
Scotland where the water level was the lowest for twenty-five
years and I did not even wet a line for a salmon in a week; bad
on the Thames, the Avon, the Wylye. Bad everywhere – so bad,
in fact, that it was a relief to be writing and not fishing.

On 10 December I felt the familiar tug of desire and took the
morning off to go to the Itchen. It was a still, overcast day. The
water was running clear and full of energy and life between the
leafless trees that crowd both banks. The stretch is full of grayling, grey shapes visible against the pale gravel, swaying in the

current as they feed. I have always found them hard to catch, and so it was this morning. But I was happy to be wading upstream and not sitting at my desk, searching the channels between the weeds and the patches of bare gravel with the nymph. The winter scene was very lovely in its muted, austere way, and it was pleasing to feel the force of the river against my legs.

Towards the top of the beat the water deepens almost to the waist. I cast in towards the bank above the trailing branches of a willow. The tuft of orange wool that I had fixed onto the cast above the nymph to act as an indicator shot down. The grayling was over two pounds, my best in a long time, and I got another almost immediately which was a little smaller. As I tramped along the path back to my car I was filled with a huge, warm glow of contentment.

Did that morning redeem my season? It did not. Did it change my view of the badness of the season? It did not. Looking back over it, the negatives still seem not so much to outweigh the positives as to overwhelm them. It takes an effort of the will to recall that I enjoyed my fishing, that I was usually glad I was fishing, that I never wished that I was somewhere else doing something else, that it was not all bad.

That is the way we anglers are, or most of us. We have an inclination towards making the worst of things, embracing miserablism verging on catastrophism. When we look back to the distant past we always see the sunlit uplands, never the sloughs of despond. Yet if I take the trouble to check what I recorded in my fishing diary three decades ago, what do I find? I am genuinely astonished by how unsuccessful I was, how often I wailed about my misfortunes and railed against the quality of fishing. Historical perspective shows beyond doubt that my fishing is much better now than it was then. Yet I cannot rid myself of this need to see darkness and impending disaster around me. And I am not alone.

A proper fishing-tackle shop is the place to experience this shared negativity at full throttle. There used to be one in my home town, Reading, where I would go on the rare occasions I needed an item of coarse-fishing gear (alas it closed in 2019). It was an excellent shop of the old-fashioned kind, in that as well as selling a proper selection of rods, reels, floats, hooks, maggots of various shades of colour and so forth, it performed an important social function. Anglers went there in the same way that drinkers patronise their local – to purchase but also to talk and be among kindred spirits.

Twelve years or so ago – I cannot pinpoint the exact time – there was one dominant issue. It arose from the sustained influx of people from the countries of eastern Europe after the EU's embrace of free movement in 2004, and it would be fair to characterise the thrust of the conversation in the tackle shop as highly xenophobic.

At that time the angling press was full of stories about the outrageous and, in English eyes, almost barbaric exploits of anglers – more like fish-hunters – from Poland, Lithuania, Slovakia, Serbia, Romania, Bulgaria and the rest. Carp ponds had been plundered. Supermarket trolleys fitted with car batteries had been used to electrocute fish. Men with spear guns had surfaced at popular club venues in front of astounded club members. Bailiffs had been duffed up when they asked to see licences. On the banks of the Thames in Reading there had been a fracas between local anglers and a gang of Poles who had been barbecuing their catch of perch and roach in full public view.

The most shocking aspect was that the target species being pillaged by these people – they were all lumped together as 'eastern Europeans' – were not salmon and trout, which were acknowledged by the British as being edible, but our coarse fish, which no true Englishman would dream of killing for the pot. The coverage, which occasionally spilled over into the national media, was exaggerated and hysterical, coloured by ignorance and prejudice. But within was a kernel of truth that came from a profound cultural divide.

I had seen something of it when fishing with my Polish friend Adam. Although he had lived in England since before my birth, he retained to the full the hunting philosophy of his homeland. With fishing as with shooting, you did it to catch, to kill, to eat. The cooking and eating were a demonstration of prowess. Otherwise what was the point? Adam combined his dedication to fishing for the pot with a deep-rooted disdain for Anglo-Saxon conventions and those who tried to uphold them. He would crack a pike over the head with his leaded priest and if an English angler objected, he would vigorously invite him to mind his own business. In the same spirit, he regarded it as right and proper that he should exceed the catch limit on stocked trout fisheries if he could; when he was caught – eventually he was banned – he blamed everything on the owner of the fishery and abused him horribly.

I had encountered this attitude on my trip to eastern Europe in 1990. Mostly I was trout fishing, and therefore the eagerness of those I fished with to kill even undersized fish was not so extraordinary. But when I got to Hungary I found they had no trout streams, so I went coarse fishing on lakes that were run by the state fishing association and were stocked on a considerable scale – mainly with silver bream, a species I had always regarded with indifference bordering on contempt. I was dumbfounded to see a lorry tipping a load of these bony and unappetising fish, plus a few carp, into a murky lake not far from Budapest; equally dumbfounded to watch every angler who caught one knock it on the head with fish stew in mind.

When I told my hosts that in England all coarse fish were returned alive, they initially thought this was an example of the famous English sense of humour. When I convinced them that I was not joking, they exploded with incredulous hilarity. What madness! Why fish?

*   *   *

By November 2017 the agenda had moved on from the slaughter wreaked by the Eastern European invasion force. There were still outrages, but they were isolated. Most of the invaders had been assimilated and had adopted the English way of returning coarse fish alive, just as they had learned the language and even – some of them – to eat fish and chips and drink ale.

But the mood in the tackle shop was no more cheerful. The gloom was focused on the condition of the Kennet, which runs into the Thames in Reading and which for generations of Reading anglers has been the coarse-fishing river of choice. There were, the regulars lamented, no decent fish left in the Kennet. The list of culprits still included eastern Europeans, but they had been supplanted at the top by otters. Yes, otters. One of the blokes had spoken to another bloke who had seen six of them in one day. Six! Did I know how much fish flesh an otter required each day to stay happy and healthy? I didn't, but I guessed it was quite a bit. Too bloody right, mate! And they eat the brain and heart and liver and other high-protein bits and just leave the rest on the river bank. How would I like to see a thirteen-pound barbel or a four-pound perch with its vital organs removed and the corpse left to rot? Not much, I said.

Again, there is a basis of fact here. Otter numbers and range have expanded hugely as a result of conservation measures and the banning of the toxic agricultural pesticides that once filtered into their food chain. In several parts of the country the release into the wild of animals reared in captivity has prompted local population spikes. And it is true that otters will help themselves to bigger, slower-moving fish if they can. A managed carp fishery, stocked with fat, ponderous, boilie-stuffed tame fish, draws them like the smell of a Sunday roast wafting from the kitchen; once they get the taste and the layout, they will kill every sizeable fish there is. This has happened at commercial carp fisheries all over the country, and it is now a routine precaution to construct the otter equivalent of a deer fence around a coarse fishery.

Otter doing what otters do.

But it flies in the face of common sense to believe that stocks of bigger fish such as barbel and chub in a highly productive river such as the Kennet should have been wiped out by a single species of predator. I fished the Kennet a lot twenty-five or thirty years ago thanks to the kindness of a rich friend who had bought a converted sawmill on a wonderful, almost untouched stretch upstream from Reading. It was the angling equivalent of the land of milk and honey; I caught my biggest pike, my biggest barbel, my biggest chub and my biggest carp there, and for a few years it was almost impossible to fail. Then, quite suddenly, the quality of fishing declined. The most obvious reason was the colouring of the water and the silting resulting from the huge increase in narrowboat traffic on the connecting Kennet and Avon canal, but there were certainly other factors at work as well – not least of them the naturally occurring fluctuations in fish populations.

Otters have re-established themselves on other major rivers – the Thames, the Trent, the Hampshire Avon for instance – without being accused by anglers of eating all the fish. Studies of their spraints show that they forage a wide variety of food sources – not least among them the hated signal crayfish, which swarm in huge numbers on the bed of the Kennet and occupy the number two position on the Reading tackle-shop hate list.

The feature common to these perceived enemies of angling – and the same applies to the cormorant/goosander menace – is that there is no simple, swift way to eliminate them. Loud and strident voices demand that 'something should be done', but no one seriously suggests bringing back DDT or the otter hounds or arming anglers with shoot-to-kill orders regarding predatory birds. As for crayfish, all efforts to control the population by trapping and culling have failed, and armies of them creep across the bottoms and beds of most of our waters devouring invertebrates, fish eggs and any other form of life they can get their horrible claws on. But populations of crayfish have stabilised, and the upside is that they have been identified as a major source of protein – not just by otters, but by fish, such as chub, with teeth to crunch their shells. We will never learn to cherish the signal crayfish as we do our little, native, highly threatened white-clawed crayfish. But our rivers and lakes are learning to live with them and so can we.

The other major source of dejection in the tackle shop had nothing to do with the state of the waters, and everything to do with the undoubted decline in the popularity of angling as the nation's second-favourite pastime. I had registered this myself as a result of regularly passing through Sonning and over the Thames during the coarse-fishing season. When we fished there in the 1960s and 70s many others did as well. Clubs controlled the main stretches of river bank and organised regular matches, but there were also places where you could fish for free. Three road bridges and a footbridge crossed the two stems of the main river and the millstream, and you could fish from any of them, as well as from the right bank where the towpath went up to Sonning Lock. In the holidays, at weekends, and on summer evenings the water margins were busy with fishermen – match anglers with their stools and boxes, lads with their dads or in groups or pairs, brothers with brothers, solitary specimen-hunters.

But over the past decade the numbers have drastically thinned. It is true that the availability of free fishing had been significantly reduced by the Environment Agency's decision to ban it along the towpath stretch over the summer – presumably because some office-bound safety person became concerned about boaters coming under fire from spinners or weights or bunches of maggots. At the same time the relentless increase in road traffic over the bridges made fishing from them both unpleasant and unsafe. But there were still places left, and plenty of fish – pike, barbel, chub, perch, even carp – but hardly anyone trying to catch them.

The figures for Environment Agency rod licences show a fall from nearly 1,300,000 in 2008–9 to a little over a million in 2017-18. According to the doom-mongers in the tackle shop, membership of the Reading and District Angling Association had halved from over a thousand a few years ago. Three or four hundred used to turn out for the big matches, one old boy told me; now it was thirty or forty, and half of them had dry nets at the end.

The old-timers may have exaggerated the scale of the decline somewhat, but the situation in Reading is mirrored elsewhere. The decline in traditional match-fishing has, by all accounts, been genuinely drastic. The days when fleets of coaches would arrive beside the Trent or Thames or Severn or Witham and disgorge armies of match fishermen with their poles and tackle boxes and buckets of maggots belong to the distant past. Where it persists, the competitive urge is more likely to be satisfied these days by the so-called commercials – small, heavily stocked still-waters where the catches are measured in tens and scores of pounds rather than ounces and drams.

A similar trend is evident in fly fishing. The age profile is steadily creeping up; at club AGMs and in tackle shops and in the angling press, the question is mournfully asked: where are the young anglers? Where are the future defenders of our waters?

The answer, obviously, is that they are not going fishing because they are doing something else. One factor is the easy availability of other forms of entertainment obtained with very little effort. Children also have less time available than they used to for open-ended unstructured pastimes such as fishing – they do more homework and go on more holidays as well as spending hours on social media.

I suspect that a more insidious influence is the irresistible rise of the protective instinct among middle-class parents, stoked by the universal mobile phone and its functions. Parents are no longer psychologically capable of sending their offspring out of the house into the countryside of a summer's morning with a picnic lunch and an admonition to be careful and to be back for supper, and then putting them out of mind until they return. A key aspect of attentive parenting requires that the offspring take part in structured, time-limited activities. The parents want them supervised by adults who have been vetted according to official guidelines. Above all, they want to know where they are at all times, and they want to be able to speak to them or text them.

They do not want them out in the woods and fields finding ways to amuse themselves. They do not want them climbing trees or poking sticks into wasps' nests or scrambling over barbed wire fences. They absolutely do not want them beside a river or lake, where the potential for death by drowning is unlimited and the likelihood of intervention remote. They do not want them impaling nasty, wriggly worms on extremely sharp hooks and leaning out over moving water to effect a cast into the eddy on the far side. They do not want them to lose track of time, which tends to happen when you are fishing.

The parents of today have taught themselves that the world

is a dangerous place. They require that their children understand it as well; and understand that the best way to counter that danger is for them never to be exposed to it or to have to work things out for themselves or to have to deal with the unexpected or to have to amuse themselves or be lost or be out of touch. They must never be left to discover something new in nature or do something incredibly stupid like fall in a river.

This is not the place to discuss how or why we should have created this entirely false but fearsome version of the world around us. The fact is that we have – and fishing is one of the many casualties.*

I have reported on these exchanges in the Reading tackle shop because they illustrate that characteristic typical of anglers of a certain age – indeed of human nature in general. It is to take the darkest possible view of whatever the challenges and problems of the moment are; to see them as posing a potentially fatal threat, or at least one of a seriousness never witnessed before.

It is nonsense, of course. No one who fishes regularly or who is concerned in any way with the aquatic environment would deny that there are serious problems: salmon farming, agricultural pollution, climate change, abstraction, eutrophication, siltation – the list is long. But the lesson of history is that things have been worse, much worse. Scroll back to the end of the nineteenth century, and – thanks to pollution and netting – salmon fishing was in a far worse state than it is now. Half a century ago many of our major rivers were still wrecked by industrial waste and raw sewage.

Historical perspective suggests that the predations of otters, cormorants and crayfish – or, indeed, immigrants from eastern

---

* One of the many unexpected side effects of the coronavirus outbreak was a surge in the popularity of angling. In the month after it was removed from the list of banned activities on 13 May 2020, more than 330,000 fishing licences were sold by the Environment Agency – well over twice as many as in the same period the year before.

Europe – represent minor injurious influences compared with the scourge of industrial pollution. I know that I frequently lament the decline in hatches of fly on my favourite trout rivers in doom-laden terms, forgetting that I can still fish and catch fish in some of the most beautiful places on the planet. It's worth trying to remind ourselves that – despite all the destruction and ruination caused by the way we live – our waters are amazingly resilient, that whatever we do can be repaired if the will is there.

Some rivers are born from lakes, but most owe their existence to a spring or springs – a mere break or tear in the earth's surface through which water stored underneath is discharged. Throughout all ages and in all cultures, springs have had sacred significance, symbolising the earth's capacity to nourish and sustain. The spring is a source of water, and also of hope and faith in a future. It sends the greatest rivers on the planet on their way – and the littlest, such as Tennyson's 'The Brook':

> I chatter over stony ways
> In little sharps and trebles
> I bubble into eddying bays
> I babble in the pebbles . . .

The brook I have in mind is born from a spring in the chalk near one of a string of villages known collectively as the Candovers – hence its name, the Candover Brook. The villages are situated at intervals along a shallow valley in the Hampshire Downs, running from just west of Alresford in the direction of Basingstoke to the north-east.

A couple of centuries ago the great social commentator, William Cobbett, rode along it on his way to Winchester on a lane of flint and chalk on which the horses' hooves made a great rattling. The stiff loam soil, he reported, was not rich for corn but never poor; it was really sheep-grazing country though. The

Candover Brook

people were very neat and habitually clean from the absence of
dust, and the buildings lasted a long time because of the absence
of humidity. Trees grew well – yews were a particular feature –
and the hazel undergrowth furnished wood for fences and wattles
for folding sheep.

Cobbett made no mention of the brook in *Rural Rides*. It may
be that he missed it, as even then – when water flows were a lot

more abundant than they are now – the Candover Brook was insignificant and tended to dry up along its upper reaches over the course of the summer. It was not until it reached Abbotstone, well down the valley, that its volume was sufficient to drive a millwheel. My own experience of it has been acquired on that lower stretch, between Abbotstone – where it emerges from beneath the lane through a tiny bridge like a half-open eye near a pair of thatched, weather-beaten redbrick cottages that were probably there when Cobbett cantered past – down to where it joins the Alre and the equally dwarfish Tichborne Brook to form the headwaters of the Itchen.

The water is unnervingly clear as it twists between beds of crowfoot over golden gravel. The natural features of its valley are remarkably unchanged – time seems to have passed it by. The meadows by the brook are the roughest grazing, pitted and gouged by the wandering feet of munching cattle and sheep. The woods and copses are where they were shown on the old tithe map, and the fields on the downs observe the medieval pattern even if the way they are cultivated does not. They are flanked by thickets of spindle, dogwood and guelder rose, and banks of hawthorn and bramble. The tranquillity belongs to another time. On a fine June day the valley is bathed in the kind of deep, soothing peace that is very hard to find today anywhere in the traffic-afflicted southeast of England. And through it, like an unclasped necklace, sparkles the brook.

The first time I tried to fish up to Abbotstone was after a very wet winter, and in several places the brook had broken out into the meadows to create mudholes and mires. In chest waders I floundered through thick, glutinous mud, sweating and cursing and at times quite unable to discern where the moving water was. Securing a firm footing to be able to cast a fly was well-nigh impossible, and on that first exploration I did not actually fish at all. I did, however, get several fleeting glimpses of surprisingly large trout fleeing upstream along a channel that was, in places, much deeper than I would have expected.

There is a mayfly hatch on the brook that gives a reasonable chance of getting after these bigger fish. The hatch is fickle – I have been there at times when it was steady and encouraging, and at others when conditions were favourable but it mysteriously failed to produce more than the odd solitary insect. My best Candover trout, a pound-and-three-quarters, came on the middle beat below Fobdown. The fly landed on a flat bridge used by livestock and when I tweaked it off, the fish came out from its refuge under the bridge to suck it down.

Historically the brook's capacity to hold fish has been adversely affected by the flattening of its soft banks by cattle, and the resulting widening and shallowing of the watercourse. Admirable restoration work has been done on the margins of several stretches, fencing them to keep the beasts off and encourage plant growth, and constricting the flow to deepen it. These stretches can hold good trout, but they are far from easy. If you wade you risk sending alarmed outriders racing upstream to warn their elders and betters of your approach. It is better to stick to the bank, but you have to keep low to avoid intruding on the trout window of vision and you must cast over a barrier of rushes to land the fly on a channel that is often not much more than a yard wide.

My successes have been outnumbered by my failures. The worst failure should have been among my greatest triumphs, and the memory of it is still painful. It was around tea-time on a lovely early June afternoon and the mayfly had obliged. They were hatching steadily in the channel between thick beds of rushes, drifting down as they struggled to free their wings from the nymphal shuck and get airborne, and being picked off with minimum expenditure of effort by the fish. I was on my knees and therefore my vision of the water upstream was largely blocked by the rushes, but I could hear the sucks and glimpse the spreading ripples left by them. Several times I snagged the fly behind me as I tried to cast, or caught the vegetation on the far side, but I kept my temper, lengthened the line in the air, and eventually managed to propel my imitation well up the channel to where the feast was in progress.

There was an audible suck and I struck. As I felt the lunge of the fish I lurched upright and forced my way through the rushes and jumped down into the stream. There was nowhere for the trout to run except up or down; instead it rammed itself into the undercut bank on the opposite side, where my nylon immediately got caught around a clump of watercress roots. I waded over, keeping the line taut. I could see the fish quite clearly a couple of feet down, its nose held in the watercress roots so that it could not escape. I should have tried to net it where it was, but I was afraid of the hook being dislodged so I made a fateful decision, which was to free the nylon from the roots by hand. Which I did, and as soon as I had a direct pull on the fish it gave a violent kick which snapped the cast.

How big? Bigger than anything I hooked on the brook before or since. Big enough to make me want to weep, and to leave a sick feeling in the pit of my stomach which returns with the memory.

I have fallen for the brook in a way I have not experienced for a long time (the feeling being like that I have had for the Loddon, the Eden and Eamont, the Suir in southern Ireland and one or two others). It is not truly pristine, in that it has undoubtedly been utilised and exploited and engineered in the past – in particular for deliberate flooding to provide early grazing for sheep. The traces of the diused channels and hatches and little bridges are there if you look for them, but overall the touch has been comparatively light and remains so. Most chalkstream fishing is highly artificial: mown banks, comfortable fishing huts, stocking, weed-cutting. The brook has had a helping hand from the conservationists, but otherwise has been left to its own devices, to fend for itself.

Apart from minnows, loaches, bullheads and the occasional eel, it holds only wild brown trout, and there are plenty of them – mostly small or very small, but with a decent proportion of half-pounders, a good few pounders, and a smattering of senior denizens. To walk down the slope from the track on the middle beat and across the meadow to the point at which the brook shows itself curling away upstream and downstream, or to climb the gate opposite the old cottages at Abbotstone and see a squadron of mayfly rising and falling in the shade of the blossom-splashed hawthorn, is to be admitted to a very precious place. There, for once, my rule about the point of fishing being fishing is suspended.

I also feel very protective towards the brook. It is so rare and vulnerable. A herd of cows can physically trample the life out of it. A pair of swans and their brood of cygnets will strip out the weed along whole stretches, leaving them bare and the fish with nowhere to hide. A dry winter and spring, followed by a hot summer, will diminish the flow to a critical level. The brook seems too small and fragile to be able to withstand any kind of ecological disaster.

But maybe it is tougher than it looks. Between the world wars it and the other Itchen headwaters as well as the upper Itchen itself were extensively fished by a man called Robert Douglas Baird, and celebrated in a modest, enjoyable book called *A Trout Rose*. Baird revealed very little of himself, beyond that he was a regular Army officer, that the fishing was owned by his cousin, and that he had written the book at the behest of his brother, who had been taken prisoner by the Germans in 1940 and wanted to be reminded of happier times.

Baird did full justice to the Candover Brook – 'the most perfect and most fascinating of all small streams', he called it. But even then, the best part of a century ago, he was anxious about the future of this vulnerable landscape. He intensely disliked the water-cress beds that had been planted along the Alre at Alresford – the precursors of today's intensive salad industry – which had oblit-erated the historic course of the river. He took a hostile view of the modern houses built down the valley at Itchen Abbas and along the road to Chilland. 'Maybe the day is not far distant,' he lamented, 'when Winchester will join hands with Alresford, when the lovely Itchen valley will be but a memory of something beautiful and dearly loved . . .'

Doubtless there were planners and other barbarians who would have cheerfully realised his prophecy had they been allowed to. And it is true that the road-builders have been allowed to destroy much of the peace of the valley below Chilland by slapping the M3 and A34 across it. But the suburban sprawl has been restrained, and by the time you get as far upstream as Itchen Stoke, just west of where the brook helps give birth to the Itchen, the snarl of motor traffic has been stilled; and on the lanes approaching the brook you are more likely to meet a tractor or a cyclist or a dog-walker than a lorry, and more likely still nothing at all.

> . . . as I travel
> With many a silver waterbreak
> Above the golden gravel
> And draw them all along, and flow
> To join the brimming river,
> For men may come and men may go,
> But I go on for ever.

And maybe Tennyson's brook will go on forever. We can hope so.

Epilogue

For weeks after the end of a summer that lasted much of September, the winds blew and the rain fell in sheets, which was excellent for replenishing parched rivers but less so for sitting beside them and engaging in the contemplative man's recreation. Then, with the leaves yellowing and the ungathered fallen apples decaying into the ground, there came a perfect early autumn day.

I had been waiting for it patiently and then slightly anxiously. I wanted to say farewell to this book about our waters and their fish by spending a few hours sitting beside one. I wanted at one level to gaze at my float and wonder what might be about to happen to the juicy wriggling worm beneath it, and at another level to consider what it all meant to me in a more metaphysical way. It had to be a suitable day, though. Storm and tempest, or a river swollen and brown with the run-off from sodden fields and the discharges from bursting ditches, would not assist quiet study.

But that morning the air was still and soft. The mist hung heavy on the woods and farmland, promising sunshine when it lifted. Where more fitting to go than that stretch of the Lea north of London that I had cycled beside and over more than two years before, when the story I wanted to tell was taking shape in my head? I would go where Izaak Walton and Thomas Barker had gone in times even more turbulent and uncertain than our own to '. . . walk the meadows by some gliding stream . . . and sit on cowslip banks, hear the birds sing and possess ourselves in as much quietness as these silent silver streams'.

It would not be as they had found it, obviously not. The Lea they knew had been engineered out of existence. But there was this stretch enclosed within the 'amenity green space' of the Lee Valley Park where the rearrangement was less heavy-handed than elsewhere; where the stream twisted this way and that between old unpollarded willows and beneath trailing willow branches, between – if not cowslip banks – at least banks spared by the flood engineer to run in a riot of nettles, willowherb, brambles, comfrey and other water-loving plants. There, I hoped, I might encounter the shadows of Walton and Barker casting with their blackthorn rods and horsehair lines as they plotted to winkle out a chub from a dark hole.

I ran into a latterday Waltonian as soon as I parked my car. He was from Romania, not far from Bucharest, and was fishing with lures for predators. He had had a couple of smallish pike, the capture of one of which he showed me on his phone. I told him I had fished extensively in his homeland, in the mountains of Transylvania, many years before, and also on the Danube delta. I said that I had never been anywhere more beautiful, and he said, 'But England is beautiful too.'

And it was, with the sun now out, lighting the silvery foliage of the willows and the darker green of the alders and giving the stream a warm, amber glow. Taking my Romanian friend's advice, I went a little way upstream to a pool of promise where I was able to settle my stool on a reasonably level bit of bank. The current ran in at the head of the pool over trailing tresses of water cabbages, slowing as the pool widened and deepened. I set up my rod, a battle-hardened eleven foot of glass fibre – the Fred J. Taylor 'Trotter', at least fifty years old – and a Mitchell 300 fixed-spool reel of a similar vintage, equally sound. I attached a cheery crimson-tipped float and stuck a lively garden worm on the hook. I had hopes of a perch, as perch are fond of worms, at least they used to be when I was a lad a long time ago.

I settled comfortably into the pattern of swinging out float and bait into the current, mending the line to keep them on the move, urging that crimson tip to tremble and dart down. The sun smiled down. I heard cyclists conversing as they pedalled, dog walkers, buggy pushers, the chatter of blackbirds. Clouds of midges pulsed above the water, lit by sunlight. A pylon's skeletal head reared over the stand of ash trees opposite, its cables looping towards the electricity substation nearby.

No perch. No bites. I moved down to the pool above the bailey bridge where I had met the Romanian. I positioned my stool on a casting platform which made for an easy cast into the current on the far side. I tried a pink North Atlantic prawn on the hook, a far cry from the slugs, snails, baby frogs and maggots recommended by Walton; then a chunk of luncheon meat stained green with halibut oil, even more outlandish. Every time the float bobbed around to the gap between the two spindly willows opposite me I tensed, expecting action. But the only action came from coots and mallards disputing their spheres of influence. Hope faded, thoughts of lunch intruded.

I reeled in and went to get my sandwiches. Beside and on the bridge were a number of warning signs reflecting the desire of the park authorities to keep the people – stakeholders, naturally – safe and within the law. One listed the dangers of taking the little stream lightly – 'Water Is Dangerous In All Weathers', it stated. Opposite was another sign warning anyone who dared go fishing in the close season (15 March to 15 June) that they would be liable to a fine of up to £50,000, which seemed quite steep. It was in five languages – English, Polish, Slovakian, Romanian and Lithuanian – reflecting the diversity of the sport's appeal.

I will not dwell in detail on my afternoon's fishing. I tried other locations, but with identical outcomes. I longed fiercely for my float to fulfil H.T. Sheringham's delicious dictum, 'pleasing in appearance, even more pleasing in disappearance'. But it failed to do so. In the last spot I tried, my boots sank deep into black, clinging mud and I made an ignominious ascent of the bank on hands and knees. Plodding back to the car smelling strongly of mud, I saw another angler in the shadow of a willow, stretched out in comfort on a reclining seat. Nothing, he said, not a touch, which cheered me a little as he looked as if he knew what he was doing. A little way further on I saw a mallard thrust its emerald-green head beneath the surface and come up with a little fish – a dace or a gudgeon – across its beak. It waggled its head, trying to get the fish straight enough to be swallowed, while gliding swiftly downstream to escape the attempts of the other ducks to dispossess it. There was a midstream fracas, in the course of which the little fish got away, and I went home.

As I write this it is raining again. Brexit is still not done, but it looks as if we will soon be turning our backs on Europe and those – like my Romanian friend – who embraced us and our ways. Two nights ago a refrigeration container was found in Essex with thirty-nine dead Vietnamese inside, and this morning a man in the newsagent's across the road from my home stared at the headlines and said, 'At least that's thirty-nine mouths we won't have to feed.'

Sometimes the world we have made seems unbearably full of horrors, and of unpleasant people saying unpleasant things. It becomes necessary to retreat to an alternative version of life. Izaak Walton found his escape from the savage fury of the Civil War at the waterside. There he was reminded of the peaceful, efficient working of the natural world around us and was calmed and strengthened.

When I was young I was cast down by fishing failure. Now, in the autumn of my days, I do not feel it in the same way. Don't mistake me – the point is still to catch fish. But I know now what I did not know then, that failure, the fishless, biteless day, is both inevitable and necessary. It makes the sweetness of success, when it finally comes, all the more intense. And it gives the opportunity to stop and look around, to wonder again at the glory of this composition: the stream hurrying over the gravel, the still water of the lake beside the beds of lilies and the spread of the willow branches, the river bursting from bare moorland over black rocks in a cloud of spray, the restless run between the beds of weed where a trout's snout will surely lift at any moment to take the invisible insect.

Don't let that ever be taken away from me.

Acknowledgements

The initial idea for this book came from Harry Marshall of Icon Films, who wanted to make a fish-based TV series, but it was not to be. I am grateful to him, and to my priceless agent Caroline Dawnay for finding someone keen to commission it – namely Myles Archibald of William Collins. I have had great support from him, from Hazel Eriksson, a most sympathetic editor, and from Sally Partington, an exceptionally rigorous and helpful copyeditor.

Andrew Douglas-Home, Andrew Graham-Stewart, and Dr Andrew Herd checked certain passages for errors – any that survive are my fault, not theirs. I am grateful to the following for their help in providing illustrations. Keith Annishaw of Angling Heritage, the angling historian John Essex, Colin McPherson, Pat Close of the Lough Neagh Fishermen's Co-operative Society, Feargal Sharkey and Chris Yates. My friend Jason Hawkes, Britain's leading aerial photographer, generously photographed the images from my old fishing books.

Many people helped me along the way, among them one of the last of the Severn lave netsmen, Mike Evans, and one of the last eel fishermen, Alan Arnold. Andrew Douglas-Home put me in touch with Ralph Holmes, one of the last Tweed netsmen and an invaluable source of information about the river. Peter Hayes entertained me for lunch at the Flyfishers' Club and provided me with fascinating information about the shadowy Sir Joseph Ball. Paul Lidgett and Nigel Hewlett of the Environment Agency filled in gaps in my knowledge about sturgeon, catfish and other exotic introductions. Mike Duddy of the Salford Friendly Anglers' Society advised me where to fish on the Irwell. Mark Walsingham told me where to find 'BB's Wood Pool. Tim Young invited me to the memorable 'The Eels Have Eyes' evening in Brentford and Joe Pecorelli patiently dealt with my questions about the current state of eel knowledge. Airlie and Mark Holden-Hindley have been unfailingly generous hosts on the Eden and Eamont.

Finally I would like to thank my fishing brothers and all my fishing pals for the pleasure they have made possible, and my wife Helen, for her tolerance of a very time-consuming passion and so much else.

APPENDIX

All the Fishes

*A listing of all the British freshwater fish, excluding
exotic ornamental imports such as golden orfe and koi carp.*

BARBEL

Its body is long and slim and powerful, with olive flanks, a white
belly and thick rubbery lips with four barbules on the upper lip
and jaw. Its distribution is limited – they are not known in
Scotland, Ireland, north-west England or south-west England.

'He affords an Angler choice sport, being a lusty and cunning
fish' – Izaak Walton, *The Compleat Angler*

'It is one of the strongest fighters of our rivers, and will do its
best to break your line by sheer force' – A.F. Magri MacMahon,
Fishlore

'He is just the chap to fight it out with you to the very last
gasp' – J.W. Martin ('The Trent Otter'), *Coarse Fish Angling*

BLEAK

Small (no more than six inches long), silvery and numerous, they
are much preyed upon by pike, perch, chub and other predators
but are of negligible sporting value. The Victorians ate them –
Harry Cholmondeley-Pennell said that eaten like whitebait 'they

make a very good dish'. The French used to scrape off their scales and turn them into imitation pearls.

BREAM
There are two species which are cousins, the common or bronze bream, and the silver bream. They are generally found in lakes, ponds, canals and slow-flowing rivers. The silver variety are smaller and not as slimy as the common and, in my admittedly limited experience, put up almost no fight when hooked. From the side they look imposingly portly, but their bodies are narrow and flat.

'Although the bream is a poor fighter it must be struck and played carefully on light tackle' – Fred Buller and Hugh Falkus, *Freshwater Fishing*

'The great objection I have to bream is the early hour at which they usually breakfast' – 'John Bickerdyke' (C.H. Cook), *Angling for Coarse Fish*

'When hooked, it shows very little fight and allows itself to be hauled to the surface without any resistance' – A.F. Magri MacMahon, *Fishlore*

BULLHEAD
Otherwise known as the Miller's Thumb, it is very small – three to four inches – with large flattened head, two dorsal fins, and sharp teeth. It is common in clean, stony streams but its presence is generally ignored as it is very hard to see and no angler would wish to catch it.

BURBOT
Once fairly common in the sluggish waters of East Anglia, the burbot – a member of the cod family – is reckoned to be extinct in Britain, although still found in Scandinavia. It is elongated and slimy and has a single barbule under its chin.

'They are such a stupid and ugly fish that I cannot advise

trouble to be taken with their dissemination' – Francis Buckland, *The Natural History of British Fishes*

CARP

The common carp originated in the Danube basin in eastern Europe and was introduced to England in the fifteenth century. Its size and tolerance of wide variations in water temperature and quality made it the favourite species for stocking artificial ponds; much later it inspired and continues to inspire obsessive devotion among a certain kind of angler. The mirror carp – which has fewer and much larger scales – is a genetically engineered mutation and grows just as large. The crucian carp belongs to the same family as the common carp, but is much smaller – a four-pounder is an exceptional specimen – and has a deeper body shape. They thrive in small ponds with reeds and lily pads. I have never caught one but there is a website, www.crucians.org, for admirers and enthusiasts.

'It is such a wily beast' – 'BB', *The Fisherman's Bedside Book*

'To hook a big one is like being jerked out of bed by a grapnel from an aeroplane' – Arthur Ransome, *Rod and Line*

'I knew it was big, and suddenly it dawned on me that it was more than that. It was tremendous' – Richard Walker, *Still-Water Angling* (on the capture of his 44-pound record)

CATFISH

The first specimens are believed to have been brought over from Germany in the 1880s by the British consul in Berlin, Lord Odo Russell, and put in the lakes in the family estate at Woburn. Subsequent stocking in other waters led to escapes, and it is believed to have established a breeding population in the Thames and Ouse. Elongated, with a wide mouth and six barbules, it can grow to a vast size in eastern Europe, where smaller specimens are highly regarded for eating.

CHAR

There are around two hundred communities of Arctic char in the deep lakes, lochs and loughs of Britain – the same species, *Salvelinus alpinus*, and a host of subspecies are found all around the Arctic Circle, across Canada and Siberia, and as far south as the Alps. It looks like a trout but with only red, orange or white spots, generally feeds in in deep water, is of very limited interest to anglers, but makes superb eating if you happen to encounter one.

CHUB

It prefers running water but is sometimes found in lakes and ponds, although not at all in Ireland, west Wales, south-west England and northern Scotland. It eats almost anything and can be caught in summer, autumn or winter; if not scared it is very obliging to anglers and held in fond regard by them.

'He is a sporting fish of a high character' – J.W. Martin, *Coarse Fish Angling*

'The chub is a much gamer antagonist than most fishing writers will allow, and in winter he is at his best' – H.T. Sheringham, *Coarse Fishing*

'Fly fishing under the boughs for chub is one of the most delightful occupations to be had on the Thames' – Francis Francis, *A Book on Angling*

DACE

A one-pound dace is a noble specimen, but what it lacks in size it makes up for in appearance – Thomas Boosey's indispensable *Anecdotes of Fish and Fishing* (1887) described it as 'a gregarious and very lively fish'. The great angler Fred Buller once caught 251 of them weighing sixty-four pounds in a single session on the Hampshire Avon.

'A shoal of dace in the streamy waters they inhabit is a pleasing sight' – Edward Ensom ('Faddist'), from *Fine Angling for Coarse Fish*

'A handsome fish, the dace, built on clean lines like a racing-skiff' – H.T. Sheringham, *Coarse Fishing*

EEL

Uniquely among our freshwater fish, the eel is catadromous – it is born in salt water, lives in fresh water, and returns to the sea to spawn. The fact that it chooses to do so three thousand miles away in the Sargasso Sea is merely one of its many peculiarities. There are a small number of anglers who target it – at night, on dark, still waters – but most rarely encounter it and find it extremely difficult to handle and unhook when they do.

'Eels are regarded by most anglers as a nuisance' – Richard Walker, *Still-Water Angling*

'Angling for eels can hardly be looked upon as a matter of any great consequence' – Francis Francis, *A Book on Angling*

'It is agreed by most men that the Eel is a most dainty dish' – Izaak Walton, *The Compleat Angler*

GRAYLING

It is a cousin of the trout and salmon, but with its underslung mouth and large dorsal fin, it looks very different. It favours the same habitat as its cousins, although its range is more restricted and it is not found in Ireland or northern Scotland. It is a wonderful fish to pursue in autumn and winter, particularly on clear streams where sight-fishing with a sunken nymph is a demanding and exhilarating way of catching them. It is highly regarded in eastern Europe as an eating fish, but generally we do not bother in Britain.

'Trout may be called handsome – grayling are beautiful fish' – E. Marshall Hardy, *Angling Ways*

'The grayling is probably the most beautifully coloured British fish' – A.F. Magri MacMahon, *Fishlore*

'I became aware that it was that rarest of opportunities, a grayling day' – H.T. Sheringham, *An Open Creel*

GUDGEON

They look rather like tiny barbel, but with two barbules instead of four and are handsome little chaps. The Victorians used to organise gudgeon-fishing parties at which a rake was used to disturb the gravel bottom, stirring up all manner of titbits and attracting shoals of fish. These parties often included women, but J.J. Manley, in *Notes on Fish and Fishing*, warned that there were risks – 'many a heart has been irretrievably lost while gudgeon-fishing', he wrote.

'A two ounce gudgeon is good, and three ounces is enormous' – Maurice Wiggin, *Fishing for Beginners*

LAMPREY

Jawless parasitic fish with a spiky tongue, of obscure habits. There are three species in Britain, two of which – the sea lamprey and the river lamprey – spawn in fresh water and spend most of their lives at sea. The third and smallest, the brook lamprey, is believed to remain in fresh water. Historically regarded as a great delicacy, they are described by Professor Magri MacMahon as 'uncommonly good' to eat, with no bones and just some bits of gristle. I have seen them writhing around on a gravel bed on the Tywi but they are not an angling fish – although Henry Lamond, the historian of Loch Lomond, refers to a fisherman striking a sea trout and catching the lamprey attached to it instead.

LOACH

There are two British species, the stone loach and the spined loach. Both are very small, with elongated bodies and six barbules around the mouth. The stone loach, which likes to hide beneath stones, is much more common than its spiny cousin which is found only in the east of England. I have never heard of anyone catching either.

MINNOW

A live minnow makes an excellent bait for a perch if you can bring yourself to put a hook through its mouth and cast it out, which I no longer can. They may be caught on fragments of worm or maggot, or in a simple trap, or even in a net if you scoop it up under a shoal. They are said to be tasty fried like whitebait, but I have never tried that.

'A minnow, a minnow, I have him by the nose' – Beatrix Potter, *The Tale of Jeremy Fisher*

PERCH

Most young coarse anglers begin with perch, which are found in almost every part of these islands, in all kinds of water. Caught in gravelly rivers, they make excellent eating when filleted and fried in butter, although I haven't had one for many years. I caught my best, a three-pounder, on fly in a Thames backwater, but they do grow up to five pounds and even bigger. Their colouring is very lovely, and they are very satisfying to catch.

'A very good and very bold-biting fish' – Izaak Walton, *The Compleat Angler*

'Not only is it handsome, but a fine sporting fish' – 'John Bickerdyke', *Angling for Coarse Fish*

'The perch is one of the very best fish from a culinary point of view' – A.F. Magri MacMahon, *Fishlore*

PIKE

The apex predator of our rivers and lakes, the pike inspires myth and legend among us almost as readily as it does fear and immediate flight in its intended prey. It feeds infrequently, and the bigger the meal it swallows, the longer the interval before it needs to feed again. In times past, live-baiting – tethering a live fish beneath a float to await destruction – was the favourite method, but this is rightly considered somewhat barbaric, and as it can be caught on a dead bait, a spinner or a large gaudy fly just as readily, there is no need to behave like a barbarian. A Thames autumn or winter pike on the fly will fight as hard, though not as long, as a grilse.

'Ever since the first pike fishing story was told there have been accounts of the pike's enormous gluttony, tales of a cunning and rapacious monster unequalled in ferocity, a veritable fish of blood' – Fred Buller and Hugh Falkus, *Freshwater Fishing*

'But a pike! Itself unpitying, unsparing, who would pity? Who spare?' – Thomas Tod Stoddart, *Angling Reminiscences*

'Like boa-constrictors they have a heavy gorge about once in two or three days or longer, then lie torpid' – Francis Francis, *A Book on Angling*

POLLAN, POWAN (AND GWYNIAD, SKELLY AND VENDACE)

All herring-like members of the whitefish genus *Coregonus* and none of any consequence to the angler. Pollan are found in several lakes in Northern Ireland and are still netted commercially on Lough Neagh (mostly illegally) – the Swiss are said to be very partial to them. Powan are quite numerous in Loch Lomond and Loch Eck in Scotland, but unknown elsewhere. Gwyniad are native to Lake Bala in North Wales, and skelly to Haweswater, Ullswater and Red Tarn in the Lake District. Vendace are found in Mill Loch near Dumfries, and in Bassenthwaite and Derwentwater in the Lake District. It would be a diverting angling challenge to try and catch a specimen of each.

ROACH

With its red-tinged fins and bright silver scales, it is a good-looking fish and very common except in Scotland and south-west England. It likes quiet water – ponds, lakes and the slower-moving reaches of rivers. The favoured angler's bait has always been maggots. Thomas Boosey quotes a reference from the *Gentleman's Recreation* to fishing for them from Tower Bridge in London with a multi-hooked handline attached to a three-pound weight.

'Of all roach-fishing I most prefer using a float in a deep, slow swim' – H.T. Sheringham, *Coarse Fishing*

'Game fighters and cunning as they are, they appeal to the sportsman' – E. Marshall Hardy, *Angling Ways*

'Bright, clean, alert and graceful. . .the roach is indeed a pretty sight' – Arthur M. Young, *The Story of the Stream*

RUDD

Deeper in the body than a roach and thicker across than a bream, it is better looking than either due to its golden, almost brassy colouring. There are no rudd in Scotland but it is abundant in reedy, muddy Irish lakes. Forty years ago or so I caught half a dozen decent rudd on a lake in Berkshire, using legered bread flake because it was too misty to see a float. I have not caught one since, but I keep meaning to try with a fly rod.

'I doubt if there is a more handsome coarse fish than the rudd' – 'John Bickerdyke', *Angling for Coarse Fish*

'Fly fishing is the most attractive method of catching rudd' – H.T. Sheringham, *Coarse Fishing*

RUFFE

Small, spiky, greedy. I caught many when I was a boy – I regret to say that a substantial proportion swallowed the hook and died as a result. I have not caught or seen one for decades, but they are there. They are often referred to as pope in the old books.

SALMON

Or more precisely the Atlantic salmon, to distinguish it from its several species of Pacific cousins. It is anadromous: it is born and spawns in fresh water and reaches adulthood at sea. The fact that it generally does not eat anything in fresh water makes the catching of it a haphazard business, which many angling writers have attempted to turn into a high science.

'To catch salmon with a fly all that need be known is how to throw twenty-five yards of line fairly straightly' – Patrick. R. Chalmers, *Where the Spring Salmon Run*

'The bold rise and the first wild rush of a twenty-pound salmon thrill through the frame as nothing else in sport does' – Francis Francis, *A Book on Angling*

'You may not have fished yourself, to do so for salmon is immensely exciting' – Prince Charles in a letter in 1969 to Harold Wilson, then prime minister.

SHAD

Shad are members of the herring family and two species, the allis shad and the twaite shad, enter British waters – principally the Severn system – to spawn in late spring and early summer. It used to sustain a small-scale commercial fishery on the Severn as far upstream as Shrewsbury – according to the eighteenth-century Welsh naturalist Thomas Pennant, it 'is esteemed a very delicate fish . . . it sells dearer than salmon'. But the building of navigation weirs on the river blocked access to its spawning grounds and it is now on the International Union for Conservation of Nature (IUCN) Red List of threatened species, although anglers fly fishing on the Wye, Usk and Tywi sometimes catch them.

SMELT

Related to trout and salmon, smelt are actually sea fish but they spawn in river estuaries. In Victorian times they were fished for as far up the Thames as Richmond. They grow no more than ten ounces in size and were once common enough to sustain commercial fishing but are now rare. I have never seen one.

STICKLEBACK

There are two species of this tiny but combative fish in Britain, the three-spined and the ten-spined. The former are more common, but both are able to live in fresh water, brackish water and the sea. According to Professor Magri MacMahon, if put in an aquarium with small goldfish, they will attack them with their spines and kill them. In spring the colouring of the males becomes more vivid, with red bellies and dark bands on their flanks, and they build nests before displaying their colours to induce the females to lay their eggs within.

STURGEON

There are accounts from all around our coasts of this huge, ponderous and primitive survivor from the early stages of evolution turning up in fishermen's nets at sea or in estuaries and causing astonishment. The biggest recorded was taken by a trawler off Orkney in 1956 and weighed 700 pounds. The Severn system and South Wales account for most of the catches – the most celebrated, from an angling point of view, being Alec Allen's on the Tywi in 1933 (see page 217).

'Do not forget that if you catch a sturgeon in Britain the fish does not belong to you but to the Crown' – A.F. Magri MacMahon, *Fishlore*

TENCH

With its stout, powerful body, deep olive-green flanks and rounded fins, the tench is a bottom-feeder most at home in reedy lakes and ponds with extensive beds of water lilies. The tell-tale sign of tench feeding is the appearance of columns of bubbles on the surface, released from the mud by their foraging snouts. Fishing for them is a peaceful and sedentary business requiring patience and an ability to stare for a long time at a stationary float, which I find I no longer have. I wish I did, for they are a very satisfying fish to catch and to look at.

'The pursuit of them involves blissful, quiet hours beside summer waters' – H.T. Sheringham, *Coarse Fishing*

'I caught my five-pounder in that witching hour when other

anglers have packed up and departed and the rats had begun to emerge from the reedy banks' – 'BB', *The Fisherman's Bedside Book*

'They are a firm and good fish to eat . . . by no means bad with parsley and butter' – James O'Gorman, *The Practice of Angling*

TROUT

Brown trout are the most widely distributed freshwater fish on earth, indigenous to Europe, North Africa and South-East Asia and established after introduction in Australia, New Zealand, North and South America, southern Africa, northern India and elsewhere. Our sea trout is a brown trout that has evolved to feed at sea but spawn in fresh water. The rainbow trout is native only to North America, but was widely introduced in Britain from the 1880s onwards, and established a handful of breeding populations – most notably on the Derbyshire Wye.

'We always say that trout are cunning but we always treat them like fools' – J.W. Hills, *A Summer on the Test*

'Trout are a first-class fish for delicate taste, sporting qualities, varied and beautiful appearance. They may be angled for in very pleasant ways. That is all.' – A.F. Magri MacMahon, *Fishlore*

'He may be justly said, as the old poet said of wine, and we English say of venison, to be a generous fish' – Izaak Walton, *The Compleat Angler*

ZANDER

A member of the perch family, zander are widely distributed in continental Europe but were largely unknown in England until the 1960s, when someone from the Great Ouse River Board decided it would be a good idea to stock them in the Relief Channel. Ninety-seven little zander were released in March 1963 and found the murky waters and abundant food source so congenial that they rapidly spread through Fenland waters and thereafter further afield. They have very large eyes – enabling them to hunt smaller fish successfully in deep, dark water and at night – and big teeth. They are highly regarded in Europe as an eating fish – I caught a smallish one on Lake Balaton in Hungary in 1990 in the middle of the night, which was certainly tasty but not wildly exciting.

Bibliography

Aston, Michael (ed.), *Medieval Fish, Fisheries and Fishponds*, British Archaeological Reports (BAR) 182(1), 1988

Baird, R.D. *A Trout Rose*, Jarrolds, 1948

Balfour, Caroline, *The Early Days of the Tweed Commissioners*, River Tweed Commission, 2007

Bazley, J.R.R., *The Art of Coarse Fishing*, Witherby, 1932

'BB' (Denys Watkins-Pitchford), *Fisherman's Bedside Book*, Eyre & Spottiswoode, 1945

—— *Confessions of a Carp Fisher*, Eyre & Spottiswoode, 1950

—— *A Carp Water (Wood Pool) and How to Fish It*, Putnam 1958

'Bickerdyke, John' (C.H. Cook), *Angling for Coarse Fish*, L. Upcott Gill, 1932

Boosey, Thomas, *Anecdotes of Fish and Fishing*, Hamilton, Adams & Co, 1887

Bracegirdle, Cyril, *The Dark River: Irwell*, John Sherratt, 1973

Bradshaw, Jane, 'Traditional Salmon Fishing in the Severn Estuary' (unpublished doctoral dissertation), University of Bristol, 1996. Available through www.aforgottenlandscape.org

Brereton, Wallace, *Irwell Gallery*, Salford History Society, 1978

Buller, Frederick, and Falkus, Hugh, *Freshwater Fishing*, Macdonald and Jane's, 1975

—— *Dame Juliana: The Angling Treatyse and its Mysteries*, Flyfishers' Classic Library, 2001

Calderwood, W.L., *The Salmon Rivers and Lochs of Scotland*, Edward Arnold, 1921

Callcut, W.G., *The History of the London Anglers' Association*, self-published, 1924

Chalmers, Patrick, *Where the Spring Salmon Run*, Philip Allan, 1931

—— *At the Tail of the Weir*, Philip Allan, 1932

—— *The Angler's England*, Seeley Service, 1938

Clifford, Kevin, *A History of Carp Fishing*, Sandholm, 1992

Coates, Peter, *Salmon*, Reaktion Books, 2006

Cocker, Mark, *Our Place: Can We Save Britain's Wildlife Before It's Too Late?* Jonathan Cape, 2018

Coopey, Richard, 'A River Does Indeed Run Through It: Angling and Society in Britain since 1800', from K.V. Lykke Syse and T. Oestigaard (eds), *Perceptions of Water in Britain from Early Modern Times to the Present*, BRIC Press, University of Bergen, 2010

Corbett, Edward, 'Angling in the Irwell', from *Anglers' Evenings: Papers by Members of the Manchester Anglers' Association*, Abel Heywood, 1880

Currie, Christopher K., 'The Early History of the Carp and its Economic Significance in England', *Agricultural History Review*, 1988

Dawson, Tom, 'Locating Fish-traps on the Firth of Forth and the Moray Firth', University of St Andrews on behalf of the SCAPE Trust and Historic Scotland, 2004. Available from www.scapetrust.org

Ellacombe, Rev. Henry, 'Shakespeare as an Angler', *The Antiquary*, 1881

Fagan, Brian, *Fish on Friday: Feasting, Fasting and the Discovery of the New World*, Perseus, 2006

Forsyth-Grant, Michael, *A Salmon Fisher Remembers*, Pentland Press, 1995

Gallichan, Walter, *Fishing in Derbyshire and Around*, Robinson, 1905

Gilbert, H.A., *The Tale of a Wye Fisherman*, Jonathan Cape, 1953

Gingrich, Arthur, *The Fishing in Print*, Winchester Press (US), 1974

Graham-Stewart, Andrew, *The Salmon Rivers of Northern Scotland*, Robert Hale, 2005

Grimble, Arthur, *The Salmon Rivers of Scotland, The Salmon Rivers of England and Wales, The Salmon Rivers of Ireland*, Keegan, Paul, Trench, Trubner, 1913

Hale, Alex, 'Fish-traps in Scotland', RURALIA Conference Proceedings, 2003

Halford, F.M., *Floating Flies and How to Dress Them*, Sampson Low, Marston, Searle and Rivington, 1886

—— *Dry-fly Fishing in Theory and Practice*, Witherby, 1989

Hall, David, and Coles, John, *Fenland Survey: An Essay in Landscape and Persistence*, English Heritage, 1994

Hayes, Peter, *Imitators of the Fly: A History*, Coch-y-Bonddu Books, 2016

Hayter, Tony, *F.M. Halford and the Dry Fly Revolution*, Robert Hale, 2002

—— *G.E.M. Skues: The Man of the Nymph*, Robert Hale, 2013

Herd, Andrew, *The History of Flyfishing*, Medlar Press, 2011

—— *The Flyfishers: A History of the Flyfishers' Club*, The Flyfishers' Club, 2019

Hills, J.W., *A History of Fly Fishing for Trout*, Philip Allan, 1921

—— *A Summer on the Test*, Geoffrey Bles, 1924

Hobson, Jeremy, and Jones, David, *Sporting Lodges: Sanctuaries, Havens and Retreats*, Quiller, 2013

Hoffmann, Richard: 'Fishing for Sport in Medieval Europe', Speculum, 1985

—— 'Salmo Salar in Medieval Scotland', *Aquatic Sciences*, 2015

Hornell, James, *Fishing in Many Waters*, Cambridge University Press, 1950

Jenkins, Geraint, *Nets and Coracles*, David and Charles, 1974

Locker, Alison, 'The Social History of Coarse Angling in England' 1750–1950, *Anthropozoologica*, 2014

Lowerson, John, 'Brothers of the Angle: Coarse Fishing and English Working-Class Culture 1850–1914', from J.A. Mangan (ed.), *Pleasure, Profit and Proselytism*, Frank Cass, 1988

—— 'Angling', from Tony Mason (ed.), *Sport in Britain: A Social History*, Cambridge University Press, 1989

—— *Sport and the English Middle Classes, 1870–1914*, Manchester University Press, 1993

Maciver, Evander, *Memoirs of a Highland Gentleman*, Constable, 1905

Mackenzie, Murdo, *A View of the Salmon Fishery of Scotland*, Blackwood, 1860

Macrae, Norman, *The Romance of a Royal Burgh: Dingwall's Story of a Thousand Years*, Dingwall, 1923

Magri MacMahon, A.F., *Fishlore: British Freshwater Fishes*, Penguin, 1946

Malloch, P.D., *Life-history of the Salmon, Sea Trout and Other Freshwater Fish*, A. and C. Black, 1912

Marshall-Hardy, E., *Angling Ways*, Herbert Jenkins, 1934

Martin, J.W. ('The Trent Otter'), *My Fishing Days and Fishing Ways*, W. Brendon, 1906

—— *Coarse Fish Angling*, W. Brendon, 1909

Maxwell, Sir Herbert, *The Story of the Tweed*, Nisbet and Co., 1905

Minnitt, Stephen, and Coles, John, *The Lake Villages of Somerset*, Somerset Levels Project, 1996

More, Prior William, *Journals*, Worcestershire Historical Society, 1914

Netboy, Anthony, *The Atlantic Salmon: A Vanishing Species?* Faber, 1968

Nicolson, Adam, and Sutherland, Patrick, *Wetland: Life in the Somerset Levels*, Michael Joseph, 1986

Noake, John, *The Monastery and Cathedral of Worcester*, Longman, 1866

North, Richard, *A Discourse of Fish and Fishponds*, London 1713 Available through archive.org

O'Sullivan, Aidan, 'Place, Memory and Identity Among Estuarine Fishing Communities: Interpreting the Archaeology of Early Fish Weirs', *World Archaeology*, 2004

Penny, George, *Traditions of Perth*, Perth, 1836

Pike, Theo, *Trout in Dirty Places*, Merlin Unwin, 2012

Pringle, D.R., 'The Privation of History: Landseer, Victoria and the Highland Myth', from Denis Cosgrove and Stephen Daniels (eds) *The Iconography of Landscape*, Cambridge University Press, 1988

Pulman, G.P.R., *The Vade Mecum of Fly Fishing for Trout*, Longman, 1851

'Q' (Sir Arthur Quiller-Couch), *The Warwickshire Avon*, James R. Osgood, 1892

Radcliffe, William, *Fishing from the Earliest Times*, John Murray, 1911

Rippon, Stephen, 'Making the Most of a Bad Situation: Glastonbury Abbey, Meare, and the Exploitation of Wetland Resources in the Somerset Levels', *Archaeology in the Severn Estuary*, 2002

Roberson, Iain, *The Tay Salmon Fisheries since the Eighteenth Century*, Cruithne Press, 1998

—— *The Salmon Fishers*, Medlar Press, 2013

Robson, Kenneth, *Amwell Magna Fishery 1831–1981*, Chesterman Publications, 1981

Russel, Alex, *The Salmon*, Edmonton and Douglas, 1864

Salter, Thomas, *The Angler's Guide*, Carpenter and Son, 1815

Scrope, William, *Days and Nights of Salmon Fishing on the Tweed*, Flyfishers' Classic Library, 1991

Sheringham, H.T., *An Angler's Hours*, Macmillan, 1905

—— *An Open Creel*, Methuen, 1910

—— *Coarse Fishing*, A. and C. Black, 1912

—— *Trout Fishing: Memories and Morals*, Hodder and Stoughton, 1920

Skues, G.E.M., *The Way of a Trout with a Fly*, A. and C. Black, 1921

—— *Nymph Fishing for Chalk Stream Trout*, A. and C. Black, 1939

Venables, Bernard, *Fishing*, Batsford, 1953

—— *The Gentle Art of Angling*, Reinhardt, 1955

Vesey-Fitzgerald, Brian, *The Hampshire Avon*, Cassell, 1950

Walker, Richard, *Still-Water Angling*, MacGibbon and Kee, 1953

—— *No Need to Lie*, Angling Times, 1964

Wentworth-Day, J., *A History of the* Fens, Harrap, 1954

Wigan, Michael, *The Salmon*, William Collins, 2013

Wightman, Andy, 'Hunting and Hegemony in the Highlands of Scotland', Centre for International Environment and Development Studies, 2004

Williams, Michael, *Draining the Somerset Levels*, Cambridge University Press, 1970

Young, Andrew, *The Natural History and Habits of Salmon*, Peter Reid, 1848

Image Credits

Chapter openers are illustrations from the ninth edition of *The Angler's Guide* by Thomas Salter, published by James Maynard in London in 1841. They were sourced from Archive.org, American Libraries Collection, with the exception of the Chapter 1 opener, which is copyright Morphart Creation/Shutterstock.

Page Source
2   Tom Fort
4   *La Pisciculture et la Peche en Chine* by Dabry de Thiersant,
     published by Masson in Paris, 1872
7   *Life on the upper Thames* by H.R. Robertson, published by Virtue,
     Spalding, and Co in London, 1875. Sourced from Archive.org,
     Harvard University
17 *The Costume of Yorkshire, illustrated by a series of forty engravings*,
     published by T. Bensley in London in 1814. Sourced from Archive.org
23 Tom Fort
25 Fox Photos/Getty Images
27 *The Berkeley manuscripts: The lives of the Berkeleys, lords of the
     honour, castle and manor of Berkeley, in the county of Gloucester, from
     1066 to 1618* by John Smyth, published by J. Bellows in
     Gloucester, 1883. Sourced from Archive.org, University of Toronto
32 Tom Fort
35 Image courtesy the Watchet Boat Museum, with thanks to John
     Eastaugh
40 Image courtesy HarperCollins*Publishers*. Photographed by Jason
     Hawkes
42 The Museum of English Rural Life, University of Reading.
     Photographed by John Tarlton
47 *Fenland Notes and Queries*, vol. I edited by W.H. Bernard
     Saunders, published by Geo. C. Caster, Market Place in
     Peterborough, 1891. Sourced from Archive.org

54 *Journal of Prior William More* edited by Ethel Sophia Fegan,
    published by M. Hughes and Clarke in London, 1914. Sourced
    from Archive.org, University of California Libraries

57 *A Concise History and Description of the City and Cathedral of
    Worcester*, printed by T. Eaton in Worcester, 1829. Sourced from
    Archive.org, The Library of Congress

62 Courtesy of the Metropolitan Museum of Art, New York.

63 Tom Fort

66 *A Discourse of Fish and Fish-Ponds* by Roger North, printed for E.
    Curll in London, 1713. Sourced from Archive.org, Oxford University

70 *The History and Antiquities of the Parish of Tottenham, in the County
    of Middlesex* by William Robinson, published by J.B. Nicholls in
    London, 1840. Sourced from Archive.org, Wellcome Library

71 As above

75 *The Compleat Angler* by Izaak Walton, printed by T. Maxey for
    Rich. Marriot in London, 1653. Sourced from Archive.org,
    Harvard University

81 *Shakespeare's Homeland: Sketches of Stratford-upon-Avon, the Forest of
    Arden, and the Avon Valley* by Henry J. Howard and Sidney Heath,
    published by J.M. Dent in London, 1903. Sourced from Archive.
    org, University of Toronto

90 age fotostock/Alamy Stock Photo

93 Chronicle/Alamy Stock Photo

94 *A History of the Manor of Beresford* by the Rev. W. Beresford,
    published by The Moorlands Press in Leek, 1908. Sourced from
    Archive.org, University of California Libraries

95 Tom Fort

102 *Izaak Walton*, a mezzotint by Samuel Arlent-Edwards, 1898. Gift
    of the artist to the Cleveland Museum of Art. Sourced from
    Wikimedia Commons

108 *Days and Nights of Salmon Fishing on the Tweed* by William
    Scrope, published by John Murray in London, 1843. Sourced from
    Archive.org, University of California Libraries

110 Lordprice Collection / Alamy Stock Photo

113 *River Angling for Salmon and Trout* by John Younger, published by
    Kelso: J. & J.H. Rutherfurd in Edinburgh, 1864. Photographed by
    Jason Hawkes

between Ross and Chepstow, published by T. Jew in Gloucester, 1839. Sourced from Archive.org, University of California Libraries

201   Image copyright the Estate of D.J. Watkins-Pitchford. From *The Fisherman's Bedside Book* by 'BB' (Denys Watkins-Pitchford), published by Eyre & Spottiswoode in London, 1945. *The Fisherman's Bedside Book* is now published by Merlin Unwin Books. Photographed by Jason Hawkes

203   Image courtesy Chris Yates. Image copyright the Estate of D.J. Watkins-Pitchford. Photographed by Jason Hawkes

208   Image courtesy Chris Yates. Photographed by Jason Hawkes

211   Image copyright the Estate of D.J. Watkins-Pitchford. From *A Carp Water (Wood Pool)* by 'BB' (Denys Watkins-Pitchford), published by Putnam & Co Ltd in London, 1958. *A Carp Water (Wood Pool)* is now published by The Medlar Press. Photographed by Jason Hawkes

220   Tom Fort

223   Tom Fort

225   Copyright Colin McPherson

226   Copyright Colin McPherson

235   Image courtesy Gairloch Museum

244   *Eels: A Biological Study* by Léon Bertin, published by Cleaver-Hume Press Ltd in London, 1956. Photographed by Jason Hawkes

249   Archivio Cameraphoto Epoche/Getty Images

255   Photo by Des McGuckin

264   Purchased from the Artist/Bridgeman Images

274   19th era 2/Alamy Stock Photo

279   Tom Fort

281   *British Freshwater Fishes* by Herbert Maxwell, published by Hutchinson & Co in London, 1904. Photographed by Jason Hawkes

282   Tom Fort

287   Tom Fort

298   *Days and Nights of Salmon Fishing on the Tweed* by William Scrope, published by John Murray in London, 1843. Sourced from Archive.org, University of California Libraries

304   Tom Fort

Index

About the Author

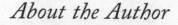

Tom Fort worked as a journalist for BBC Radio News in London for more than twenty years. He was fishing correspondent for the *Financial Times*. This is his ninth book – the others include *The Book of Eels*, *Downstream* and *The A303: Highway to the Sun*.